DOGLO D0282931 L

A Complete Guide to Dog Care

J.M. Evans and Kay White

HOWELL
BOOK HOUSE

New York

HOWELL BOOK HOUSE
A Simon & Schuster / Macmillan Company
1633 Broadway
New York, NY 10019

MACMILLAN is a registered trademark of
Macmillan, Inc.

Library of Congress Cataloging-in-Publication data
available on request.

ISBN 0–87605–633–8

Manufactured in Singapore

10 9 8 7 6 5 4 3 2

Contents

List of figures

List of tables

Introduction

We know that the friendly, uncritical companionship of a dog can be a valuable morale booster and an aid to relaxation to help counter the stresses imposed by life today. We need dogs as never before, but we need dogs which are kept properly — healthy, well-behaved dogs which are not permitted to annoy other people, dogs which are valued by their owners and kept until the end of their days as important members of their household.

Owning a dog is a privilege and one which many people have to deny themselves through limitations on housing, exercise areas, working hours and even because of the frank anti-dog attitude taken by a small segment of our society.

The authors, both of whom have had wide experince with a variety of dogs, and who value dogs as important parts of their lives, want to share some of the knowledge they have gained over the years, to make dog ownership smoother and more rewarding.

We believe that the book tells you the things the other books leave out. We hope that you and your dog owning friends will refer to *The Doglopaedia* frequently and, with this in mind, we have cross referenced extensively throughout the text to make retrieval easy.

Choosing a dog is a very personal matter and difficult to cover in a limited space, but we have outlined in concise tables the advantages and disadvantages of puppies and older dogs, mongrels and pedigree animals, rescued dogs and surplus kennel dogs. It is important that the right dog goes into the right home so that the pet can integrate without problems. We trust this information will make it easier for you to choose the dog that will suit your home and family.

We examine anatomy and physiology, to show you how your dog, small or large, is built and how its systems work. We show you how the dog thinks, how it learns and how you can teach it acceptable behaviour in the correct way — too many people are, unwittingly, teaching their dogs to do the things they *don't* want them to do! We believe that you can teach your dog to behave acceptably with just a little magic and no shouting or bullying.

The 'What ifs' in Chapter 17 are unique, for we have looked at illnesses and injuries through the signs the owner will see, and advise on the action to take. Another exclusive feature are the boxed history tips given for many illnesses, to help you give the most important information to the veterinary surgeon when you take your dog for consultation. We know only too well how easy it is to become tongue-tied and flustered, so we remind you of the things you wanted to ask the vet, and we explain the jargon that vets tend to use in reply.

We hope that if you follow the advice given, the veterinary surgeon will be able to use his skill to best effect to help your dog. Similarly, the section which deals with post-surgical nursing will save you anxiety and promote the dog's smooth recovery and, incidentally, win you the approbation of your veterinary surgeon, if you look after your dog in the professional way we have described.

Accidents and misdemeanours occur in the best of managed households and even the most well behaved dogs sometimes get it wrong; consult our 'What ifs' around the house for those problems other books gloss over — like the best way to clean up vomit and how to introduce your dog to a new kitten. We believe in facing the practicalities too, and we hope this part of the book will prove particularly useful.

Because we want you to enjoy your dog, we have included a list of the activities you can undertake with your pet. Some of them may not have come to your attention before and we have indicated where you may find a 'way in' to many of these activities which, like the dog itself, may become a vital part of your life.

Our intention is that *The Doglopaedia* should fill the role of a knowledgeable dog-owning friend, forever at your elbow to answer the questions that don't get answered elsewhere and, most importantly, to help you, your family and your dog to enjoy a happy, lifelong relationship.

SECTION ONE

DOG MANAGEMENT

Choosing and caring for a dog

Nutrition and feeding

1
Choosing and caring for a dog

Choosing a dog

There is an infinite variety of size, shape, coat texture and inherited ability in the pedigree breeds which have been developed by knowledgeable dog breeders over the years.

In the past, breeds were developed to encourage an ability for certain types of work, such as herding, tracking game, retrieving, guarding or as warning watchdogs. The characteristics which made the dogs suitable for these jobs are still present today, although the majority of dogs are kept in idleness and boredom.

Although your selection of a companion dog may be based on the fact that you admire its looks, do not forget that its behaviour patterns as a domestic pet will be strongly influenced by the work it once did. For instance, the hound may be difficult to halt or recall when it is following scent; the untrained gundog will flush and pursue game, perhaps to your cost and embarrassment, and the dog specifically designed to dig and to work underground will exercise its talents in your flowerbeds.

The dog whose looks you admire may be completely unsuitable for the place in which you live and for your life style. An example would be the Beagle living in a house which has more ground than can be effectively fenced. Although this breed has appealing looks, is of a convenient size and has an easy-to-care-for coat, its ancestors were pack hounds and were bred to follow scent — all day if necessary. Your pet Beagle will do the same unless it is very securely fenced in.

The result could be that you are labelled as antisocial, a careless owner whose dog is a nuisance, even though your pet is perfectly charming when at home. Table 1.1 will help you choose a dog with behaviour traits suitable to your circumstances and lifestyle.

The decision to buy a dog is an important one, because it implies a commitment to look after a dependent creature for at least the next 10 years. The dog's needs and comfort must be considered in relation to all the activities the family likes to undertake. The house and garden will no longer be immaculate once the dog arrives. The dog which sheds hair constantly may make a great deal of housework and so become an intolerable nuisance through no fault of its own.

It is far better to be realistic about the amount of commitment you are prepared to make than to be in the unhappy situation of having bought the wrong type of dog.

The right dog for you

The important matters to consider are size, coat type, dog or bitch, adult or puppy, pedigree or mongrel, what you require it for — just as a pet or as a guard dog — and were to obtain it from. The following notes and Tables 1.2 and 1.3 give pointers to the things you should consider when making your choice.

Size

Giant breeds
Magnificent animals, often gentle in temperament and very quiet and restful in the house, making themselves quite small in their own corner. However, they do need a lot of room in a car and everything, from collars to veterinary treatment, costs more. They need more food, more medication and boarding kennel costs are higher. Giant breeds tend to be short-lived.

Large breeds
May be boisterous in play, and aggressive with other dogs if not properly controlled. Large breeds which have full swishing tails can do a lot of damage within the home.

Long haired dogs
May need up to an hour's grooming *every day*. Professional trimming for Poodles, Bichons and Terriers is a regular expense.

Medium sized dogs

Suit many families, their homes and their cars. There is plenty of choice within this group.

Small dogs

This category tends to be noisy. Small terriers bred to be vermin exterminators have quick snapping jaws which may make them unsuitable as pets for small children.

Very small toy dogs

Dogs under 10lb/4.5kg in weight are not really suitable for the rough and tumble of family life. Toy dogs tend to become devoted to one or two adults who handle them carefully.

Coat type

There is an infinite variety of coat type in dogs, from the absolutely hairless, naked-skinned Chinese Crested, through to smooth-coated dogs like Bull Terriers; thick, double weatherproof coats like Labradors'; Spaniel-type silky coats; harsh, bristly Terrier coats; curly, non-shedding Poodles; rough, wiry Wolfhounds; to the dogs with very deep, corded coats like the Komondor and the Puli.

All dog hair tangles and matts more quickly than human hair. Smooth-coated dogs require minimal grooming and mud dries on them quickly if they have been swimming or wallowing. All coat types will require some attention. Dogs such as the Old English Sheepdog and the Afghan will need to be brushed and combed daily in order to keep the skin healthy and the coat clean. Long-haired dogs tend to smell when they are wet or damp.

Poodles and Bedlingtons will require clipping and bathing every 6–8 weeks. Unless you are a budding hairdresser you will need to make regular appointments with a poodle parlour if your dog is to look its best. Many terriers will need handstripping twice a year.

In a companion dog it is possible to have the long coat of some breeds clipped right down, and this 'new look' can be very attractive, especially on the Old English Sheepdog.

A long-haired dog is a big commitment in time and requires somewhere convenient to do the grooming. A bench of suitable height, with conveniently placed hooks to tether the dog while you work, makes things easier, but the main problem is hair flying about. You will not want to groom the dog in your living room or kitchen.

Dog or bitch

This is one of the major decisions when you are considering acquiring a dog, and it is better to come to a majority agreement within the family **before** you start looking for an adult dog or puppy. If you take a dog, or a bitch, just because there was only one sex available at the time, you may find that the animal you bought does not fulfil your needs.

In the smaller breeds, character and size do not differ very much between the sexes, but you may find that the males in small terrier breeds are the ones which tend to be hypersexed, as are some mongrels.

In the larger, guarding breeds, males tend to be significantly larger in size, more dominant in temperament, and require firm handling. Bitches in general are more biddable, more sympathetic and kindly with children, and often intuitively quicker to define their owners' wishes. On the other hand, bitches can experience mood swings and variable temperament during the oestrous cycle. If you want a dog as a permanent companion to be available for anything the family wants to do, then the male is perhaps more suitable, unless there are definite plans to control oestrus in the bitch.

In the bleeding phase of heat, the bitch must be confined to an easily cleaned room, which usually means leaving her in an 'isolation situation' in the kitchen during the evenings — unless the whole household is willing to sit with her or to have the furniture covered with old sheets. Entire bitches are not very suitable for obedience competition, gun dog work, etc as they have to be withdrawn when they are 'on heat', and perhaps also during a false pregnancy.

In beauty competitions the entry in dog classes is usually lower, so giving better odds on a prize, but the male which fails to win has really no future at all, whereas the bitch can be mated to a dog which excels where she fails in conformation, colouring, etc. There is no absolute rule about showing bitches in season, but the practice is frowned upon.

The casting vote in the choice between dog and bitch often lies with the sex of the animals which are constant visitors to the house. It may not be a happy situation to have a male if mother-in-law often brings her bitch to stay — but if she happens to own a Rottweiler dog, you may be in for trouble in the future if you get yourself a 'stallion' Boxer, as the two males will eventually dispute the territory and inevitably fight. Some consideration may also be given to the dogs belonging to neighbours — male rivalry, or bitch/male sexual attraction can lead to human disputes.

One or more dogs

Do not obtain more than one dog simply because you think they will be happier together. Dogs are very content to have just the attention of people. It is, of course, not possible to give as much time to each individual dog if you have more than one. It is also difficult to avoid favouring one dog more than the other. Remember too that the dogs will sort out a pecking order between themselves, with you as the pack leader; all may be well when you are present but in your absence things may go wrong. We are not happy to advise the novice owner to have more than one large dog of the type bred for guarding. Many of the unfortunate attacks on children have been by a pack (two or more) of such dogs running amok in the absence of the owner. Think very carefully before you have two or more dogs of the guarding breeds, especially if you are an inexperienced dog owner.

Puppy or adult?

In essence, your decision on whether to buy a puppy or adult dog should be influenced by three considerations:

- Have you the time, the commitment and patience to educate a young puppy for domestic life? Will there be someone with the puppy for the majority of the day, so the puppy can be prevented from making behaviour errors which become increasingly hard to eradicate?

- Are you keen to shape the dog the way you want it to be, or would you rather take on an adult and possibly have to find out why it became unacceptable in its previous home?

- Have you the patience to wait for the right litter to be born? Instant puppy availability is seldom possible.

If you decide to buy a puppy, it is preferable to take it into your home when it is 6–8 weeks old. Unless the breeder is able to give a lot of time to socialising and educating each puppy in the litter separately, it does a prospective companion dog no good to be kept with its mother and litter mates after the age of 9 weeks.

Purebred or mongrel?

There is no special magic about mongrels, although they can make absolutely splendid companion dogs and family pets. An adult mongrel can be a good choice if you do not have the time to raise a puppy. Mongrels are, after all, derived from what we know as pedigree breeds, and indeed many people delight in speculating on the ingredients which went into the delightful mongrel they own.

Because mongrel litters are almost always accidentally bred, the puppies are cheap or given away, and so are more likely to be taken on impulse. This is obviously not a good way to acquire a living creature which deserves just as much consideration as the most expensive and rare purebred puppy.

Among the disadvantages of taking on a mongrel puppy must be the gamble on eventual size, coat type and temperament, and also the fact that as mongrel litters are seldom purpose-bred, the mother and puppies may not have received as much care as a planned pedigree litter would do. Also, mongrels are by no means free of the diseases which affect their more aristocratic brethren although the principle of survival of the fittest may mean that the puppy has a big helping of hybrid vigour.

On the other hand, if you take an adult mongrel from a rescue home, you will have a good idea of its size and will no doubt already have fallen for its looks. But remember it may already have had a traumatic life which will affect its health, its temperament and confidence in humans. It may have a behaviour problem that could be difficult to cure. Despite good looks, it is wise not to select a dog that cringes at the back of the kennel and is over-fearful or one that is over-bold and barks and growls. Take your time when selecting and if you have any doubts, go back another day.

If you do choose a mongrel puppy, it is even more imperative to get a veterinary check on your purchase and to start a worming and vaccination programme straightaway.

Behaviour traits

When choosing a pedigree dog it is important to consider how its likely behavioural traits will fit in with your needs and lifestyle. For example if you are very houseproud it would be far from sensible to choose a breed that is likely to be destructive. Similarly if you live in a built-up area, noisy, yappy dogs and those that are inclined to wander are certainly best avoided. If young children live in your house or are frequent visitors then obviously you should choose a breed that is most likely to be trustworthy with children, and so on.

With this in mind we carried out a survey involving almost 200 people concerned with dogs, including veterinary surgeons, veterinary nurses, breeders, boarding-kennel owners, dog judges and behaviour consultants. We asked them to rank the breeds in respect of the positive behaviour traits noted below.

By pooling their views we were able to give an indication whether dogs and bitches in the breed are likely to be average, worse or better than the overall average for the particular behaviour trait. Details are given in Table 1.1.

We were surprised at how consistent the findings were, but having said that it is important to note that individual dogs do vary from the norm for the breed. This should always be borne in mind.

We hope that this information will help you choose a breed that is most likely to fit your requirements and circumstances. But do remember that much can be gained by looking closely at the behaviour of the puppy's mother and father, if this is possible.

Table 1.1 can be read across to obtain a picture of the behaviour traits of a particular breed, or downwards to allow a comparison of different breeds in respect of a specific trait.

The behaviour traits we asked our judges to score for each breed were:

- **Protective behaviour:** Breeds that are likely to instantly sound the alarm when they hear something unusual and bark at intruders were ranked above average.
- **Disinclination to wander:** Breeds that prefer to be with their owner and are content in a smaller territory were ranked high.
- **Lack of destructive behaviour:** Above average breeds are those that are unlikely to ruin furniture, paintwork or car upholstery.
- **Quietness:** Quiet breeds that are not inclined to be yappy or prone to excessive barking were ranked high.
- **Trustworthiness with children:** Above average breeds are less likely to need constant supervision when with young children.

> We strongly recommend that someone capable of restraining the dog should always be present when any dog is close to babies, toddlers or children under 12 years of age.
>
> Dogs should not be left alone in cars with children. Even though they might not bite, they can still cause unintentional injury in defending 'their' territory.
>
> Children should be taught not to play tug-of-war or any rough games with dogs.

- **Friendliness to other dogs:** Breeds that are less likely to be aggressive to and dominate over other dogs rank high.

Those people involved in the survey were asked to regard the behaviour trait described as being a desirable one.

Obtaining a puppy

Consult a veterinary surgeon about any hereditary diseases in the breed of your choice, and what clearance certificates you should ask for.

Try to see as many dogs of the breed as possible — at dog shows and in the homes of people that own them. You may find that the dog you admire outdoors is not the dog you would want in your own sitting-room.

Ask your veterinary surgeon if there are any reliable local breeders.

Buy as close to home as possible.

Be prepared to wait for the right puppy from the right breeder. The majority of buying mistakes are make because of the impulse for an 'instant puppy'.

Buy from the breeder, *not* from a dealer. Places which advertise several breeds at the same time are likely to be dealers who buy in puppies from several different sources. The risk of infectious disease and stress-induced illnesses is high when puppies have made long journeys at an early age, and been mixed with other litters.

Do not take offence if the breeder cross-questions you about your lifestyle and the way the dog will be kept. It is done partly to protect you from making a mistake in buying a puppy which will not suit you.

Never buy a puppy because you feel sorry for it. If a puppy is sickly, the breeder is the best person to look after it and to decide what its future is to be.

Never buy a puppy which is cheaply priced because it is deaf, lame or has some other disability or illness. It could prove to be very expensive in the end.

Be cautious about buying a puppy with an umbilical or inguinal hernia. Get a veterinary surgeon's opinion on the puppy.

The puppy should come from clean premises, where there is not an overpowering smell of urine and faeces. It should be in a well-lit but shaded room, with enough space to move about.

It is best not to buy a puppy unless you have seen the mother of the litter and found her to be an agreeable dog in reasonable health after her litter. Furthermore, it is sensible to ask if you may make arrangements to go to see the sire of the litter.

Try to take your puppy as early as possible, ideally from $6^1/_2$ weeks. The puppy will fit into your home and family best while it is still very young.

Expect to pay a deposit on the puppy of your choice — about 20 per cent of the purchase price. The balance is payable when you collect.

When you collect your puppy

Expect to receive:

- A signed receipt for your payment.
- The puppy's signed pedigree.
- A diet sheet stating what foods, when and how much the puppy is fed.
- Hints on grooming and the tools to use.
- Some notes on the care of the specific breed.
- Some article — a piece of cloth will do — which has been in the nest with the bitch and puppies and will convey a comfort-smell to the puppy.

If the puppy is a pure-bred you should be given a registration application (completed and signed by the breeder) or registration document paper with transfer of ownership.

Initial budgeted costs

There is a considerable initial expenditure on any puppy very soon after purchase.
Among the immediate expenses will be:

- Transfer of ownership for purebred puppies.
- Full course of vaccinations and worming. Tattooing or electronic identity implant.
- Collar and lead.
- Insurance premium for veterinary fees and Third Party insurance, if available.
- Possibly a folding wire crate, preferably for an adult size dog.

While the puppy is very young, a bed can be made from a cardboard carton, and bowls can be appropriated from the household stock, but as a medium to large or giant breed grows, it will be necessary to buy the dog's own equipment. Large breed puppies cost a lot to feed during the growing phase.

Continuing costs

Your continuing commitment to the dog will include feeding, boarding kennels during your holidays, the amount of the exclusion on veterinary fee insurance (about the cost of an initial consultation), booster vaccinations, contraceptive measures for a bitch, renewal of collars, leads, bowls etc, and bedding.
Remember:

- Some of these expenses will vary according to the size of the dog you choose, so be prepared.

- Weight for weight, the running costs of a mongrel are the same as those of a pedigree dog. Only the initial purchase differs.
- Rail travel:

All these costs must be considered before you purchase a puppy. Be sure you can cope before you buy.

Equipment

Collars

A very young puppy should wear a soft collar for short periods every day. Always remove the collar when the puppy is unsupervised as it could easily get hung by the collar on a cupboard handle, for instance, or get a paw caught in the collar.

Neck size enlarges rapidly as the puppy grows. Care should be taken that the collar is neither too loose nor too tight. Slip collars which slacken round the neck when the lead is not held taut are unsuitable for use in urban situations.

Many people now choose to let their dog wear a leather harness so that the lead attaches to the centre bone and does not pull on the neck.

Choke or check chains have been found to cause extensive bruising on dogs' necks, and they should not be used. It is not wise to leave a loose neck chain on a dog which is running free outdoors or in the house, as the slack may catch on a projecting object and strangle the dog.

Many breeds look best in their own specific type of collar. Ask the breeder to show you the kind of collar traditionally worn by your breed.

Every dog must by law have some means of identification attached to the collar when outside the home. Check frequently to make certain that engraved discs are still readable and bear the correct address. It is convenient to use a cylinder containing a slip of paper to bear the address if you are travelling with your dog on holiday. Electronic tagging with microchips is now available and can help identify your dog should it be lost or stolen. Many veterinary surgeons have the equipment needed to 'chip' animals and many rescue centres and police stations have 'readers'.

Leather collars become hard and uncomfortable if they are allowed to get wet. Test the collar and the 'D' ring often to make sure it is still adequately strong.

Anti-flea collars contain a small amount of highly poisonous chemical. Do not risk compounding the chemical action by spraying the dog with anti-flea spray as well, or by hanging anti-fly strips above its bed or spraying the room with an insect killer.

Anti-flea collars should be taken from the packet and aired for a day or two before being put on the dog. Children should not be allowed to handle these collars, either on or off the dog, and the collar must not be allowed to become wet.

If the dog's skin shows any sign of allergic reaction in the area of the collar, remove it at once and consult a veterinary surgeon.

Anti-flea collars do not have a strong enough fastening to be used with a lead.

The Halti head collar

A modern idea in dog control aids, especially useful for dogs which tend to lunge at passers-by, is the Halti head collar, made of strong nylon tape and designed by an animal behaviourist on the principle of the head collar used on unbroken foals. The control point is under the dog's chin rather than around the neck. The Halti is well tolerated by most dogs and offers the owner greater security when leading a strong animal.

Leads

The most important part of a lead is the hook which attached it to the collar. Check the hooks and the 'D' rings which attach them to the lead frequently.

Also check the stitching on the loop handle. A saddler will re-stitch it for you if it is becoming frayed. Many accidents happen because the collar or the lead broke at the critical moment.

A helpful modern invention is the Flexi-lead, over 30 ft of lead contained in a box-like handle. The length of the lead the dog is allowed is controlled by the handler, so allowing it a lot of freedom or bringing it up close to heel. This can be a most useful aid in controlling dogs which will not come when called because their attention is held by something which interests them. Flexi-leads should not be used in towns as accidents have been caused by pedestrians walking into the extended lead.

Beds

Every dog should have its own bed, in a quite warm corner of one room in the house. The dog can then be told to go to its bed to prevent it from being a nuisance. A collapsible wire crate can serve a useful purpose to contain dogs as it is easily erected wherever it is needed, even in the garden and around the swimming pool.

A puppy's first bed should be a cardboard carton, placed inside the wire crate.

A suitable bed for the next stage is the oval or round rigid polystyrene bed. This is an economical choice as it is easily cleaned, light to move and almost indestructible.

In general, woven wicker baskets are not really suitable as they are most inviting to chew, and can be difficult to clean and disinfect properly. However many owners find them very convenient especially for dogs of the smaller breeds. If such baskets are used they should be thoroughly scrubbed regularly and put out in the sunshine to dry and air. For older dogs a bean bag filled with polystyrene beads offers warmth, comfort and support, and this type of bed does not harbour parasites. Buy one with the strongest inner cover you can find, which allows for topping up with extra beads, and which also has a washable top cover.

Crates for dogs

Call it a dog crate, or an indoor kennel, or even a cage, this portable house is one of the 20th century's best inventions for dogs.

Crate training a puppy

- Allow the puppy free access in and out of the crate and praise him when he goes in voluntarily.
- When the puppy is used to the crate it can be left with the door shut for up to an hour at a time and the pup taken out at regular intervals.
- Most dogs will soon come to regard the crate as their den and will happily use it in their owners' absence.
- The door should be left open if the dog is to be left alone for any length of time.

The dog's natural instincts are to find a den, a place which offers protection, and we have yet to meet a dog that does not take instinctively to a crate even if not encountered until middle to old age.

The use of a wire mesh crate to train new puppies and restrain older dogs where necessary is standard practice in the United States and is now beginning to find favour in the UK. Breeders, exhibitors, veterinary surgeons and groomers already use crates as a matter of course.

Crates are made of wire panels that fold down to the size of a suitcase for carrying. Most models have a metal tray floor and they are quick to erect.

Buy the size your dog will need when adult: if necessary partition off some space with cardboard. Leave the crate door open to start with. Put in soft bedding (the breeder may have given you a piece of used bedding with the litter smell on it). Show the pup that this is his bed, feeding place and is where his toys are.

The door can be shut when the pup goes in to sleep. This helps in house-training, as few puppies willingly soil their beds. When your pup wakes and whines to attract your attention, you know you should take him outside. It is more constructive to prevent the puppy soiling indoors than correcting him after an accident has occurred.

When you are busy in the kitchen and handling hot dishes, you and your puppy will be much safer if he is in his crate. Being in the crate is much more friendly than shutting the puppy in a separate room.

As crates are portable, it is easy to take it into the sitting room when you have guests. The puppy can be the centre of attention with no risk of being hurt or of annoying non-doggy people. Put the crate in a shady place in the garden when unfamiliar children come to play or when you are using the swimming pool (if you are lucky enough to own one).

The crate will serve the dog all his life: on holidays, when you go visiting and when your dog is ill and needs protection, rest and nursing.

If you need to convince yourself how user-friendly a dog crate is, you may be able to borrow one from your breeder or veterinary surgeon. Dogs know instinctively that this is the nearest thing to a primitive den that will come their way in the domestic setting.

Use the crate sensibly. Do not confine a pup in it for more than two hours at a time: puppies need frequent periods of activity as well as plenty of sleep. Try to be in the same room as the crated pup as much as possible so it does not associate separation anxiety with being in the crate. Ensure that the crated dog has enough air but is not in a draught and that the crate is shaded from direct sunlight in summer.

Blankets

The most hygienic and work-saving blankets for dogs are those made of porous polyester fur fabric which is warm, long-lasting, very easily washed and quickly dried. Dogs will not chew this fabric as they do woollen rugs. The blankets are white or pale beige, so you can easily see when it is soiled. As these items are easily transportable, you can train your dog to sit upon it wherever it may be laid. This can be very useful when travelling or visiting friends. Manufacturers advertise in the canine press, or the blankets can be obtained through pet shops.

Care of puppies

The following hints should ease those anxious but happy days when a new puppy first joins your household.

Before you bring a puppy home, make a small fenced off area in the kitchen in a warm draught-proofed corner, to contain the puppy's bed, and a paper covered area for toilet purposes. A den of this kind gives the puppy security, and also keeps it from getting underfoot when you are busy. Later the puppy's bed can be in the same corner with the fencing dispensed with. Panels intended for enclosing compost heaps make good indoor fencing and are useful in the garden later; although a purpose-built dog crate as described earlier is the most ideal.

Although the puppy appears to be delighted with its new home, there is bound to be inner stress at the complete change of environment. Do not ask too many people to see the puppy and keep it quiet for a few days while it adjusts to the immediate family.

Eight-week old puppies tend to play for half-an-hour and then sleep for an hour-and-a-half at a time. Long periods of rest are essential for the development of a healthy body and good temperament. Do not disturb the puppy until it wakes naturally. If during play periods the puppy appears to be getting over-excited, remove it from stimulating circumstances, give it a hot-water bottle (well wrapped) and a comforting toy, and allow the puppy to be quiet. Over-stimulation in puppy days can produce a hyperactive, restless dog which is not pleasure to own.

Feed the puppy at regular times with small amounts of food, perhaps four or five times daily with the first meal being early in the morning and the last at bedtime. Keep to the foods advised by the breeder for at least the first two weeks in your home. See also Chapter 2.

Observe the puppy closely, and regard any deviation from normal as quite serious in the very young puppy. Ask for veterinary advice quickly, as young puppies can deteriorate very rapidly. As the puppy grows older, veterinary attention for illness should still be a matter of urgency, remembering that the first 6-12 months of a puppy's life are the most traumatic for illness and accidents.

Take veterinary advice on the vaccination programme to be followed and present the puppy at the surgery at the correct time. Take precautions to avoid picking up infection from other dogs until two weeks after the final vaccination. See also Chapters 7 and 11.

Follow the worming programme advised by the veterinary surgeon faithfully.

Do not be in too much hurry to take your puppy out on a lead. Walking on the lead should be carefully and properly taught by a responsible adult, so that the puppy realises that pulling is never allowed. Do not permit children to drag the puppy around the roads on a lead in the guise of training it — bad habits may be instilled and the puppy's neck may be irrevocably harmed by tugging on the collar.

House-training

Everyone wants their puppy to be reliably house-trained as soon as possible, but it is unkind and brings disappointment to expect too much too soon.

Eight-week old puppies have very little bladder control — achieving elimination outside means that someone responsible must be watching the puppy all the time so that success can be praised instantly.

Getting the puppy to eliminate in the garden means going out with the puppy every hour on the hour during the day, and staying out, encouraging it, until success is achieved. Putting the puppy out on its own is quite useless.

It may be better to allow the puppy to use newspaper indoors (which good breeders will have trained it to do) for a week or so, if the weather is bad when you bring the puppy home. You may then make quicker progress when you are able to take the puppy out every time it needs to go, when the weather is kinder to both of you. It is in any case unrealistic to hope for 100 per cent day and night house cleanliness before the age of 5-6 months, and if that seems a long time, remember that children take much longer.

Bitches

Although bitch owning can involve some additional problems and responsibilities, many owners consider that these are far outweighed by the benefits. In comparison with dogs, bitches are generally:

- More companionable
- More biddable
- Less likely to roam
- Less aggressive, particularly to other dogs.

The attentive bitch owner should have at least a fundamental knowledge of the matters described in this chapter, so that correct action can be taken should any problems occur, of if any differences from the normal are observed. The informed owner will know when to seek advice from a veterinary surgeon or breeder, how to describe the problem, and understand the advice given so to implement it effectively.

Heat in bitches

Signs and frequency

Most bitches reach puberty when they are between 6-7 months of age, but possibly as early as 4 months or as late as 2 years. At this time the bitch's vulva will become enlarged and a varying amount of blood-stained fluid is passed — the bitch is said to have 'come on heat' or to 'be in season'.

Some bitches may show signs of abdominal discomfort, increased excitability, and be less inclined to eat for a few days before heat commences. Bitches become attractive to dogs, usually from the first day of heat, but mostly they are not interested in their admirers until 7-10 days have passed. At this stage the bitch is equally anxious to escape to meet the male.

Conception is more likely to occur if mating takes place 10-12 days after the first obvious signs of heat are noticed, but can sometimes occur at earlier or later matings. Most bitches will subsequently come 'on heat' at intervals of 6-9 months throughout the rest of their lives — there is no equivalent to the menopause. See Table 1.4.

False pregnancy

This term is used to describe the condition in which bitches show the signs of pregnancy, nursing and lactation, and yet have no puppies, either because they have not been mated or have failed to conceive. The signs occur late in meta-oestrus, ie 1-2 months after the bitch has been on heat, and vary in type and severity from one bitch to another. Characteristically, however, most bitches will produce milk and display obvious maternal behaviour. Many of them show nervous signs including panting and breathlessness. A lot of bitches will carry shoes and other toys around the house and collect them in their bed. In severe cases, some bitches will actually strain as if they are producing a litter. Once a bitch has had false pregnancy she will probably have it again after each heat with the signs becoming progressively more severe on each occasion. With regard to treatment, it is worth noting that the condition is really a normal occurrence in that something like 60 per cent of bitches have false pregnancy to a degree. Indeed, in the wild state or in a breeding kennel false pregnant bitches will be capable of nursing a litter from a bitch that has died, so the condition serves a useful purpose. Thus if the signs are mild it is probably better not to give treatment. The nervous signs will disappear more quickly if the bitch is denied sympathy and if toys and brooding objects are removed. Less milk will be produced if the carbohydrate content of the diet is reduced, if the bitch's water intake is reduced somewhat (she must not of course be denied access to water entirely for long periods) and if the amount of exercise is increased.

If the signs are severe and the above action does not lead to an improvement, veterinary assistance should be sought. A course of hormone tablets or a hormone injection may help and in some cases it may be considered necessary to bathe the mammary glands to help the milk to be reabsorbed. Sedatives may be required to control the nervous signs, especially if the bitch is disturbed and cannot rest. Veterinary surgeons often advise that bitches that have a severe false pregnancy or that suffer regularly in this way after each heat be spayed, since bitches that do not come on heat do not have false pregnancy. The chemical control of heat by giving regular hormone injections can help to reduce the incidence of false pregnancy and may be advocated in some cases.

Pyometra

Definition:
Accumulation of large amounts of fluid in the uterus usually occurring 1-2 months after a bitch has been on heat.

Cause:
Not entirely clear, but probably brought about by hormone imbalance.

Signs:
Drinking excessively, frequent urination, depression often with a raised temperature. Abdominal distension. In 'open' cases there is a thick red-brown evil smelling discharge from the vulva. The condition is usually seen in older bitches that have not had puppies, but exceptions do occur.

Treatment:
If a bitch owner suspects that his pet is suffering from the condition, it is most important to seek veterinary advice without delay, since an emergency operation involving surgical removal of the uterus and ovaries may be needed to save the animal. Some open cases, that is those with vaginal discharge, can respond to medical treatment.

Mating

Readers are strongly advised to seek advice from their veterinary surgeon and/or an experienced dog breeder and to read specialist books that are available on this subject before they have their bitch mated. It is important that the bitch is mated at the right time if she is to conceive. A recently developed test, Premate, is available which allows veterinary surgeons to determine from a blood sample the optimum time to mate bitches. This test is particularly useful in bitches which have failed to conceive previously or where it is necessary to travel a long distance to the stud dog. In maiden bitches an experienced dog should be used. Mating with a suitably selected and screened sire is necessary if congenital abnormalities, such as umbilical hernias, poorly formed joints, etc are to be avoided. It is also important to establish wherever possible that there is every chance that homes will be able to be found for the puppies. Where this is not the case it is very often kinder to reduce the size of the litter by putting down some of the puppies at birth. Owners wishing to breed from their bitch should also be fully prepared to look after her throughout pregnancy, which lasts for about 9 weeks (57-69 days) and to cope with the whelping, and be prepared to help the bitch nurse her puppies and to feed, clean and handle them at least four times a day after weaning until they are ready for permanent homes. Puppy rearing is a full time job that carries a great number of responsibilities, thus in general it is better left to experts. There is no truth in the old wives' tale that having a litter of puppies is good for a bitch.

Note:

The muscles in the vagina contract at the end of coitus preventing the dog's penis from being withdrawn. This constitutes the 'tie' that is a desirable feature of mating that mostly, but not always, occurs. The dog will step over the bitch, or be turned by handlers into this position so that the animals are tied back to back. There is no point in trying to separate the animals that are locked in this way, since the dog will be released in good time. Buckets of cold water thrown over the animals simply wet them and do little to speed up the process of separation.

Mismating

What if my bitch is mismated?

It is very important to act immediately, as an injection to avert pregnancy needs to be given within 4 days of the mating. Visit your veterinary surgeon at once.

The effect of the injection will be to reverse the dominating hormones of the bitch's oestrous cycle, so that she will begin her heat all over again. Even more vigilant control will be needed, as the bitch may be even more willing to be mated on a second occasion.

More positive control methods must be used in future, as it is dangerous to the bitch's health to rely on averting the pregnancy after mismating.

Unexpected pregnancy

What if my bitch is found to be pregnant unexpectedly?

Your veterinary surgeon will advise you if it is possible and wise to spay the bitch, removing the uterus and foetuses surgically.

If this is not a practical proposition, or if the bitch is wanted for breeding in future, the only option is to allow the pregnancy to proceed, and whelping to take place naturally, but resolving to cull the litter down to a maximum of two puppies which should be left to assuage the bitch's maternal instinct and to utilise the milk supply.

It may be difficult to persuade a veterinary surgeon to cull the litter, as their training is orientated to preserving life, but if the litter cannot be reared conveniently, and there is no assured market for the puppies, it is kinder to have them destroyed soon after birth, rather than allow them to swell the thousands of unwanted dogs already hoping that someone will give them the right kind of home.

Rearing a large litter properly is also an expensive exercise, and there can be no hope of recouping the cost of a litter of crossbreeds and mongrels.

Mammary tumours

A high percentage of bitches will develop mammary tumours (growths in the mammary glands) as they get older although, as mentioned later, heat control does help reduce the incidence. It makes sense therefore to inspect the mammary glands of bitches at least four times a year. This is preferably done when the bitch is on heat and about 1 month later. If lumps are felt, their size should be recorded and monitored carefully under veterinary supervision and advice taken about their removal before the tumour has a chance to spread to other parts of the body. Fortunately many of the growths are benign and are relatively easily removed, provided they have not been allowed to grow too large and action is taken before the skin over them has become thin and ulcerated.

Heat control

There are many reasons why bitch owners should control heat in their pets. However, the most important are:

1. To gain a health advantage — the chance of the bitch developing uterine problems, mammary tumours and false pregnancy will be reduced.
2. To prevent unwanted pregnancy.
3. To make the pet more consistently companionable — during heat and other stages of the cycle (especially if the animal suffers from false pregnancy) a bitch's temperament will be changed.
4. To make owning a bitch more convenient — to avoid problems of messy bleeding, unsightly vulval swelling, attractiveness to dogs and the need to keep the bitch confined twice a year.

Remember, in most bitches heat lasts for 3 weeks and occurs twice a year — it may last longer and occur more frequently in some. Thus bitches are not 100 per cent fit and are less enjoyable companions for about 3 months in every year.

Sprays and lotions which claim to disguise the odour of a bitch in heat are largely ineffective, and even seem to be recognised as a heat indicator by keen and experienced male dogs.

Chlorophyll and other specially prepared tablets are also a waste of money and in addition to not deterring males, will certainly not prevent the bitch itself from trying to meet the opposite sex.

Various contrivances based on knickers and sanitary pads are obtainable and are considered useful by some bitch owners to prevent the bitch staining furniture and carpets.

Heat control can be achieved by spaying or by chemical methods using an artificial hormone similar to that contained in the human contraceptive pill. Each has advantages and disadvantages and thus the matter should be discussed with a veterinary surgeon so that the most appropriate action can be chosen to suit the particular animal and circumstances.

It is important to realise that the choice will be different for different breeds of dogs and will vary according to the owner's needs. By and large, however, small Terrier type bitches do not have too many problems associated with spaying, but in bitches of the large breeds, and especially Old English Sheepdogs, difficulties like incontinence occur quite commonly after the operation.

Coat changes can occur in Spaniels and in bitches with short hair and spayed bitches tend to be less trainable and less efficient at guarding their territory. In some cases bone growth may be adversely affected. Unfortunately no operative procedure can be guaranteed to be completely safe and problem-free, but thanks to modern anaesthetics and techniques few difficulties arise when young healthy bitches are spayed. Spayed bitches do have some tendency to put on weight after the operation, but this can usually be easily prevented by reducing the amount of food given and by avoiding the temptation of giving titbits.

Whelping

Pregnancy usually lasts about 63 days from the day of mating, but may be as short as 57 or as long as 69 days.

If you are aware of the pregnancy during its late stages (the last 2-3 weeks), the bitch will appreciate being fed about a quarter to one-third more food than normal, and also being given her daily intake in several small meals during the day. Her appetite may be

Figure 1.1 Whelping – if a bitch needs a little help! (a) Giving assistance during the birth of a puppy; (b) coping with the umbilical cord.

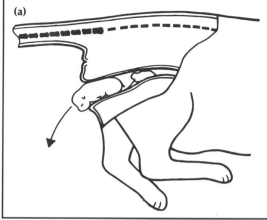

Hold the puppy's head, or hind legs if it is coming backwards, in a clean, dry face flannel. Pull gently downwards and backwards away from the spine. Don't use force and try to pull at the same time as the bitch strains.

Break the cord with your fingers, or cut with clean scissors, $1^1/_2$-2 in from the pup, without pulling on the puppy's stomach wall. Use clean hands and wash them afterwards.

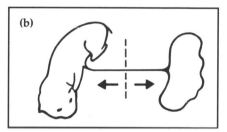

variable and she may vomit in the mornings. It is normal for a bitch to refuse food entirely for 24 hours when whelping is imminent.

Provide a cardboard box of appropriate size in a secluded, darkened and warm place in which the bitch can whelp. Plenty of clean newspaper should be available to line the box, and it is normal behaviour to the bitch to shred up this paper during the early stages of whelping.

Stage I of labour may last from 2 to 24 hours. During this stage the bitch will be restless and may pant compulsively.

Stage II begins with the first big expelling contraction or straining movement and it is as well to make a note of when this occurs.

If the first puppy has not appeared after an hour, the veterinary surgeon should be contacted by telephone for advice.

Normally a dark coloured sac of fluid will appear at the vulva ahead of the first puppy, which will be wrapped in another fluid-filled membrane. The puppy should be born very soon after this stage is reached. If not, gentle assistance, in the form of gentle traction downwards and backwards, may be given as indicated in Figure 1(a). The bitch should tear open this sac at once, to release the puppy and will proceed to lick it clean and dry. If the bitch cannot do this, it must be done for her, and the puppy held upside down to allow any fluids to drain from the lungs.

A further expelling movement should bring the placenta, or afterbirth — a piece of liver-like tissue. The bitch will instinctively eat the placenta and make an attempt to clear up the fluids which will have escaped during the birth of the puppy. Green and brown staining from these fluids is normal. If the puppy remains attached to the placenta and the cord is not severed by the bitch, this can be done by tearing it with the fingers, taking care not to pull on the puppies' abdomen, as indicated in Figure 1(b).

It is wise to keep a note of the number of placentas passed, there should be one for each puppy. A retained placenta can be dangerous — contact your veterinary surgeon if you think all have not been expelled soon after whelping is finished. A delay of more than 1 hour in births, when there are obviously more puppies to come, should be reported to the veterinary surgeon for advice.

It is always wise to ask a veterinary surgeon to call at the house during the 24 hours after whelping to check the bitch and to put down any puppies which, perhaps because they have some congenital abnormality, need to be culled.

Some veterinary surgeons feel that they have more assistance at their disposal, more convenient equipment to hand, and can make better use of their time, if all their patients are brought to them at the surgery. Parking problems in large towns also add to problems with housecalls.

If you are required to take a litter, or a sick dog, to the surgery, make up a bed which will protect the car and keep the dog warm. In the case of a dog which may have an infectious illness, or where puppies are unvaccinated, do not take the animals into the waiting room, but ask the receptionist where the vet would prefer to see the dogs.

It may be possible to give puppies their first vaccinations in the car to avoid their meeting other dogs which may be carrying infections.

Further reading
The Book of the Bitch, J M Evans and Kay White (Howell Book House USA, Ringpress Books UK)
The Technique of Breeding Better Dogs, Dr. Dieter Fleig (Howell Book House, USA Ringpress Books UK.)

Male dogs

Entirety

It is essential when choosing a male puppy to ensure that it is **entire,** ie that it has two testicles descended into the scrotum.

The testicles may retract temporarily in a young puppy and the seller may be optimistic that the puppy will become entire in time, but a veterinary surgeon can give you an informed opinion when the puppy is about 8 weeks old.

Dogs which are monorchids — more correctly termed unilateral cryptorchids, that is with only one testicle descended into the scrotum — can sire puppies, but as the condition is hereditary such a puppy is an unwise buy.

Cryptorchidism is important to the buyer even if there is no intention of using the dog at stud. A testicle retained within the abdomen is particularly susceptible to growths (tumours) which can affect the whole hormonal system, and may be life-threatening if they spread to other parts of the body. Consult your veterinary surgeon as an early operation may be required.

House-training

Male dogs are often slower to house-train than bitches. Dogs squat to urinate until they are adolescent, when the customary leg-raising posture is adopted to facilitate territory marking.

Male adolescence

In late puppyhood, during the adolescent phase, a young male may experience an upsurge of hormones making him indulge in excessive sexual behaviour. If the dog is suitably discouraged (see Chapter 4) this behaviour will often prove only transient.

A survey carried out in 1977 among dog owners visiting veterinary surgeries for any reason revealed that 52% of dogs under 1 year of age and 65% of older dogs had annoying hypersexual traits. The fact that such behaviour is tolerated is even more remarkable as many of the dogs showed two or more hypersexual traits and one dog displayed no less than six!

But what behavioural traits are we talking about? In short, three main signs:

• Mounting people and inanimate objects
• Aggression, particularly towards other dogs
• Urination about the house (territory marking)

and three minor signs:

• Wandering
• Excitability
• Destructiveness

All of these are obviously both worrying and potentially embarrassing.

What makes some dogs hypersexed? Fundamentally, sex drive in male animals is controlled by the male sex hormone, testosterone (which is produced by the testes), and/or areas in the cerebral cortex in the brain. In some dogs, the hormones are more important and in others the animal is motivated principally by its brain. Furthermore, it is always worth noting that the hypersexual traits noted above can be learned behaviour and that they can be perpetuated by inappropriate training.

Quite obviously treatment and prevention must be aimed at reducing the production of testosterone, at calming the cerebral cortex and applying corrective training (or at least not reinforcing the behaviour by any sort of reward). Often, all that can be achieved by castration and/or the use of synthetic hormones, coupled with a determination by the owner to teach the dog that such behaviour does not pay off.

A number of scientific publications have been written on this subject and veterinary surgeons in practice are familiar with what can be done.

If your dog is a problem in this respect, it's well worth talking to your vet since a course of tablets, a series of injections, or possibly a relatively simple operation may be all that is required to give you some peace and save your dog from frustration.

Wandering

Male dogs are more motivated to wander from home than females. Security of gates and fencing of a height to enclose the dog is essential. For dogs with the inclination to dig or burrow, fencing must be buried in the ground. If you live on an estate or in a place where wandering dogs can be a problem to themselves or passing traffic, it makes sense to obtain a breed that is happier staying close to home.

Use at stud

It is unwise to allow a dog to be used at stud to oblige a casual request. Unless a dog is a show winner there is not likely to be a regular demand for his services and, in this case, it is better for the dog **never** to have had stud experience.

It is unfair to keep a male dog, which is not to be used at stud, with entire bitches which are undergoing regular oestrous cycles.

The owner of a pet male will be wise to 'screen' bitches which may accompany visitors to the house, and request that they be left at home if they are coming into oestrus. An encounter with such a bitch on his own territory can be upsetting to the male and will almost inevitably lead to territory marking, even indoors, which may get the male into undeserved trouble.

Contraceptive measures for male dogs

Hormones

Consult your veterinary surgeon about a hormonal preparation which may be given by injection to male dogs to mimic the effects of castration in respect of behaviour. However, such injections may not affect fertility.

Vasectomy

In this operation the tubes that transport sperm from the testicles are cut, so rendering the dog unable to sire puppies, but still able and willing to perform a mating act. Such a dog is sometimes used as a 'teaser' in breeding kennels. Since this operation does not affect the dog's behaviour, it will still be interested in mating bitches and may still roam, so it is not of relevance in the domestic situation.

Castration

Castration involves removal of the testes from the scrotum, leaving the dog with an empty scrotal sac which is not unsightly. Although the operation is carried out under general anaesthesia it does not require abdominal surgery and healing is usually rapid. The operation is performed:

(a)   To render a dog sterile when his services as a stud are unwanted.
(b)   In dogs that have developed testicular tumours.
(c)   To help overcome hypersexual behaviour which has persisted beyond adolescence, particularly interdog aggression and the tendency to roam to seek out bitches.

It is as well to remember that the traits mentioned above may have become a learned behaviour which may persist even after castration. In some cases it may take as long as 4-6 months before the effect of castration becomes apparent.

Guarding ability, intelligence, playfulness and owner-affection are not usually significantly altered in males castrated after puberty. There is a tendency for castrated dogs to put on weight if the amount of food given is not reduced and an adequate amount of exercise given.

Elderly dogs

We have to thank the high nutritional standards of commercially prepared dog foods, the modern effective vaccines, and the tremendous advances in veterinary knowledge for the welcome news that dogs are living longer, giving an average 2 to 4 year increase on the expected lifespan of 20 years ago.

The life expectancy of dogs differs widely, ranging from 7 to 10 years in Bulldogs and the giant breeds, to well into the late teens in some Spaniels and small Terriers. Longevity is to some extent a hereditary factor, as well as depending on good care by the owner and freedom from congenital factors which may shorten life.

Greying of the muzzle and eyebrows is seen in some dogs as early as 5 years old, but this does not signify that the dog is to be regarded as old at that stage. In extreme old age the whole coat may become dusted with white hairs, or even white all over.

Old dogs have a capacity for deep and prolonged sleep; take care not to startle an elderly pet as it may respond with a growl or snap which was not really intended. Their years should be respected and they should not be teased by puppies, cats or children.

There are many ways in which the quality of life of an old dog can be increased, often just by a little forethought and consideration on the part of the owner. The following hints may be of help.

- Avoid turning an old dog out on winter mornings and evenings. The shock of very cold air can precipitate drop attacks and strokes.
- Avoid boarding an elderly dog in kennels. Stress can trigger a latent illness.
- Keep distemper/parvovirus/hepatitis/leptospirosis boosters up-to-date. An elderly dog can lack immunity to these diseases.
- Have teeth attended to regularly to make eating easier and to prevent halitosis.
- Have anal sacs checked regularly. Blocked sacs are uncomfortable for the dog as well as unpleasant for the owner.
- If the dog is unable to take much exercise, keep the food intake down, but offer small amounts more often, so that the dog does not feel its pleasures are taken away. An overweight dog is more prone to heart disease. Your veterinary surgeon may advise you to feed one of the special diets that are available for old or obese dogs. The use of such foods can help prevent some of the problems that beset older dogs.
- Bearing in mind that old dogs are not as mobile as before, take care that they do not sit on cold damp concrete, or in full sun, for too long. Put rugs and beds in favourite sitting-places, so that they are convenient to go to.
- Take care that an old dog does not sit or lie on rough surfaces, as elbow and hock callouses can become painful and even chronically ulcerated.
- Do not allow an old dog to get too far away on walks. They can easily become lost though being disoriented when sense of smell, sight and hearing is deteriorating.

Special care for the older dog

- **Water**
  Monitor the amount of water being drunk daily.
  Consult veterinary surgeon if there is an increase without apparent cause.
  If necessary, offer the dog water, as it might be too lethargic to help itself.

- **Food**
  Provide food of consistency and at temperature which dog prefers. Slightly warmed food can be more appetising.
  Trial and error will show which type of bowl is most convenient for the dog to eat from — mouth dexterity is not as good as in the young. Raising the bowl on a step or platform can help as bending the neck may be painful.

- In some situations it may be advisable to change the dog's diet. For example a reduction in the protein and salt content may be beneficial. Your veterinary surgeon will advise and may prescribe a specially prepared commercial diet for your dog.

- Observing and caring for your elderly dog can be interesting and rewarding in terms of the dog's visible gratitude for the arrangements you make for its comfort and for the many ways you will be able to devise for continuing to enjoy the companionship which you have valued for so many years.

- Remember dogs live for now rather than for yesterday or tomorrow. This makes being old and caring for the old so much easier in the dog than in the human. Some specific aspects relating to the care of elderly dogs are noted in the previous table.

Dogs and the law (UK)

There are a number of laws which apply to dog ownership. They are intended to protect dogs from cruelty and misuse, to protect livestock and wild animals from dogs and to protect people from annoyance by badly-kept dogs.

In addition, many local authorities make their own bye-laws concerning fouling of footpaths, roads and parks where dogs must be kept on leads, and public buildings into which dogs may not be taken. The notion that Cavalier King Charles Spaniels are permitted by law, dating from the time of Charles II, to flout any such laws, is a complete myth.

Food shops and restaurants are encouraged by the Food Hygiene Regulations 1970 to ban dogs from their premises.

Large land-owners such as the Forestry Commission also create bye-laws prohibiting the chasing of deer, game birds, etc by dogs on their land.

Licences

Three activities require licences from the local authority, and involve inspection of the premises concerned. The licence cost is determined by the local authority.

- **The Breeding of Dogs Act 1973**
  Owners of more than two bitches from which puppies are bred for sale require a licence.

- **Boarding Establishments Act 1963**
  Anyone who boards animals for payment, whether in a private house or a kennel, requires a licence and will be inspected by the local authority.

- **Pet Animals Act 1951**
  Anyone buying in animals for re-sale, or breeding quantities of animals for sale may be required to take out a licence to keep a **pet shop**, whether the premises are a conventional shop or not.

- **Selling dogs**
  Dogs and puppies may not be sold in the street or any public place, or to a child under 12 years old, or in conjunction with a rag or old clothes dealing business.

- **Buying dogs and puppies**
  In general the law decides that it is up to the buyer to be careful what he buys, and livestock is bought 'as seen' without any warranty. However, if the buyer states that the puppy is wanted for a particular purpose, eg for showing or breeding, and in due course the dog does not fulfil that purpose, the buyer may have a claim under the Sale of Goods Act 1979. If a pedigree is given with a puppy, it must be signed and correct. It may be regarded as an offence of obtaining money by false pretences to give an incorrect pedigree; pedigrees can be checked at the Kennel Club.

The dog owner's responsibility

Your dog must not be a nuisance to neighbours or other persons. Nuisance may be defined as persistent and prolonged barking, trespassing on other people's property, threatening or attacking people, or obstructing access to a public place or roadway.

Your dog must wear a collar bearing your address at all times when outside your property, except when working as a gundog, or herding sheep or cattle.

Tail docking

In July 1993 it became illegal for anyone other than a veterinary surgeon to dock a puppy's tail at any age — even soon after birth. This traditional right is now denied to dog breeders or anyone else not holding a degree in veterinary surgery. Anyone who docks tails is now liable to prosecution by the RSPCA on a charge of cruelty as are people with puppies which were obviously docked after July 1, 1993.

Dangerous Dogs Act 1991

This emergency legislation was hurriedly formulated after an unusual spate of attacks by dogs bred and trained for fighting at secret meetings and displays. The dogs, often English bull breeds interbred with imported American Pit Bulls and known as Pit Bull Terriers, were subjected to a number of punitive restrictions, whether or not they had been involved in any fighting incidents.

From August 12 1991, it became an offence, carrying a penalty of £2,000 fine and/or 6 month's imprisonment, to take a designated fighting dog on to the streets unless it was muzzled and leashed. These dogs, estimated to number 10,000 at the time, may not be sold, given away, bred from or advertised; these restrictions being designed to allow the American Pit Bull to die out.

The importation to Britain of Pit Bull Terriers, Japanese Tosa, Fila Braziliera and Dogo Argentino was also made illegal.

After December 1 of that year (later extended to March 1 of the following year) it became an offence for anyone to own a fighting dog which was not neutered, registered, officially tattooed with a number and insured for third party risks.

One section of the Dangerous Dogs Act 1991 affects all dogs. If someone complains to the police that any dog has *given them reasonable grounds for apprehension*, that dog can be seized by the police and taken away to await a court hearing, possibly eventually to be destroyed. The owner is not told where the dog is held and is not allowed to visit it.

A Labrador dog in its own garden behind a fence barked at a passerby who complained. This dog faced a destruction order just for noisily protecting his own property. A Pekingese was arrested in similar circumstances.

A well-known Queen's Council has described this Act as almost a charter to help ill-disposed neighbours to harass dog owners. Nevertheless, it is essential that dogs of all kinds and sizes are kept on leads and under control so that no-one, however great their fear of dogs, can say that the dog threatened them or gave them occasion to feel fear.

For further reference: *Your Dog and the Law*, Godfrey Sandys-Winsch (Shaw & Sons Ltd).

USA

The complexity of the modern world exerts a very strong influence on dogs, their owners and the general interaction of dogs and society. This is fully demonstrated by the numerous laws in effect throughout America which relate to the keeping and control of dogs. Certain laws protect dogs from people and people from dogs. There are laws on the books to provide legal remedies for the destruction by dogs of public and private property and laws to mandate acceptable standards of dog-keeping in a community. Because of the great size and diversity of the North American continent and the tremendous number of large and small communities, laws will vary based on the character and needs of the particular city or town. It would be impractical to cite specifics in this book, but certain generalities must be included in this discussion.

Wherever dogs are kept, owners should take care that they are not allowed to roam unsupervised. Dogs at large are in serious danger of death, injury or theft and may also foul or destroy lawns, gardens or outdoor furniture. Unsupervised dogs can kill or injure pets or livestock and may attack people. In cases where small children or frail elderly are set upon by one or more wandering dogs, the outcome can be disastrous.

Dogs running at large may be seized by authorities and, under certain circumstances, humanely destroyed. A farmer discovering a dog worrying livestock may legally shoot the dog to death without any legal penalty. The owner of an unsupervised dog would probably be held liable for loss and damage to property.

Responsible dog owners obey the law by providing secure exercise areas on their own property for their dogs and keeping them on leash in public places. When responsible dog owners do take their pets out in public, they are prepared to clean up and properly dispose of any of their dogs' faeces. Many American communities have enacted laws obliging owners to do so. To the great credit of dog owners, most willingly comply with these local measures; those who do not give the majority a bad name. If your locality has clean-up and/or leash laws, be an exemplary citizen and comply fully at all times. Dog owners can also run foul of the law if their dogs are allowed to create an annoyance by incessant barking. This can especially be a problem in densely populated areas such as large apartment buildings. In this connection, if you rent your living quarters, check your lease to be sure you can keep a dog at all. Many landlords have a no pets clause in their leases and you can find yourself dispossessed if you acquire a dog over the landlord's objections. If you are planning to get a dog, find out in advance what all your civic responsibilities as a dog owner will be and be prepared to meet them. Otherwise, don't become a dog owner.

Generally, dogs are not allowed in food markets, restaurants and office buildings. Dogs are also not allowed on some forms of public transportation at all; with others they are allowed if confined to a carrier. These rules of public access do not apply to guide dogs for the blind, hearing dogs, service dogs for the disabled and certified therapy dogs.

Most communities require that dog be licensed, but the manner in which licenses are issued will vary. It is best to inquire of the town or the local animal control officer for specific details. Communities will also vary regarding the number of dogs which can legally be maintained on one's property. A kennel license is usually required for anyone wishing to breed dogs as a hobby and the owner is wise to cover him or herself by taking one out.

Any business dealing with dogs is subject to the normal laws of the community in this regard. Pet shops, boarding kennels, grooming parlors and the like must all comply with any regulations governing zoning, cleanliness, humane treatment and all the other many factors which will be involved here.

In recent years some municipalities have enacted a 'puppy lemon' law for the protection of buyers. Under this law, a newly-purchased puppy deemed unsaleable for any reason upon veterinary examination, may be returned to the seller for a full refund or the seller is liable for the puppy's veterinary expenses up to the full purchase price of the puppy. In this connection, buyers as well as sellers have a duty to know their rights as well as their obligations.

Many communities are also enacting dangerous dog laws. Unfortunately, there are too many misguided persons in this world who keep aggressive dogs for all the wrong reasons, not the least of which is pit fighting for wagering. Even in our technologically enlightened age, we have still not fully purged ourselves of the lust for blood sports.

The whole subject of dogs and the law is very complex as you can see. Readers in North America are recommended to acquire a copy of The Complete Guide to Dog Law (New York, Howell Book House, 1994) by Deidre E. Gannon, Esq. for a more complete view.

The fundamental rules of dog ownership

Buster, the character on the left, has been created to illustrate the Golden Rules of Dog Ownership in a way that children can readily understand.

The children of all dog owners should be encouraged to follow these principles so that they can enjoy 'their' Buster to the full and so that he fits properly into society. Buster appears later in *The Doglopaedia* (See Chapter 5).

Buster

- likes his own warm basket or box where he can lie quietly out of the way.

- loves going for regular interesting walks whatever the weather.

- adores riding in the back of the car, but likes some fresh air and to be left in a shady spot.

- likes to jump onto beds and chairs but knows it is not allowed.

- much prefers his own drinking and eating bowl as he knows he shouldn't eat from people's plates.

- likes titbits as a reward when he has behaved especially well.

- enjoys visiting food shops but knows it is forbidden.

- likes showing off how obedient he is by sitting, staying and walking to heel.

- is proud of his vaccination certificates.

- But most of all, he wants to be loved and to be part of the family.

- doesn't like having his ears and tail pulled.

- hates being left alone for long periods or being shouted at and kicked.

- is frightened of eating crunchy bones as he knows they could make him gravely ill.

- is upset if he makes a mess on the pavement or in a playground by mistake.

- dislikes being dirty and having a tangled coat.

- is afraid of busy roads so prefers to be on the lead in traffic.

- hates not going away with the family but knows that sometimes he has to go to a good kennel where he will be well looked after.

- dislikes not having an identity disc on his collar in case he gets lost.

- is worried if he is let out on his own, in case he gets run over, upsets other people or can't find his way home.

Useful names and addresses (UK)

Veterinary bodies and associations

British Small Animal Veterinary Association,
Kingsley House, Church Lane, Shurdington, Cheltenham, Glos, GL15 5TQ
Tel: 01242 862994

British Veterinary Association,
7, Mansfield Street, London, W1M 0AT
Tel: 0171 6366541

Royal College of Veterinary Surgeons,
32 Belgrave Square, London, SW1X 8PP
Tel: 01712354971

Welfare Associations

RSPCA
Causeway, Horsham, West Sussex, RH12 1HG
Tel: 01403 264181

Blue Cross
1-5 Hugh Street, Victoria London, SW1V 1QQ
Tel: 0171 8345556

National Canine Defence League
17 Wakeley Street, London, EC1V 7LT
Tel: 0171 8370006

People's Dispensary for Sick Animals,
Whitechapel Way, Priorslee, Telford, Shropshire TF2 9P0
Tel: 01952 290999

Guide Dogs for the Blind Association
Hillfields, Burghfield, Reading, Berks RG77 3YG
Tel: 017535 55711

Hearing Dogs for the Deaf
London Road, Lewknor, Oxon, OX9 5RY
Tel: 01844 353898

Dog Press

Dog World
9 Tufton Street, Ashford, Kent TN23 1QN
Tel: 01233 621877

Our Dogs
5, Oxford Road Station Approach, Manchester, M60 1SX
Tel: 0161 2362660

Kennel Gazette
Kennel Club, 1 Clarges Street, Piccadilly, London, W1Y 8AB

Dogs Today
Pankhurst Farm, Bagshot Road, West End, Nr Woking, Surrey GU24 9QR

Your Dog
Emap Apex, Apex House, Oundle Road, Peterborough, PE2 9NP
Tel: 01733 898100

Charities
Animal Health Trust
PO Box 5, Newmarket, Suffolk OB8 7DW

British Veterinary Association Animal Welfare Foundation
7, Mansfield Street, London, W1M 0AT

USA

Veterinary schools and associations
American Veterinary Medical Association (AVMA), 1931 North Meacham Road, Suite 100, Schaumburg, IL 60173-4360
American Association of Animal Hospitals (AAHA), PO Box 150899, Denver, CO 80215-0899
Association of American Veterinary Medical Colleges, Lester M. Crawford, DVM, 1101 Vermont Avenue, N.W., Suite 710, Washington, DC 20005-3521
Auburn University, College of Veterinary Medicine, 180 Greene Hall, Auburn University, AL 36849
University of California-Davis, School of Veterinary Medicine, Davis, Ca 95616
Cornell University, NY State College of Veterinary Medicine, Ithaca, NY 14853-6401
University of Pennsylvania, School of Veterinary Medicine, 3800 Spruce Street, Philadelphia, PA 19104-6047
Tufts University, School of Veterinary Medicine, 200 Westboro Road, North Grafton, MA 01536

Animal welfare associations and humane societies

American Humane Association (AHA), 63 Inverness Drive, E., Englewood, CO 80112-5117
American Society for the Prevention of Cruelty to Animals (ASPCA), 441 E.92nd Street, New York, 10128
Humane Society of the United States, 2100 L Street NW, Washington, DC 20037
The Delta Society, PO Box 1080, Renton, WA 98057
The Latham Foundation, Latham Plaza, Clement & Schiller Streets, Alameda, CA 94501-1397
Morris Animal Foundation, 45 Inverness Drive, E., Englewood, CO 80112
Therapy Dogs International, 6 Hilltop Road, Mendham, NJ 07945

Major dog publications

AKC Gazette, 51 Madison Avenue, New York, NY 10010
Dog Fancy, Fancy Publications, 3 Burroughs, Irvine, CA 92690
Dog World, McLean Hunter Publishing Corp., 29 N. Wacker Drive, Chicago, IL 60606
Dogs in Canada, 89 Skyway Avenue, 200, Etobicoke, Ont, Canada M9W 6R4

Major registering bodies

American Kennel Club, 5580 Centerview Drive, Raleigh, NC 27606
Canadian Kennel Club, 89 Skyway Avenue, 200, Etobicoke, Ont, CANADA M9W 6R4
United Kennel Club, 100 East Kilgore Street, Kalamazoo, MI 49001

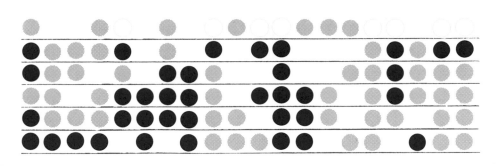

Bulldog · Bullmastiff · Bull Terrier · Cairn Terrier · Cavalier King Charles Sp. · Chihuahua · Chinese Crested · Chow Chow · Clumber Spaniel · Cocker Spaniel English · Collie · Curly coated Retriever · Dachshund (Min) · Daschshund (Standard) · Dalmatian · Dandie Dinmont Terrier · Deerhound · Dobermann · English Setter · English Springer Spaniel

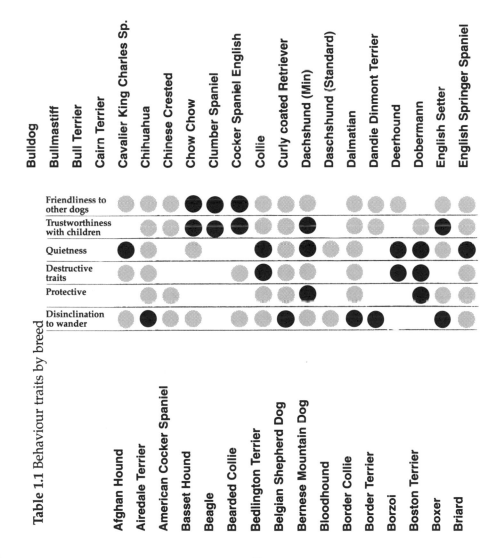

Friendliness to other dogs · Trustworthiness with children · Quietness · Destructive traits · Protective · Disinclination to wander

Table 1.1 Behaviour traits by breed

Afghan Hound · Airedale Terrier · American Cocker Spaniel · Basset Hound · Beagle · Bearded Collie · Bedlington Terrier · Belgian Shepherd Dog · Bernese Mountain Dog · Bloodhound · Border Collie · Border Terrier · Borzoi · Boston Terrier · Boxer · Briard

29

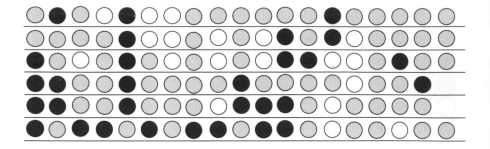

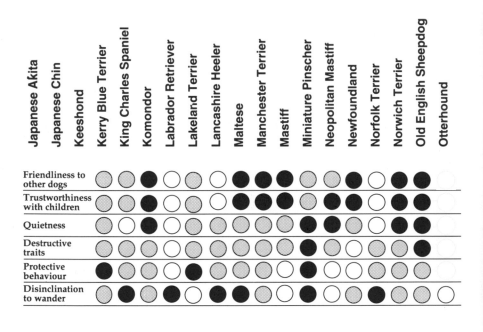

Above average score

Average score

Below average score

Schnauzer (Standard)
Scottish Terrier
Sealyham Terrier
Shetland Sheepdog
Skye Terrier
Soft Coat Wheaten Terrier
Staffordshire Bull Terrier
Sussex Spaniel
Tibetan Spaniel
Tibetan Terrier
Weimaraner
Welsh Corgi (Cardigan)
Welsh Corgi (Pembroke)
Welsh Springer Spaniel
Welsh Terrier
West Highland White Ter.
Whippet
Yorkshire Terrier

Papillon
Parson Jack Russell Terrier
Pekingese
Pt. Basset Griffon Vendeen
Pharoah Hound
Pointer
Poodle (Standard)
Poodle (Toy)
Pug
Puli
Pyrenean Mountain Dog
Rhodesian Ridgeback
Rottweiler
St Bernard
Saluki
Samoyed
Schipperke
Schnauzer (Giant)
Schnauzer (Min)

Table 1.2 Obtaining a purebred dog

	Pedigree puppy from 6½ weeks	Pedigree adult direct from first owners	Pedigree adult from breed rescue service	Pedigree adult kennel surplus animal
Purchase price	Average £150–£300 ($250–$500); rare breeds up to £1,000 ($1,650). Resale value drops sharply after 16 weeks except for major show winners.	Nominal price unless major show winner.	Donation requested. Home probably inspected before you are considered for ownership.	Nominal (negotiable).
Maintenance costs	High in first year then levels out according to size and grooming needs.	Average for breed.	If medical history unknown, there may be hidden costs. May need rehabilitation and careful feeding.	Average for breed.
Precautions on purchase	Essential to see the dam. Visit the sire if possible, also see adolescents in the breed. Consult vet about possible inherited diseases, and suitability of the breed as a pet in your home and locality. See also Table 1.1.	Ensure that the seller has the right to dispose of the dog, and that no breeding term agree-ments are unfulfilled. Check health record with veterinary surgeon who has attended the dog, or ask your own vet to contact the first owner's vet.	Try to find out as much as possible of the dog's background. As it may be possible for a previous owner to try to reclaim the dog, get a signed statement that it has been made over to you by the rescue organisation.	Consider deeply whether a dog which has only lived a kennel life will make a suitable pet. Do not expect to you for removing it from the environment it grew up in.
Pedigree, registration and transfer of ownership form	Signed pedigree should be given at the time of purchase. Delay not uncommon for Kennel Club forms.	Pedigree should be supplied. Obtain a transfer of ownership from from the Kennel Club and request first owners to sign it. Transfer to your ownership as soon as possible.	Pedigrees not given with rescued dogs, even if the rescue society has them.	Pedigree may be withheld to prevent future breeding.
Vaccinations necessary	Full course as recommended by veterinary surgeon.	Vaccination certificates should be available. Boosters if due.	Full booster vaccinations.	Vaccination certificate should be available. Boosters, if due.
Insurance and veterinary fees	Can be enrolled from the age of 8 weeks. Claims payable from 2 weeks thereafter.	Enrol at once if under 8 years old. Previous illnesses may be subject to exclusion.	Enrol at once if under 8 years old.	Enrol at once if under 8 years old. Previous conditions may be subject to exclusion.

Table 1.2 (continued)

	Pedigree puppy from 6½ weeks	Pedigree adult direct from first owners	Pedigree adult from breed rescue service	Pedigree adult kennel surplus animal
Possibility of breeding	Bitches: possible under the guidance of original breeder. Males: No demand for services unless a major show winner. Stud use inadvisable in a companion dog.	Bitches: on veterinary advice only Males: no demand. Inadvisable in a companion dog.	Not advisable and many services forbid it. You and your home may be subjected to periodic inspection to see if the dog is happy.	Failure to breed easily is a probable reason for disposal. Not advisable.
Health status to be expected	Should be in first class condition. Parents should have been screened for hereditary diseases and copies of current certificates given. Illness may already be in incubation stages and/or may be brought on by stress at change of home.	Life history of illness should be supplied. Veterinary check advisable before dog is acquired. Ask when oestrous period due and if contraceptive medication has been given.	Veterinary check advisable before dog is acquired. May need a lot of care or veterinary attention if dog has been deprived or cruelly treated.	Should be in first class condition. Bitches: ask for record of oestrous periods and/or contraceptive medication used.
Feeding	As prescribed by breeder for first 2 weeks. Feed 4/5 times a day. Make feeding changes gradually.	Feed what the dog has been accustomed to for 2 weeks. Make changes gradually.	Rescue kennel should advise what suits the dog.	Feed as the kennel did for 2 weeks for possible. Change gradually to domestic type feeding.
Temperament	According to breed and inherited traits. See Table 1.1	Make in-depth enquiries about phobias.	Rescue service should screen but may have an over-optimistic viewpoint because of familiarity with the breed.	May alter considerably when kept as a single pet.
House-training	Quick to average, influenced by owner's dedication and weather conditions.	Should be house-trained but may lapse initially in unfamiliar conditions.	May lapse in house-training through time spent in kennels.	May not have been trained; may be difficult to train in adult life. Probably been used to having access to run throughout daylight hours.
Suitability as pet in average domestic situation	High/medium/low according to breed and inherited characteristics.	Probably good. May be mentally disturbed for weeks/months through changing homes.	Unknown. May be a delinquent which may or may not reform even with training.	May be unhappy as a sole pet. May be claustrophobic and orientated only to other dogs.

Table 1.2 (continued)

	Pedigree puppy from 6½ weeks	Pedigree adult direct from first owners	Pedigree adult from breed rescue service	Pedigree adult kennel surplus animal
Behaviour faults to watch for	Biting, snapping when restrained, excitability, furniture gnawing. Hypersexuality in males.	May be no faults, but may be almost untrained. May be aggressive over food and feeding bowls, towards other animals or certain categories of people, especially men and children. Seek veterinary advice regarding behaviour modification techniques.	May be none at first but behaviour patterns will emerge as the dog becomes confident in your home. Close observation of reactions and caution is advised. Inappropriate behaviour should be corrected promptly.	May show phobias and fears, timidity or aggression at removal from supportive pack situation and complete change of environment. May have no urban lead training or familiarity with traffic.
Activities with your dog	Beauty shows right up to Championship Show level; Agility and Obedience competitions; sponsored walks; swims; water rescue in appropriate breeds.	All shows if dog is registered.	Agility, Obedience, etc.	Unlikely to be suitable for top-class shows, probably not suitable for competitive obedience.

Table 1.3 Obtaining a mongrel dog or cross-bred

	Mongrel puppy from 6½ weeks	Cross-bred puppy	Mongrel adult from Rescue Society
Purchase price	Low. Average £30. ($50). Do not accept bull breed crosses	£40–£60 ($70–$100)	Average £30 ($50) donation.
Maintenance costs	High in first year, then levels out according to size.	High in first year then levels out according to size.	Average. Medical history unknown; there may be hidden illness or disability.
Precautions on purchase	Make sure the puppy is weaned and can eat solid food. See dam/sire if possible. Buy from the premises where the puppy was born. Do not buy a puppy which has made a long journey or changed ownership already, as risk of infectious disease is increased when puppies are moved between dealers.	Find out the breeds of the parents and how/why cross was made. Take veterinary advice on suitability of the cross. See also under Mongrel puppy.	Consult with kennel staff about the suitability of the dog for your family. Have they tested its reactions to children, old people, men/women, ethnic minorities?

Table 1.3 (continued)

	Mongrel puppy from 6½ weeks	Cross-bred puppy	Mongrel adult from Rescue Society
Possibility of breeding	Not advisable. Consider neutering of both sexes.	Possibility of breeding back to one of its component breeds, but very little chance of selling a whole litter.	Consider neutering of both sexes to curb desire to wander as dogs and bitches may have had mating experience..
Vaccinations necessary	Full course as advised by veterinary surgeon.	As for mongrel puppy.	Full booster course unless rescue society has given current vaccination.
Insurance for veterinary fees	As for pedigree puppy.	As for pedigree puppy.	Enrol at once if under 8 years old.
Health status to be expected	May be problematical. Worming routine will be necessary; check for fleas, lice etc and get veterinary advice for de-fleaing.	Skin and coat may give problems through crossing of coat types.	Probably average health but early neglect or ill-treatment may predispose to ill-health in middle to old age.
Feeding	As pedigree puppy.	As pedigree puppy.	Feed small meals frequently until you can assess the state of the dog's digestive system. May be compulsive eater and/or may be inclined to eat its own faeces.
Suitability as pet	Unknown quantity. Will require supervision and good fencing as parents may have been habitual vagrants.	May be difficult to train. Looks may favour one parent but behaviour traits the other.	Can be very successful but may be difficult to convert into a well-mannered pet.
Temperament	May be hyperactive.	Inherited behaviours may be in conflict, eg guard dog crossed with gun dog.	Long-term kennelling in a rescue kennel can alter the temperament, encouraging barking, hyperactivity or aggression.
House-training	Average to short time to house-train.	As mongrel.	May be difficult to house-train.
Behaviour faults to watch for	Extreme submission or aggression. Tendency to wander. Scavenging. Excess barking.	As mongrel.	Probably chronic escaper. May have nervous or aggressive reaction to other dogs or even to familiar people handling certain articles such as brooms.
Activities to undertake with your dog	Exemption, beauty and fun shows; obedience tests; agility; sponsored walks.	As mongrel.	Exemption, beauty and fun shows; obedience; sponsored walks.

Table 1.4 The oestrous cycle

Stage of cycle	Duration	Comment
Pro-oestrus	Average 9 days	This stage is the beginning of heat. The vulva is swollen and there is blood-stained discharge. Although the bitch is attractive to dogs she will not allow them to mate her.
Oestrus	Average 9 days	This stage is defined as the period when the bitch will accept the male. The vulva is much enlarged and turgid. The discharge is straw coloured rather than blood stained. Ovulation occurs about 2 days after the start of oestrus.
Met-oestrus	Average 90 days	The stage occurs in the unmated bitch and hormone changes equivalent to those seen in pregnancy occur. At the end of this stage the bitch may show signs of false pregnancy. The beginning of this stage and its end are not marked by any obvious external signs.
Anoestrus	Variable – but on average $2^1/_2$ months	The duration of anoestrus largely determines how frequently the bitch will come in season. This is the period of sexual inactivity between cycles.

Table 1.5 Care of the elderly dog

	Signs	Action	Comment
Deterioration of general health	Loss of energy, poor coat, dullness, body odour, weakness	Veterinary consultation, possibly complete blood profile to monitor function of body organs	Laboratory screening of a small blood sample may reveal need for dietary adjustment and mineral/vitamin supplementation
Senility	Increased demand for owner's company, disorientation, restlessness	Veterinary check; medication may be necessary	The old dog will have good days and worse days; with sympathy and tolerance the old dog will still have a happy life
Loss of hearing	Increased barking, altered voice, failure to respond to call	Veterinary check to eliminate ear disease	Once aware of the disability, the owner should take special care to keep the dog close on walks and to protect it from danger; 'fetch' rather than call the dog
Deteriorating sight	Bluish film over the eyeball, scars on eye surface, blundering into furniture, reluctance to go out at night and/or in bright sunlight	Veterinary check to see if treatment will improve the condition	A partially or even completely blind dog can live a contented life in familiar surroundings provided care is taken not to move furniture etc, and to protect the dog from danger. Unless there are particular risks in its environment or to people likely to come into contact with it, a dog should not be destroyed solely because it is blind.
Incontinence	Wet beds, puddles where dog sits down	Veterinary consultation to check for disease; medication may be necessary but 'leaks' may be due to reluctance to rise from bed	Cover cushions with plastic bags and lay porous polyester fur rug on top so that dog is not lying in a puddle
Reduced bladder capacity	Dog asking to go out several times a night or puddles in the room where it sleeps – often on the doormat	Veterinary surgeon may prescribe a medicine which will help regulate urination pattern but often little can be done	Lapses of house-training must be excused in the very old

Table 1.5 (continued)

	Signs	Action	Comment
Constipation	Irregular passage of faeces, difficulty in passing faeces, difficulty in adopting normal excretory posture	Increase fibre in diet, via bran biscuits or grated vegetables and apples; medicinal paraffin (up to 1 tablespoon/15ml) may be given as lubricant	Faeces should ideally be passed twice a day and at least once daily
Changed coat character	Even smooth-coated dogs tend to an over-growth of coat in old age; nails grow at an accelerated rate	'Strip' thickened areas of coat regularly; give more frequent baths and face washes; regular clipping of nails by veterinary surgeon makes walking more comfortable	Sunflower oil (1 teaspoon–1 tablespoon/5–15ml according to size), given in the food, helps prevent dryness of coat
Tooth decay	Painful eating, refusal of hard biscuit, unpleasant mouth odour	Veterinary consultation	Extraction of decayed teeth can make a great improvement in total health
Digestive problems	Vomiting of food or saliva and bile; diarrhoea; constipation	Revert to puppy feeding regime of 3–4 small meals daily. Seek veterinary advice on diet – less protein may be needed.	Cooked eggs are the most easily digested form of protein. Special diets are available through veterinary surgeons.
Inappetence	Total food refusal	Seek veterinary advice if no food taken for 48 hours	Complan, Brands Essence and sponge cake are useful invalid foods.
Reduced mobility	Difficulty in rising from bed, tottering gait, unable to use hind legs	Veterinary consultation, since it is possible to effect an improvement by medication	Warmth, via a heated pad, a comfortable bed (polystyrene bean bags are good), a coat to be worn even indoors and hand massage of the limbs all help to increase mobility. Make sure to protect from dangerous falls; put a barrier across the stairs to prevent the dog climbing and falling down. Gentle exercise should be given whenever the dog feels able to go for a walk

2
Nutrition and feeding

Nutrient requirements
Choice of foods
Practical feeding
Obesity

The food eaten by different dogs varies considerably yet the majority grow well and remain healthy. This is because dogs, like any other animal, have requirements for specific nutrients rather than particular foods and provided these needs are met, the source (prepared petfoods, fresh raw materials or a mixture) is not particularly relevant.

Although the dog is a member of the mammalian order Carnivora, in a nutrition sense it is more accurately defines ad omnivorous, since it is able to survive on a diet made entirely of materials of animal or vegetable origin. Like the cat it is equipped with strong, sharp teeth designed for tearing and cutting meat, but unlike the cat it has adapted a much more flexible and varied diet than one consisting largely of animal tissues.

The key to proper feeding is a 'balanced' diet; one which contains appropriate quantities of all essential nutrients, neither too little nor too much. It also embraces other important characteristics of foodstuffs often taken for granted – palatability, digestibility, concentration and safety. A food may appear to be suitable on paper because chemical analysis shows that it contains all the essential nutrient in the right proportions, but if it is not palatable enough to be eaten, or if the nutrients are bound in such a way to prevent their digestion and absorption, it is not the balanced diet it appears to be. Similarly the food must be sufficiently concentrated to allow the dog to take in enough to meet its particular nutrient needs, and should be free from any toxins, bacteria or parasites which might harm the dog.

Nutrient requirements

Dogs need proteins, fats, minerals, vitamins and water. They can also utilise carbohydrate although it cannot strictly be described as essential. Most foods contain a mixture of some or all of these nutrient classes and therefore careful combination of different foodstuffs will result in a suitable diet. Nutrients are required in the diet in different quantities. As shown in Table 2.1, a dog needs 20 times as much protein as calcium and 100,000 times as much protein as riboflavin (vitamin B$_2$). Even so, if any essential nutrient is missing or present in insufficient quantity, the whole diet will be inadequate.

Energy

In addition to providing specific nutrients, food also provides energy or calories. Energy is needed not just for muscular activity or exercise, but also for maintenance of body temperature and for processes necessary for life such as breathing and heart function. Even a sleeping dog uses energy.

There are many factors which affect energy requirements. Puppy growth, pregnancy and lactation increase the requirement, but for normal adult dogs the most important factor is body weight. Figure 2.1 shows that although larger dogs have a greater requirement, this is not strictly in proportion to their bodyweight. A range in energy requirement is shown to allow for other influences such as age, sex, level of activity and environmental temperature.

Figure 2.1 Factors determining energy requirements.

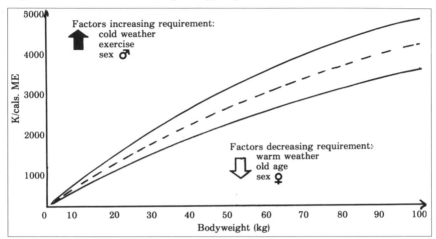

The energy requirements of every dog will change through its lifetime. Figure 2.2 gives a theoretical example of a typical Labrador Retriever bitch, showing energy intake and bodyweight through puppyhood, two litters, a period of working and into old age. While many dogs will not experience such large fluctuations, it is important that owners recognise that needs may vary through the dog's life cycle and that food intake will need to be adjusted accordingly.

The energy in food comes from protein, fat and carbohydrate which are oxidised, or burned, in working tissues to release energy. Each gram of protein and carbohydrate provides about 4 kcal while fat supplies double that amount. Excessive intake of any of these nutrients will lead to the accumulation of energy as body fat, inadequate energy intake will result in poor growth (in puppies) and weight loss (in adult dogs). It is, therefore, important to provide the correct number of calories for the particular dog at the specific stage in its life cycle, taking into consideration its lifestyle and the environment in which it lives.

Protein

Proteins are very long molecules made up of chains of many small units called amino acids – rather like a string of beads. There are about 20 different amino acids, but since each combination produces a protein with specific characteristics, there is an almost infinite variety of proteins. Proteins are essential constituents of the cells which make up the body tissues, having several important functions in the regulation of metabolism (as enzymes and some hormones); in a structural role in cell walls and muscle fibre, in transport of essential materials, and in the body's defence against disease.

The protein requirements of growing puppies and pregnant and lactating bitches are greater, weight for weight, than normal adult dogs. This is because protein is necessary

Figure 2.2 The history of energy requirements for one bitch

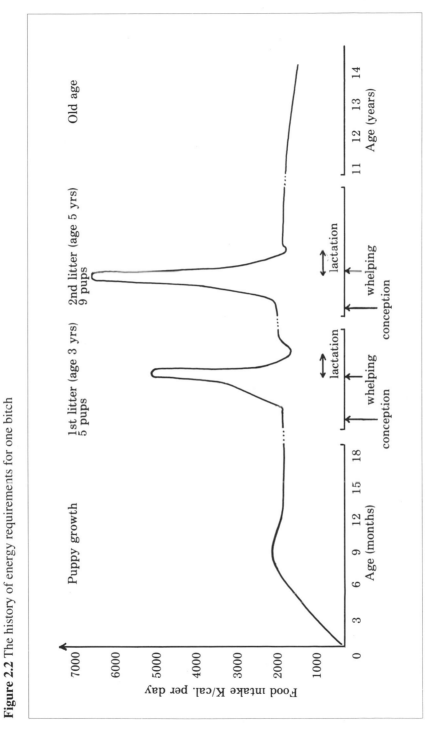

for the synthesis of new tissue, and for the production of milk. However, even adult dogs need to replace protein broken down and lost from the body every day, mostly in the urine but also in faeces and in hair growth.

Protein quality is an important consideration in the selection of foodstuffs and is governed by two factors – digestibility and the amino acid profile. Digestible protein is that part which is absorbed through the gut wall into the body and not lost in the faeces. The digestibility of protein in the dog can vary from as low as 50 per cent in some cereals up to 95 per cent for milk or egg protein. The amino acid profile reflects which of the 20 amino acids are present in the protein. This is particularly important as 10 of these are essential to the dog. Essential amino acids cannot be synthesised in sufficient quantities by the body and must, therefore, be provided in the diet. Non-essential amino acids are equally necessary, but can be synthesised if sufficient raw materials are present (in the form of excess amounts of other amino acids and non-protein nitrogen). Milk and eggs contain the greatest proportions of essential amino acids; cereals the least. This does not mean, however, that dogs should be fed entirely on meat, milk and eggs but that judicious mixing may be necessary if cereals form a large part of the diet.

Protein deficiency can result from either insufficient dietary protein or from a shortage of particular amino acids. The observable signs are largely non-specific – poor growth or weight loss, loss of appetite, rough and dull hair coat and increased susceptibility to disease. Table 2.1 shows that the recommended protein allowance is 22 per cent of the dry matter of the food. This is an extremely generous allowance and covers all stages of the life cycle including puppy growth and breeding. In fact, assuming a good quality protein is fed, 10 per cent would probably be quite adequate for non-breeding adult dogs.

Protein which is surplus to the body's requirements is *not* laid down as additional muscle but is converted to fat and stored as adipose tissue. Feeding extra protein to produce 'body' will only produce fat.

Fat

Fat has several roles in the nutrition of the dog: it is a very concentrated source of energy, it enhances the palatability of many foods and it serves as a carrier for the fat-soluble vitamins A, D, E and K. Its most important function, however, is as a source of the essential fatty acids, particularly linoleic acid, which are used to form part of the cell walls and which are necessary for the synthesis of prostaglandins. Linoleic acid deficiency results in a coarse dry coat, thick dandruff, skin lesions and in reproductive failure. Dogs with this deficiency usually respond quickly to dietary supplementation with sunflower oil which is a rich source of linoleic acid.

Fat is well digested by healthy dogs. The Alaskan Husky's traditional diet is seal meat which is two thirds fat and these dogs thrive despite adverse environmental conditions and hard work. However, any diet with a very high fat content may need supplementation with other nutrients – such diets will be eaten in smaller quantities, therefore other nutrients should be present in higher proportions to ensure that daily requirements are met. It is important to note that diets containing very high levels of polyunsaturated fats may become rancid with the destruction of nutrients, particularly vitamin E.

Carbohydrates

It has been assumed for many years that while dogs are good at utilising carbohydrate as an energy source, it is not an essential dietary requirement. This is because dogs are able to synthesise their glucose requirement from dietary fat and protein if these are present in sufficient quantity. However, recent work in the USA has indicated that some pregnant bitches need a dietary source of carbohydrate in order to produce healthy puppies. It is difficult to reconcile this with what we know of the dog's evolutionary history, as the prey which formed the diet would contain very little carbohydrate. Whether this finding is confirmed or not is largely academic, as the majority of dogs are traditionally fed diets which contain large proportions of carbohydrates as biscuit or meal.

There are three major groups of carbohydrates in foods: sugars, starches and the indigestible polysaccharides like cellulose. Sugars are easily digestible and are palatable to dogs which tend to have a 'sweet tooth'. Starches are long chains of the simple sugar units. They are easily digested by enzymes (amylases) in the digestive tract after the starch is degraded by cooking or crushing. Untreated starch is much more difficult to digest and dogs fed on raw potatoes or uncrushed cereal are likely to suffer from diarrhoea and flatulence as the starch passes undigested to the large intestine where it is fermented by bacteria.

The indigestible polysaccharides can be collectively grouped under the title of 'dietary fibre' or 'roughage'. This passes through the digestive tract relatively unchanged, adding bulk. Because it acts like a sponge retaining water, it tends to reduce the incidence of constipation (by keeping stools soft) and diarrhoea (by mopping up surplus fluid). Although many benefits associated with the intake of high levels of dietary fibre have been described in man, these are mostly associated with diseases not commonly seen in dogs. The action of fibre in the human gut is through a reduction of transit time (the time taken for food to pass through the digestive system) and the dog already has a much shorter transit time than man. It seems likely therefore that if there are any uses for dietary fibre in dog nutrition, these are limited to the management of constipation, diarrhoea and diabetes and possibly obesity.

The incorporation of high levels of fibre in the diet of normal dogs may decrease the availability of absorption of other nutrients, especially minerals. It will also markedly increase faecal volume; consequently not more than 10 per cent of the dry matter of the food should be made up of dietary fibre (less than this for puppies).

Vitamins

Although required in very small amounts, vitamins are necessary for normal health and function. A vitamin is an organic compound which plays an essential part in the regulation of various metabolic pathways and is broken down in the process. Vitamins are distinguished from other compounds with similar functions in that the animal is unable to synthesise replacements and must obtain a dietary source.

It is usual to describe the different vitamins by the major specific sign of deficiency. Thus vitamin A is popularly associated with sight, since deficiencies lead to an impairment of vision; vitamin E with reproduction; and so on. This is an over-simplification since deficiencies of all the vitamins have signs in common, particularly poor appetite, general loss of condition and poor growth. Table 2.2 shows those vitamins which are needed by dogs (note dogs do not require vitamin C) and their dietary source, main functions, signs of deficiency and problems associated with excessive intake.

Vitamins are classified according to their solubility in either water or fat. This apparently arbitrary division has practical nutritional consequences. The water-soluble vitamins are not retained in the body when given in excess and are lost in the urine. Since they are not stored, regular intake is necessary. Conversely, the fat-soluble vitamins A, D, E and K are retained when fed in excess of requirements. While daily intake of these vitamins is necessary, there is a danger of accumulation following prolonged overfeeding. Vitamins E and K are unlikely to be toxic, but overfeeding of vitamins A and D has been shown to have serious results, principally malformation of the bones (vitamin A) and calcification of the soft tissues (vitamin D). It is understandable that owners who want to do the best for their dog are tempted to give generous supplements 'just to make sure' but the outcome may be tragic. Most diets need no supplementation, but where this is necessary great care should be taken to ensure that the manufacturer's instructions are followed closely and that the same vitamin is not being given several times under different proprietary names.

Minerals

Dogs require about 20 minerals, but some are needed in such small quantities that the absolute requirements have not been established. These trace elements are present in most common foodstuffs and deficiencies are most unlikely. Minerals have three important functions:

- as structural components of bones and teeth (calcium, phosphorus and magnesium);
- as soluble salts which control fluid balance (sodium chloride in blood and extracellular fluid; potassium, magnesium and phosphorus inside body cells);
- in enzymes and other proteins (such as iron in haemoglobin).

Table 2.3 gives details of the minerals required by dogs. Again, many are toxic if given in repeated overdoses and indiscriminate supplementation should be avoided. Some breeders believe that the larger breeds have special requirements for calcium and phosphorus as these are the principal mineral constituents of bone. However, the greater total food requirement of these dogs will ensure appropriate calcium intake, provided the diet is balanced.

Water

Water should be considered in conjunction with feeding. A shortage of water leads to illness and death more quickly than that of any other nutrient and a fresh supply of drinking water is an essential part of a dog's diet.

Water is necessary for many different functions in the body. It is used as a transport medium (blood), the route for elimination of toxic wastes (urine), for heat loss (evaporation), to allow the chemical reactions necessary for life (in digestion and within the body cells) and many other functions. Water balance is controlled within quite narrow limits, and since some water loss from the body is obligatory, daily intake is essential.

Water is taken into the body in several forms: in fluid drunk, as a part of food and in the water released when protein, fat and carbohydrate are broken down. It is lost in faeces, urine, by evaporation (mainly from the lungs), and in the milk of lactating bitches. The precise daily requirement of each dog will depend on its particular situation and therefore a plentiful supply of clean drinking water should always be available.

Choice of foods

There are many different ways of satisfying the need for nutrients. For dogs these fall broadly into two categories – the use of prepared petfoods and of home-made diets. Neither of these methods is frankly right or wrong, each having different advantages and disadvantages.

Prepared petfoods

Prepared petfoods from reputable companies provide a correctly balanced diet – guaranteed nutrition, good palatability and digestibility, suitable energy density and safety, in addition to convenience. They also offer variety without loss of consistency. Table 24 shows the main categories of prepared food, classified according to method of preservation, together with typical ingredients and characteristics. Most of the dogs in the population are normal adult dogs and the majority of foods are intended to meet the needs of this group. More specialised foods are readily available to meet the requirements of other lifecycles stages, such as puppy growth.

Foods for adult dogs can be divided into complete and complementary (those intended to be mixed with other foods, eg canned food with biscuit. This diversification is not as complicated as it may seem at first sight; the label should specify the intended role, give a guide to quantity and may also state how the food has been developed and tested. Complete diets are carefully balanced to provide for all a dog needs, and do not need supplementation. Dog owners should be careful when choosing products to make sure that they are comparing like with like. The contents are often expressed in different ways. To avoid confusion, the current tendency is to express the amounts of nutrients present in the food in relation to the kcal provided (usually the amount per 400 or 1000 kcal).

Although not necessary, complete prepared petfoods *can* be supplemented with fresh foods in the firm or left-overs of food prepared for the family, or table scraps. If this is done the amount of prepared petfood could be reduced proportionally; this extra source of nutrients should not make up more than 15-20 per cent of the daily intake.

Fresh foods

Considerable skill is necessary to put together a satisfactory diet from fresh raw materials. It is not enough simply to buy 'meat', whether best steak or pet mince, on the assumption that this is the natural diet of a dog. As a hunter the dog did not restrict itself to the muscle meat of its prey, but in the whole body, so obtaining minerals, vitamins and even roughage from the bones, brains, skin, gut and gut contents. Muscle meat alone cannot form a balanced diet as it contains inadequate amounts of calcium, iodine, copper and the fat-soluble vitamins. It is possible to calculate that to meet its calcium requirement, a half-grown Labrador Retriever would need to eat seven times its own bodyweight in lean meat every day! Nevertheless, meat (including offals and tripe) is an excellent source of protein and, with careful supplementation, can form the basis of a reasonable diet. Table 2.5 shows the main groups of foods commonly used for pet feeding, with a summary of their nutrient content. Do remember that the same food type can vary greatly in quality from one source to another and, in the case of meat, from one cut to another. As a consequence, digestibility and calorie content can be very variable, making the formulation of a suitable diet using fresh foods very difficult if not impossible.

Other raw materials have different problems. For example, cow's milk contains the milk sugar lactose in substantial quantities, bitchs' milk contains little and many puppies lose the ability to digest lactose after weaning. When fed cows' milk, such puppies (and adult dogs) develop severe diarrhoea as a result of lactose intolerance. Eggs, when fed raw in substantial quantities, may cause a vitamin deficiency; this is because raw egg white contains a substance called avidin which binds biotin (a water-soluble vitamin) and makes it unavailable. Heating destroys avidin and therefore eggs should be fed cooked. Mineral availability can be a problem when some cereals are fed, as one of their constituents binds to certain minerals, limiting their availability.

Although there are some materials which can be fed raw, cooking is advisable for most foods, particularly meats. Cooking will kill most bacteria and parasites and will improve the digestibility of some materials. However, over-cooking should be avoided as this will reduce the food value of proteins and destroy vitamins. Minerals and vitamins may be lost if the cooking water is discarded.

The same principles of hygiene should be employed in the preparation of food for pets as for the family. The list in Table 2.6 gives some reminders of basic principles. These include care in purchase, storage, preparation and feeding.

Supplementation

As mentioned earlier, most prepared petfoods, when fed as directed, require no additional supplementation. The larger manufacturers have large analytical laboratories which run continuous checks on the mineral and vitamin contents of their foods, and also conduct long-term feeding trials. Home-made diets based on offal and fresh meats usually do require some supplementation, even when a good quality biscuit or meal is fed. The dangers of excessive supplementation have already been outlined, these are real dangers and should not be ignored.

Table 2.7 shows the various supplements available to dog owners. These range from proprietary vitamin supplements to herbal remedies, stopping just short of witchcraft. Some, such as garlic tablets and raspberry powders, have little scientific basis but are quite harmless.

Practical feeding

Adult dogs

The majority of dogs are normal, healthy, non-working, non-breeding animals. These are by far the easiest to feed, having the least demanding nutrient requirements, and in general their problems are those of over-feeding rather than nutrient deficiencies.

Adult dogs will thrive on all diet types from complete dry foods, canned foods alone or with biscuit, carefully constructed home-made mixtures of fresh foods. Sudden changes in diet should be avoided as this may lead to diarrhoea and if a new food is introduced it should be done gradually over 5-6 days. Dogs left in boarding kennels or taken on holiday should be fed their usual food if possible, as a change of diet adds to the stress involved. Adult dogs need to be fed only once a day, preferably at the same time, at the convenience of the owner. Some dog owners routinely fast their dogs on one day a week and while this practice is not recommended for all dogs, it appears to have no ill effect on those involved.

The quantities of food required depend on several factors including temperature. Dogs living outside in winter will require more food to maintain bodyweight than in other seasons. In very hot weather, water supply is a critical factor since the dog relies on panting, with evaporation of water from the respiratory tract and tongue, to lose heat and maintain body temperature within normal limits.

Dogs which are working also have higher energy needs than pet dogs of the same size, sex and age. This group includes police and army dogs, sheep dogs and, of course, sledge dogs. They are usually fed after a day's work, when they are tired, and should be given a palatable, more concentrated food to ensure that their energy requirements are met in a reasonable amount of food. Extensive exercise increases energy requirement, particularly in a cold climate. Pedigree Chum Formula Activity Plus is an example of a prepared food designed to meet the needs of dogs in this group.

Pregnancy and lactation

Just as a human mother-to-be is often mistakenly encouraged to 'eat for two', many dogs are overfed in pregnancy. In dogs the fertilised eggs are not attached to the wall of the uterus until 2-3 weeks after mating, later than in other mammals, and the additional demand for nutrients is negligible until the sixth or seventh week of gestation. In the last 3 weeks of pregnancy the foetuses grow rapidly. The provision of extra energy and nutrients is thus important at this stage. Failure to supply sufficient food will affect the condition of the bitch and eventually the puppies will suffer, being born at best small and at worst malformed or dead.

If the bitch is a reasonable weight at mating, well-covered but not fat, no changes need to be made to her normal balanced diet until the sixth or seventh week after mating. Although about 30-40 per cent more food will be required during the last days of pregnancy, it is a good idea to scale this so that the amount increases gradually. A 10 per cent increase per week from the sixth or seventh week is a practical and appropriate scheme, and experience has shown that this results in healthy puppies of good size and a bitch whose weight after whelping is little different from weight at mating.

It may be necessary to divide the allocation into several small meals towards the end of pregnancy as the uterus takes up more and more space in the abdomen, limiting the volume of the stomach. The specially concentrated diets widely available are ideal; a diet of canned food balanced for adult maintenance is too dilute and bulky.

There may be some loss of appetite immediately before whelping. This is quite normal but if it persists into lactation, veterinary attention should be sought as

Figure 2.3 Growth of pups *in utero*.

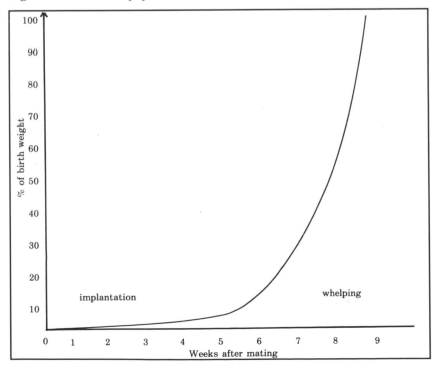

inappetence at this time may be associated with a variety of clinical conditions and; in any case, prolonged food deprivation will limit milk production. Lactation is the most nutritionally demanding stage of a bitch's lifecycle. Dogs' milk is very concentrated (having twice the energy, dry matter, protein and fat of cows' milk) and requires a considerable amount of food and energy to produce. It has been shown that at peak lactation, some bitches produce up to 7.5 per cent of their own bodyweight in milk every day. Even though the majority produce around 4 per cent, this is still a considerably output. During the third and fourth weeks after whelping, a bitch may need as much as four times her normal daily intake. The exact quantity depends on the size of the litter and whether the pups have any other source of nutrients in addition to the bitch's milk. The food may need to be divided into several small meals and should be concentrated and palatable. Some dogs may be left to determine their own intake, but others will overeat if allowed to eat to appetite and a careful watch of intake and bodyweight will be necessary. An unlimited supply of fresh drinking water will also be necessary.

Weaning should be a gradual process. An abrupt separation of bitch and puppies may lead to mastitis in the bitch and a check in growth of the puppies. Puppies may be offered small amounts of soft food from as early as 2 weeks of age, but only if they show an interest. Much will depend on the size of the litter and the milk supply of the bitch and however early the puppies take alternative foods, the bitch's milk should remain the prime source of nutrients until the puppies are at least 4 weeks old. Gradual separation and withdrawal of the bitch will allow her milk supply to dry up without the use of medicaments and allow the puppies to adapt to their new food naturally. It may be advisable to cut the bitch's food down to half the maintenance level immediately after total separation but if the bitch has lost condition during lactation she will need additional food to bring bodyweight back up to normal as soon as her milk supply has diminished and weaning is completed.

Puppies

Puppies have special feeding requirements. They require large amounts of food in relation to bodyweight, but their stomachs have very limited capacity. Very young puppies need 2-3 times as much food as an adult dog of the same weight (comparing, for example, a 7kg (15lb) Boxer puppy with an adult Cairn Terrier, Figure 2.4) because they need to supply energy for maintenance and activity in addition to the materials for growth. It is very important to allow such puppies the opportunity to satisfy their needs, despite the small capacity, and for this reason the total food allocation after weaning should be divided into 4-5 meals spread as far apart as possible throughout the day, and a more concentrated food, such as Pedigree Chum Puppy Food or Pedigree Formula Junior used. As the puppies grow this can be cut down to 2-3 meals and eventually to the single meal of the adult.

The question of exactly how much food is difficult to answer in general terms. The values in Figure 2.4 are derived from the National Research Council's recommendations, but these are intended only as a guide and individual puppy's needs will vary. It is now known that to cram food into puppies, or to allow free access to a palatable diet in an attempt to achieve very rapid early growth may lead to bone disorders, especially in the larger breeds. On the other hand puppies need to grow quickly enough to fulfil their genetic potential for size before the bones lose their ability to increase in length. As with many aspects of nutrition, it is a question of moderation and balance and it is ultimately the responsibility of the owner to assess the health and condition of their dog, taking advice where appropriate from other owners and breeders and, of course, their veterinary surgeon.

Figure 2.4 Energy requirements at different stages of lifecycle.

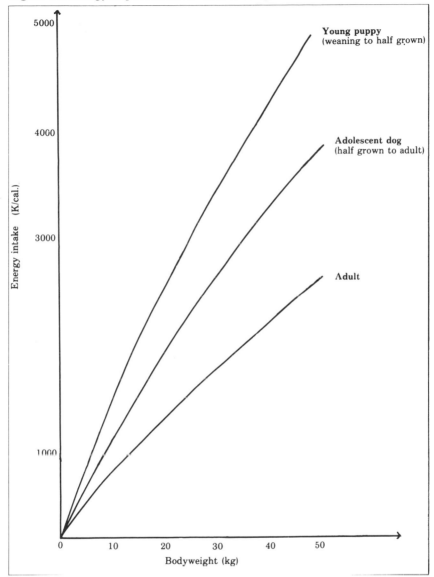

Not all foods are suitable for puppies. Volume should be limited and therefore the food may need to be more concentrated than some of the foods available for adult dogs. Similarly some of the dry foods fed to adult dogs may come in pieces that are too large and hard for puppies to eat or be insufficiently digestible. Recently introduced specially formulated dry foods overcome these problems. In addition to larger quantities of food, puppies need a greater concentration of protein in their diet than adult dogs. Most of the canned foods contain adequate levels of protein and the proportion of biscuit can be adjusted. There are also specialist canned puppy foods designed to provide all the nutrients in a form which is easily eaten and digested.

Contrary to some schools of thought, milk is not an essential food for puppies as it provides nothing which cannot be obtained from other foods. However, for puppies which can tolerate it, milk may make a useful supplement to the feeding regime.

Any changes which are made to the diet should be made gradually to avoid stomach upsets. Overfeeding may also cause diarrhoea because of the strain on the digestive system. A puppy, whatever its age, should be fit and lively, not fat and lethargic.

Old and sick dogs

There is often much that an owner can do to give nutritional support to dogs which are ill. For example, during convalescence the provision of an appetising food which is carefully balanced is essential to the proper recovery of the dog. There are proprietary diets made specially for this purpose and your veterinary surgeon will be glad to give advice.

Specific illnesses require special dietary treatment. For instance, diabetes requires consistent energy and carbohydrate intake; nephritis (kidney disease), a reduced protein diet containing protein of an especially high quality; and some forms of heart disease, a low salt diet. All of these are likely to be needed in conjunction with other treatment and veterinary surgeons will often give dietary advice and prescribe a special proprietary diet together with specific medicines.

Old dogs suffer from a variety of different problems, each requiring specific nutritional support. Some of these may be contradictory, and this is why it is difficult if not impossible to design a diet which is suitable for all old dogs. Common problems of old dogs include the diseases listed above, in addition to obesity and constipation. As dogs become older their energy requirement decreases (partly through lack of activity, partly through a drop in metabolic rate) but often their intake remains unchanged.

Obesity, with all its complications, covered later in this chapter is a very unpleasant condition and it is worth making strenuous efforts to prevent it. Slimming programmes should be under veterinary guidance and specially formulated diets with reduced calorie content can be obtained from most veterinary surgeons.

Constipation occurs as the muscles in the intestines become more sluggish and it may help to add a little wheat bran to the food.

Some old dogs suffer a temporary loss of appetite. While it is inevitable that they will lose weight because of inadequate energy intake, it is possible to ensure that the vitamin and mineral intakes are kept up by careful supplementation of the food eaten, or by dosing with tablets under veterinary guidance in extreme cases where no food is taken.

For old dogs and sick dogs the guidelines are the same as for every other group discussed earlier – provide a specially formulated diet which is palatable, digestible and which has the appropriate nutrient content for such dogs. Look at the condition of the dog and if in doubt, consult a veterinary surgeon. If prepared foods are used, it can be helpful to seek advice from the manufacturer.

Snacks and treats

A number of snacks and treats for dogs are produced by Pedigree Petfoods and other companies. These can be used as complimentary foods or as training aids (rewards). It should be noted that these do represent a source of calories and the amount of food fed should be reduced accordingly to prevent excessive weight gain.

Tips for reluctant eaters

1. Make sure that the diet is complete and balanced. Where appetite is depressed, additional vitamins and minerals may be given, provided there is no clinical contraindication.
2. The diet should be highly digestible.
3. The diet should have a high nutrient density, minimising the amount that the animal needs to eat.
4. Feed on a 'little and often' basis, dividing the total daily intake into 3-4 meals.
5. Temperature has a marked effect on palatability and warming the food can help considerably with tempting inappetent animals to eat. Where necessary, warm the food to 38°C (100°F), but no more.
6. Include animal fat in the diet providing there is no contraindication. In addition to being a rich source of energy, it helps to increase palatability.
7. Remove food that is not eaten after 10-15 minutes; fresh food offered later is likely to prove more acceptable.
8. Small pieces of some commercial dog 'treats' mixed with the food will often encourage dogs to eat more rapidly.
9. Dry cat food sprinkled on or mixed with the food often helps.

Obesity

The cause

Obesity is the single most common nutritional problem faced by dogs and people in the developed world. Estimates vary, but about one third of the populations of each species in these countries can be described as obese.

The cause of obesity is quite simply eating more than is needed by the body, resulting in storage of the excess as fat in adipose tissue. There are many theories to explain why some animals eat more than others and why some appear to need less than others, but the fact remains that if calorie intake exceeds requirement, for whatever reason, the result will be the accumulation of fat and a gain in bodyweight.

Why is obesity a problem? The definition gives the answer – obesity is an excess of body fat to the extent that normal body function is impaired. Unfortunately it is a problem which develops gradually so that owners often notice no change from day to day in the health and size of their dog. The problem is often confronted only when the veterinary surgeon is approached when the dog has become severely incapacitated by its weight problem.

Associated problems

The major conditions associated with obesity are:

- orthopaedic problems (arthritis)
- congestive heart failure
- breathing difficulties
- reduced liver function
- reproductive problems
- diabetes mellitus

- impaired digestive function (flatulence)
- increased surgical and anaesthetic risk
- reduced resistance to disease
- heat intolerance
- skin disease
- reduced life expectancy.

Some result from the additional weight putting strain on some of the body's systems (for example locomotor and breathing problems), others to the insulating effect of a thick fat 'jacket' (heat intolerance). The list above shows just how important the prevention of obesity is, and why it is worth slimming an obese dog rather than allowing it to waddle on in discomfort to an early death.

Obesity is easy to recognise. Not only is the behaviour of an obese dog characteristic (see Table 2.8) but the visible signs are obvious. Conventional wisdom has it that a dog whose ribs are visible when moving is not obese; this is all very well for short-haired breeds but less useful for those with long flowing coats. If the ribs can be felt easily under the coat then it is unlikely that the dog is obese. Feeling other areas may also help, for example fat may accumulate along the spine and around the base of the tail. It is also helpful to observe the dog's silhouette. The abdomen should be flat or concave, not pendulous. Old photographs of the dog can help uncertain owners check the condition of their dog. A seriously obese dog should receive immediate veterinary help but if the dog is only showing a tendency to gain weight, a careful watch on the diet should suffice until the next routine surgery visit.

Treatment

The aim of any slimming diet is to reduce fat content of the body with as little effect as possible on the 'lean body mass' (muscles, organs). The lean body mass determines the resting metabolic rate (the rate at which energy is used) and therefore undue loss will not only weaken the body but reduce the amount of food needed to maintain the final bodyweight, increasing the risk of further weight gain. It has been shown in man that too rapid weight loss results in excessive loss of lean tissue and therefore a slow but steady reducing regime is recommended. Ideally the aim should be to lose weight at the rate of 15 per cent over an 8-14 week period.

It is not essential to buy special foods. Providing the total energy (or calorie) content of the diet is carefully reduced, the dog's normal diet can be used quite successfully. There are, however, certain pitfalls and owners should be aware that some dietary components, eg fat, contain more calories than others (Table 2.9). It may help to reduce the biscuit component of the diet as this will have a disproportionally large effect on energy density without significantly affecting total bulk. A sprinkling of wheat bran on top of the food is also reputed to have an effect on satisfying hunger, although the use of bran should be restricted as it does provide some calories. Carrots contain few calories and can be used to bulk up the diet.

Compliance is the major difficulty when owners try to slim dogs on the food they are normally fed – and specially formulated slimming diets available from veterinary surgeons do have many advantages over home-made preparations. Not only do they contain all the nutrients required for normal health but by providing bulk without calories their composition is controlled and constant. This makes adjusting the intake to achieve a reasonable rate of weight loss much simpler. These diets are only available from veterinary surgeons who will provide advice, feeding guides and very informative literature. Owners of obese dogs should always present their dog for a full veterinary check before a slimming diet is started, to ensure that there is no underlying disease problem.

Figure 2.5 Energy requirements for maintenance and weight reduction.

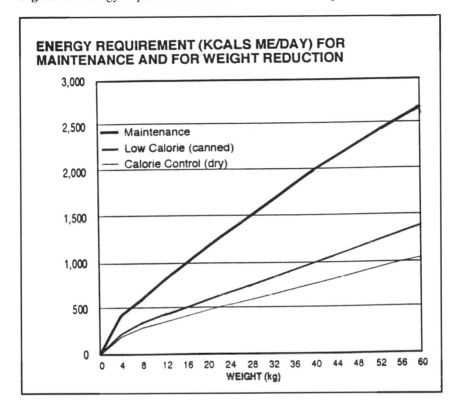

ENERGY REQUIREMENT (KCALS ME/DAY) FOR MAINTENANCE AND FOR WEIGHT REDUCTION

Whatever the diet and its source, there are some guidelines which will help increase the chances of success:

1. **Establish a goal**

    Decide how much weight needs to be lost (by consulting a veterinary surgeon, a breeder, or breed records). Don't forget individuals vary in optimum weight. Make a note of the current weight and the target weight.

2. **Decide on a dietary regime**

    It may take several attempts before appropriate quantities are established, but the first step is to try the amounts recommended in Table 2.10 and Figure 2.6. Whether a prepared slimming food is used, or a modification of the dog's normal diet, the recommended quantity should be fed for 2 weeks *exclusively* and then the dog reweighed. If the weight loss is not sufficient, the diet should be adjusted (reduced by 20 per cent, for example) for the next 2 weeks, and so on.

3. **Weigh the dog regularly**

    It is necessary to monitor the dog's progress carefully. Some dogs will sit on bathroom scales, others may have to be held by owner and then the owner's weight subtracted. Once a week (preferably at the same time of day) is quite frequent enough as there will be some fluctuation in bodyweight from day to day. Keep a graph of bodyweight plotted against date. Figure 2.7 gives a hypothetical example of the progress of one overweight female Labrador.

4. **Aim for gradual weight loss**
   Gradual weight loss with retraining of appetite is more likely to result in permanent weight loss than a starvation diet followed by a return to the previous diet. For example, a reasonable rate of loss is a 15 per cent reduction in 8-14 weeks.

5. **Encourage exercise**
   Exercise alone will not result in sufficient weight loss for most dogs. However, as an adjunct to a decrease in food intake it can only help. **NOTE:** Do not *over*exercise grossly obese dogs as this may put intolerable strain on heart and lungs. Gentle exercise (eg walking) is the order of the day for dogs more than 25 per cent over their target weight.

6. **Make it easy for the dog**
   A reduction in calorie intake below expenditure must inevitably result in hunger. It is important that the owner of a would-be slim dog appreciates this – it is no good feeling sorry for your dog and offering snacks and titbits as a peace offering, this will only make the problem worse. There are certain manoeuvres which may appease hunger. These include the addition of materials which give bulk but are poorly digested. Dividing the food into two or three small meals may also reduce hunger and inadvertently help to stimulate weight loss. Raw or cooked carrots will offer little in the way of calories but some satisfaction. A smaller feeding bowl can help if it deceives the dog into thinking it's getting a full helping, but it will also help ease the owner's sense of guilt!

7. **Convince your friends**
   There will always be people who cannot resist appealing eyes and a soulful expression, people who belive it is cruel to 'starve' a dog. If you live next to one of these people it makes it even more difficult to achieve satisfactory weight loss, for as soon as your back is turned, your dog will be fed biscuits and scraps and be beating a path to your neighbour's door for food. It is necessary to convince everyone who comes into contact with this dog that it is in its *own* interest that it should lose weight.

Prevention

By far the best way to eliminate obesity from any population is to prevent it rather than attempt to cure it. There are difficulties in this, however, particularly since the gradual onset means that owners slowly become accustomed to their dog's fatness and never see a sudden change. Nevertheless it is still entirely preventable. Glandular obesity, a defect which slows metabolism, is very rare and it is possible, with a sufficiently small food allowance to prevent even these dogs from becoming obese.

Each dog is different. Wide ranges are deliberately given on manufacturers' feeding guides to allow for this, and it is the responsibility of the owner to determine their dog's needs precisely. Fatty snacks and titbits which may tip the balance from weight stability to weight gain should be avoided for all but the most active dogs. If any titbits, snacks, treats or table scraps are fed, the normal ration should be reduced accordingly.

Some dogs are more susceptible to obesity than others. These include particularly castrated dogs, spayed bitches, older dogs, dogs of old or obese owners and dogs of certain breeds (Labrador Retrievers, Dachshunds, Cocker Spaniels and Collies). Owners of dogs in these categories need to be particularly careful, but even dogs outside these groups can become obese if not properly fed. There is a well-known saying that fat babies make fat adults, and that may be true for dogs too. In man the theory was that a fat child made excessive numbers of adipocytes (fat cells) which predisposed him to obesity as an adult, but this theory has now been largely discredited. It is more likely that the fat puppy gets accustomed to overfeeding and as a result begs for more food than thinner companions.

Figure 2.6 The history of weight loss in one dog

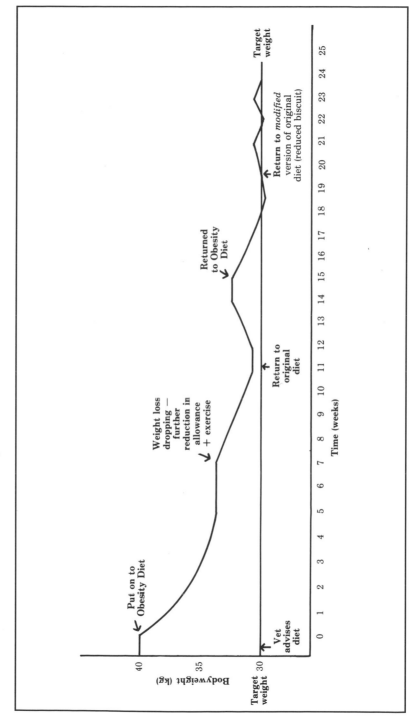

Table 2.1 Recommended nutrient allowances for dogs*

Nutrient	Unit	Allowance per 100g DM or per 400kcals
Protein	g	16
Fat	g	5.5
Linoleic acid	g	1
Calcium	g	1.1
Phosphorus	g	0.9
Potassium	g	0.6
Sodium chloride	g	1.1
Magnesium	mg	40
Iron	mg	6
Copper	mg	0.73
Manganese	mg	0.5
Zinc	mg	5
Iodine	mg	0.15
Selenium	µg	11
Vitamin A	IU	500
Vitamin D	IU	50
Vitamin E	IU	3
Thiamin (B_1)	mg	0.1
Riboflavin (B_2)	mg	0.25
Pantothenic acid	mg	1.1
Niacin	mg	1.2
Pyridoxine (B_6)	mg	0.12
Biotin	µg	10
Folic acid	µg	22
Vitamin B_{12}	µg	2.7
Choline	mg	125

IU = International Units

* Taken from the UK National Research Council (1974) Nutrient Requirements of Dogs, to allow for dogs at all stages of the lifecycle.

Table 2.2 Vitamins

Vitamin	Dietary source	Main functions	Results of deficiency	Results of excess
Fat-soluble				
Vitamin A	Fish oils, liver, vegetables	Vision in poor light, maintenance of skin	Night blindness, skin lesions	Anorexia, pain in bones (malformation)
Vitamin D	Cod-liver oil, eggs, animal products	Calcium balance, bone growth	Rickets, osteomalacia	Anorexia, calcification of soft tissues
Vitamin E	Green vegetables, vegetable oils, dairy products	Reproduction	Infertility, anaemia, muscle weakness	Not known in dogs
Vitamin K	Spinach, green vegetables, liver, in-vivo synthesis	Blood clotting	Haemorrhage	Not known in dogs
Water-soluble (B group)				
Thiamin (B_1)	Dairy products, cereals, organ meat	Release of energy from carbohydrate	Anorexia, vomiting, paralysis	Not known in dogs
Riboflavin (B_2)	Milk, animal tissues	Utilisation of energy	Weight loss, weakness, collapse, coma	Not known in dogs
Niacin	Cereals, liver, meat, legumes	Utilisation of energy	Anorexia, ulceration of mouth (black tongue)	Not known in dogs
Pyridoxine (B_6)	Meat, fish, eggs, cereals	Metabolism of amino acids	Anorexia, anaemia, weight loss, convulsions	Not known in dogs
Vitamin B_{12}	Liver, meat, dairy products	Division of cells in bone marrow	Anaemia	Not known in dogs
Folic acid	Offal, leafy vegetables	As above	Anaemia, poor growth	Not known in dogs
Pantothenic acid	Animal products, cereals, legumes	Release of energy from fat and carbohydrate	Slow growth, hair loss, convulsions, coma	Not known in dogs
Biotin	Offal, egg yolk, legumes	Metabolism of fat and amino acids	Loss of coat condition (scaly skin, scurf)	Not known in dogs
Choline	Plant and animal materials	Nerve function	Fatty infiltration of liver, poor blood clotting	Not known in dogs

Table 2.3 Minerals

Mineral	Dietary source	Main functions	Results of deficiency	Results of excess
Calcium	Bones, milk, cheese, white bread	Bone formation, nerve and muscle formation	Poor growth, rickets, convulsions	Very high levels – bone deformities
Phosphorus	Bones, milk, meat	Bone formation, energy utilisation	Rickets (rare)	Symptoms of calcium deficiency
Potassium	Meat, milk	Water balance, nerve function	Poor growth, paralysis, kidney and heart lesions	Muscular weakness?
Sodium/chlorine	Salts, cereals	Water balance, muscle and nerve activity	Poor growth, exhaustion	Thirst, high blood pressure (if intake maintained)
Magnesium	Cereals, bones, green vegetables	Bone formation, protein synthesis	Anorexia, vomiting, muscular weakness	Diarrhoea
Iron	Eggs, meat (liver), green vegetables	Part of haemoglobin (oxygen transport)	Anaemia, low resistance to hookworm infection	Weight loss, anorexia
Copper	Meat, bones	Part of haemoglobin	Anaemia	Anaemia in other mammals, hepatitis in Bedlington Terriers
Zinc	Meat, cereals	Digestion, tissue maintenance	Hair loss, skin thickening, poor growth	Diarrhoea
Manganese	Tea, nuts, cereals	Fat metabolism, many enzyme functions	Reproductive failure, poor growth	Poor fertility in other mammals, albinism, anaemia
Iodine	Fish, dairy produce	Part of thyroid hormone	Hair loss, apathy, drowsiness	In other animals, symptoms similar to deficiency
Cobalt	Organ and muscle meat, milk	Part of vitamin B_{12}	–	Not known in dogs
Selenium	Cereals, fish meals	Associated with vitamin E function	Muscle damage	Toxic

Dogs may also require molybdenum, fluorine, tin, silicon, cobalt, nickel, vanadium and chromium in very small amounts

Table 2.4 Prepared petfoods

Type of food	Feeding	Major ingredients	Comments
Dog biscuits/meal	Complementary – to be mixed with canned food or fresh meat	Cereals, some have minerals and vitamin supplementation	Cheap source of roughage and energy. May have low palatability.
Dry complete foods	May be fed alone, only water required	Cereals, animal and vegetable protein concentrates, fats, vitamins and minerals	Cheap feeding regime, but may be problems with palatability and digestibility, particularly in loose mixed diets. Extruded kibble products are better in these respects.
Semi-moist foods	May be fed alone, only water required	Some cereals, protein concentrates, fats, vitamins and minerals	Higher water content leads to softer food which is more palatable
Canned foods	Mostly complete but some are complementary and need to be fed with biscuit	Meat, poultry, minerals, vitamins, some cereals or soya	Soft moist texture, high palatability, even when mixed with biscuit. Canning process very effective preservation. Loaf or chunks in gravy presentations meet animal preferences

Table 2.5 Fresh foods

Food	Source of	Seriously deficient in	Comments
Meat (lean beef, mince, chicken)	Protein, fat, some B vitamins, some minerals	Calcium, phosphorus, iodine, copper, fat-soluble vitamins, biotin	Variable quality, palatability and digestibility
Tripe	Protein, fat	Calcium, phosphorus, many trace minerals, most vitamins	Quality may vary depending on source
Liver	Protein, fat, fat-soluble vitamins, B vitamins	Calcium, phosphorus, other minerals	Excessive amounts might lead to disease
Milk	Most nutrients		Some dogs cannot digest the lactose in milk
Eggs	Most nutrients		Raw egg white may lead to biotin deficiency
Bones	Calcium, phosphorus, magnesium, protein	Fat, vitamins, some minerals, essential fatty acids	Only feed large uncooked bones. Restrict to one weekly as high ash content may cause intestinal problems
Bread/cereals	Carbohydrate, protein, some minerals and vitamins	Fat, essential fatty acids, fat soluble vitamins	High levels of phytate may restrict absorption of minerals

Table 2.6 Storage and preparation of fresh foods

Purchase
1. Make sure materials are fresh and have been stored in clean area. For meats check colour and smell.

Storage
1. Meats should be refrigerated or frozen. If meat is refrigerated, it should be used within one or two days of purchase. Frozen meat should be thawed slowly, used immediately and not refrozen after cooking.
2. Store dry materials in secure containers away from rodents and check for mites which will reduce food value. Do not keep indefinitely as vitamin potency will be reduced.

Preparation/serving
1. Cook meat to destroy parasites and bacteria. Do not reheat cooked meat after cooking. Cool before feeding.
2. Always use clean utensils and bowls which have been thoroughly rinsed to get rid of all detergent.
3. With the exception of dry foods, remove and discard uneaten food after 30 minutes.

Table 2.7 Dietary supplements

	Nutrient	**Dosage**	**Dangers**
Proprietary supplements	Minerals and/or vitamins	As directed	Toxic in excess
Yeast tablets	B group vitamins	As directed for man but scale to dog size by weight	None
Cod liver oil	Vitamins A, D, E	Less than 5 ml/week for largest dogs	Toxic in excess
Vegetable oils	Essential fatty acids	1% of dry matter of diet (5% of meat diet)	Can become rancid with time
Bone meal	Calcium, phosphorus	$^1/_4$ oz/lb meat	Excess may cause malformed bones
Seaweed tablets	Iodine	As directed	Little
Garlic tablets	?	?	?
Raspberry tablets	?	?	?

Table 2.8 Characteristic behaviours of overweight dogs

Eating behaviour	• eats food very quickly and asks for more • begs for food at family mealtimes
Activity	• sleeps rather than plays • refuses to walk more than short distances • pants heavily if made to run • has difficulty negotiating steps and slopes
Effect of weather	• seeks shade, pants and sprawls out in warm weather

Table 2.9. Energy content of different foods

Food	Energy content kcal/100 g
Canned dog foods	75-100
Puppy food (canned)	110
Dog biscuits and meals	340-390
Complete dry foods	330-390
Fatty mince	180-220
Liver	158-180
Dressed tripe	70-90
Green tripe	100
Milk	65
Bacon	400-500
Cheese	300-450
Chocolate	500

Table 2.10 Suggested calorie requirements for obese dogs

Starting weight		Target weight		Canned food	Dry food
kg	lb	kg	lb	kcal/day	kcal/day
5	11	4.25	9	167	209
10	22	8.5	19	281	352
15	33	12.75	28	381	477
20	44	17	37	473	591
25	55	21.25	47	559	699
30	66	25.5	56	641	801
35	77	29.75	66	720	900
40	88	34	75	795	994
45	99	38.25	84	869	1086
50	110	42.5	94	940	1175
55	121	46.75	103	1010	1263
60	132	51	112	1078	1348

Dog management

SECTION TWO

DOG BEHAVIOUR AND TRAINING

Motivation and intelligence

Training and dog behaviour

Mishaps and problems

3
Motivation and intelligence

> **The family pack**
>
> **The senses**
>
> **Behaviour patterns**
>
> **Body language**

By understanding the nature and motivation of their pet owners will ensure that training and living with a dog is an easy, fulfilling and pleasurable experience.

In the 20th century we have a situation where dogs bred for working and sporting activities are commonly being chosen as pets. Such dogs need to adapt to a role of relative idleness, thus there is a need to find ways to compromise between the life the dog is equipped to live and the one in which the domestic pet finds itself. Some small dogs have been deliberately bred for a 'toy' or pet role, but it is still necessary for owners to remember that they nevertheless retain the basic instincts common to the canine species as a whole and to act accordingly.

The family pack

Dogs are not solitary animals. By nature they prefer to live within a family or pack structure. The pack provides moral and physical support, and also protection for its members. For dogs below the rank of pack leader, the pack also supplies leadership and direction, and takes decisions for its members. Dogs respond very well to being provided with a framework of guidelines within which they must live. The dog which is allowed to do just as it likes is not a happy dog.

When a dog lives within a canine pack it will dominate some of the pack members but will defer to others which are above it in the pack hierarchy. Ambitious dogs and bitches will make intermittent bids to improve their ranking, even challenging the pack leader, with the hope of usurping the position themselves.

Domestication has not altered the dog's desire either to be in charge or to accept being dominated by a person it respects. **The pack of the pet or companion dog is its owner and the immediate family of people and animals with which it lives.**

In a wholly canine pack, leadership is somewhat flexible, in that a slightly lower-ranking dog than the pack leader may assume leadership in some particular situations. In the domestic pet we see a typical example of this in the dog which is dutifully obedient within the home but which pulls continually on the lead and so dominates a walk when out of doors. The dog is taking decisions and imposing its will on the handler — this dog is pack leader in taking a walk. **It is important that the dog's owner shall be the pack leader in all situations** and be aware that dogs of all sizes and characters may make periodic bids for supremacy, especially during adolescence. The concept of pack behaviour and submission to the pack leader is inherited by puppies at birth, and is reinforced by their mothers. While the litter is in the nest, the mother is the only pack leader and all the puppies defer to her. But in adult life in the full canine pack, and in a canine/human pack family situation, there will be several individuals who are above the dog in ranking and yet who also defer to the pack leader. **It is important that in the canine/human pack, the dog should not be allowed to consider itself superior to any of the human members of the pack.** If other animals are kept, the dog may assume dominant or submissive ranking with them, but it must not be dominant to any human.

The bitch is able to use sharp and immediate physical punishment, often preceded by warning growls at her puppies. An adult pack leader subdues and disciplines the pack most frequently by eye contact and body language, with some vocalisation (growling) and there is rarely need for physical conflict except where an individual makes constant bids to assume power.

By observing the way a canine or wolf pack is disciplined we can discover how to build a rewarding and agreeable relationship with the family pet (see also Chapter 4).

The senses

Puppies are born relatively immature compared to a human baby. In the first 4 weeks of life they develop eyesight, hearing, mobility and adult vocalisation, as well as their first set of teeth. Some important features in respect of the senses are given in Table 3.1.

Behaviour patterns

General habits

Although dogs have been domesticated for thousands of years, they are still in many ways close to the primitive animal. Many of the actions and behaviour patterns which are natural behaviour to the dog can be unpleasing to us and the the community when we keep dogs as pets. Although dogs can be trained to modify some of these unwelcome behaviour patterns it may well be cruel to go too far in trying to eradicate them altogether. It is, however, antisocial to allow some 'natural' behaviours to go unchecked. Dogs, like people, must learn to control certain natural behaviours if they are to integrate properly into society.

It is a natural behaviour for a dog

* to investigate any unfamiliar object, animal or person by vigorous sniffing and possibly by urine marking. Information about other dogs is obtained by sniffing at their genitals and/or faeces and urine.
* to re-mark with a stream of urine key points and objects if another dog has been on the territory.
* to help itself to any edible object left within its reach — this is *not* stealing.
* to dig, either for vermin or to bury bones and trophies.
* to appropriate any object bearing the fresh scent of the owner or close members of the family.
* to be possessive about food and toys unless trained from an early age to give up possessions to those above it in the pack hierarchy.
* to flush out game birds and rabbits and to give chase if not restrained.
* to feel lonely and to bark as a means of gaining attention and company.
* to feel jealous of newcomers to the family, especially if more notice is taken of a new puppy or a new baby than is given to the resident dog.
* to lick the muzzles of dogs, and to attempt to lick the faces and hands of humans. This is a sign of submission and affection. Puppies lick the dam's muzzle to induce her to regurgitate food for them.

- to jump up to greet familiar humans, in an effort to get as near the face as possible.
- to need to chew hard objects, especially at 4-8 months old, while teething. Chewing on bones or hard objects also alleviates boredom.
- to eat the faeces of other species, especially cow manure, horse droppings, cat faeces and rabbit pellets.
- to roll in obnoxious, highly odorous substances, such as the carcasses of carrion.

Bitches

Bitches come into season for the first time at between 6 and 18 months of age and heat occurs at about 6-monthly intervals for the rest of the bitch's life, unless the reproductive cycle is controlled by chemical means (your veterinary surgeons will advise) or unless the bitch's ovaries and uterus are removed (spaying). See also Chapter 1.

Where bitches are kept together it is likely that they will stimulate each other to come into oestrus. Bitches often engage in mock-mating play with each other. This is harmless provided it does not provoke irritability and fighting.

It is *normal* for bitches to vary in temperament at different stages of their cycle. This must be borne in mind when training bitches and when looking for signs of disease.

It is natural behaviour for a bitch to seek to escape and to invite a dog to mate her when she is at the fertile peak of her heat period. This behaviour pattern must be prevented for social reasons (she may cause a road traffic or some other accident and, of course, give birth to unwanted puppies).

The options are:

1. Keep the bitch under the strongest supervision. This means ensuring that doors and gates are shut *all* the time, which can be difficult especially when there are young children in the home.
2. Having the bitch's uterus and ovaries removed (spaying).
3. Averting the season by chemical means. If you want to take this option, see your veterinary surgeon well ahead of the time your bitch is expected in season.

Males

Male dogs are usually capable of siring a litter from between 6 to 10 months old and until late middle age.

A dog at the height of its fertility will mate several bitches every week, if the opportunity is available, but eagerness to perform the mating act is no guide to the dog's fertility. A veterinary surgeon can perform a sperm count on stud dogs as a positive check on fertility if it is needed.

It is a natural behaviour for a male dog with a high libido to escape to track down a bitch on heat, sometimes over quite a long distance from its home. This behaviour is accentuated if the dog has had an occasional mating experience, so it is better not to allow a pet dog to be used at stud in order to oblige a friend. Owners of dogs which have started wandering in search of bitches should seek veterinary advice without delay since early treatment with hormones or possibly castration may be indicated. See also Chapter 1.

Elimination behaviour

Adult dogs pass faeces two to three times a day depending on what is fed. Puppies defecate on average four to five times a day, again depending on what is fed and how often. In general terms, foods high in protein are likely to be low residue producers, while some of the cereal-based complete diets produce a large volume of faeces.

Some foods, for example carrots, nuts, dried fruit, some beans and flaked maize, are not well digested by the dog and may be seen unchanged in faeces. The colour of faeces is related to the type of food eaten. The dog's food is normally digested and faeces eliminated within 12-24 hours of feeding, but when a small indigestible object has been swallowed, it may take 2-3 weeks or even longer for it to appear in the faeces.

Young puppies urinate very frequently, as many as 10 times a day. Adult dogs urinate about three times daily, excluding territory marking behaviour and the message-leaving urination of a bitch coming on heat.

Both dogs and bitches should have full control of urine and faeces by the age of 6 months, except possibly during illness. Very old dogs may become incontinent. If a puppy continues to dribble urine after the age of 6 months and when house-training is understood, veterinary advice should be sought, as a malformation of the urinary system is not uncommon and may need to be corrected by surgery.

The urine of most bitches will burn patches on the lawn, and the stream of urine from an adult dog will kill plants and shrubs. The only remedy is to pour cold water on the place as soon as possible after the urine has been passed. See also Chapter 5.

Adult bitches are often very particular about the surface on which they will urinate. Some will only use their own garden. Many more will only use the surface (grass, concrete, gravel etc) to which they are accustomed. When away from home a bitch may resist passing urine for as long as 48 hours, although drinking normally. The only remedy is to give her every opportunity to empty her bladder in conditions as near as possible to those with which she is familiar at home, and eventually she will have to give in. It can be very useful for their owners to train dogs and bitches to urinate to the sound of an undulating whistle, as horse owners often used to in the past.

Very submissive puppies may have an involuntary emission of urine at moments of great fear or great pleasure, for instance when when greeting their owner. Some bitches will continue this behaviour past puppyhood, and this may be a sign that the bitch is becoming too low in the pack structure, or that more orders are being given her than she is capable of comprehending. Such a bitch should have her ego built up by brisk praise and encouragement of good behaviour rather than sympathy or scolding when she dribbles urine.

Body language

A dog's emotions and intentions can be judged by observing the way it stands, how it holds its ears and tail and by other tell-tale signs. Good dog owners will observe their pet carefully and continually so that they can interpret what dogs are 'saying'. The details given below will serve as a guide and hopefully help observation of the individual pet.

The head

(i) *The ears* are pricked or erect when alert or listening intently, but held back to the head as an indication of submission or pleasure, and also when the dog is ready to attack. Other body signs help to distinguish the dog's intentions.

(ii) *The eyes* are narrowed and half-closed in pleasure or submission.

The leader of a dog or wolf pack often exerts control by means of eye contact alone. The superior dog will give a lower ranking animal, which is perhaps contemplating some forbidden behaviour, a long hard stare. The submissive dog will lower its head and turn away, to avoid meeting the pack leader's eyes. The dog which means to challenge the pack leader will return the stare, often for several minutes, until one or the other mounts a physical attack.

Lower ranking dogs also recognise and appreciate a soft-eyed glance of approval from the pack leader. Direct eye contact from human to dog should be avoided where a dog is known to have aggressive tendencies. Frequent, gentle eye contact between dog and owner signifies acceptance of the current behaviour pattern and is very beneficial to the relationship.

(iii) *The mouth* in some breeds, particularly Labradors, is opened to show the teeth in an almost human one-sided 'grin' of friendly greeting. Both lips are drawn further back and more of the teeth are exposed in the snarl of aggression.

Body posture

Body posture is used to convey mood by all dogs. When expressing aggression, a dog seeks to make itself look as large and as frightening as possible. It stands on its toes, the chest thrust forward, and some of the hair is held erect, often the ruff around the neck and a wide band of hair right down the spine. The tail is held stiffly in line with the back and may wave gently, but *is not wagged*. It is a mistake to assume that because the tail

Figure 3.1 Body language

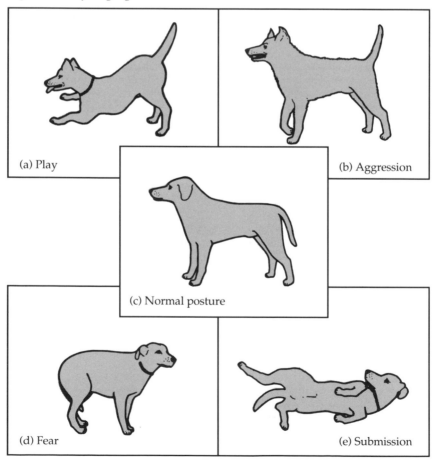

(a) Play

(b) Aggression

(c) Normal posture

(d) Fear

(e) Submission

is moving, the dog is ambivalent about its attitude or is, after all, friendly. The head is usually lowered, and barking stops when an attack is imminent. The dog which assumes an aggressive stance while barking with mouth wide open is probably fearful and will back away when challenged.

A submissive dog will adopt a posture the opposite of that described above.

Vocalisation

(i) *Growling* is used to communicate with other animals and people. The dog owner should be aware of the difference between the low throat murmur of pleasure and 'conversation' made by some dogs when being petted, and the true rumbling growl used as a warning that an attack will be made if the offending behaviour of human or dog is continued. *Never challenge or tease a growling dog.*

(ii) *Roaring* with mouth wide open, and mock biting without clenching the jaws, is a play sequence between dogs, and dog and human. This mode of play should not however be encouraged with children or by older people with fragile skin, and extremely cautiously, if at all, with the guard dog breeds.

(iii) *Howling,* always done from a standing position, produces a sound that carries a long way. It is used as a distress call and for dog/dog communication, never in connection with aggression.

The tail

Tail wagging and the angle at which the tail is carried are prime methods of communication used by dogs. The angle at which the tail is held is usually determined by conformation and breed habit, but in general the tail held at 45° or higher to the spine expresses alertness and interest. The tail clamped low over the anus expresses a fear posture, while extreme nervousness brings the tail right down between the legs with the hindquarters at the crouch.

Note that Whippets and Italian Greyhounds naturally carry their tails in the fear position.

Dogs wag their tails to signify pleasure — puppies as young as 4 weeks old will wag their tails while eating. Dogs whose tails are docked very short will express pleasure by gyrating their whole hindquarters.

Summary

By observing closely the dog's signals the informed owner will be able to identify dogs that are fearful and submissive from those that are aggressive (see Figure 3.1).

Submission

Submissive dogs approach from the side, never head on. The tail is held low, the body crouching with the rear end held high. The animal will try to lick the face or hands of the dominant dog or person and may roll on its back to expose its groin. In many dogs there is a one-sided grin and most dogs will wag their tails in friendly greeting with the tail held parallel to the ground.

Fear

Fear is expressed by shaking, shivering, a look of apprehension, hiding beneath furniture and keeping the head low. Some dogs may urinate involuntarily. Extreme pleasure may also produce a body tremor but is accompanied by tail wagging.

Aggression

Beware of dogs that are standing tall, waving their tails slowly, having both lips drawn back and are uttering a low, threatening growl. Such animals are best ignored and eye contact avoided. Dogs have a very well-developed 'fight or flight' mechanism, which, coupled with extremely acute hearing and quick reaction time, enables them to get out of a danger zone very quickly, and also to mount an attack with hardly any warning if the opportunity presents itself. Veterinary surgeons and breeders learn to read the premonitory tell-tale signs early and so are prepared.

Getting it right

(i) *Move carefully.* Their very quickness of reaction may sometimes lead a dog to misinterpret the intentions of children or adult strangers. An arm raised in greeting may appear as a threat to a dog, a child's high-pitched screams may offend or over-excite the dog.

(ii) *Don't stare and run away.* Since a dog's natural instinct is to chase, an animal or person running away is a target to be caught and brought to the ground. It is helpful to teach children to move slowly when in contact with animals and to walk away deliberately without looking at the dog rather than running away if they think that a dog is threatening them. This tip may prevent a disaster.

(iii) *Stand up naturally.* Dogs expect humans to be upright or sitting down. A person who falls to the ground is vulnerable to attack, especially where several dogs are working as a pack.

(iv) *Speak to dogs.* Because a dog's sight is poor in certain lights, a dog may fail to recognise a friend until they speak or come within scenting distance. Always warn a dog of your presence, by speaking gently, especially if the dog is sleeping. If you know the dog's name, use it.

The well-informed dog owner will help his pet 'get it right' by communicating through voice, movement and, where appropriate, touch. With a little thought and by talking to dogs as one would a child, situations of conflict can be easily averted.

(v) *Familiarise your dog with possible frightening situations.* Dogs are wary of loud noises, sudden currents of air (sometimes even high winds), people with unusual or distorted voices, people with unusual body outline (eg carrying a sack), people with hesitant or lame walk, or an object or place associated with an unpleasant happening. They will also react strongly to a fear scent left by other dogs, eg at a veterinary surgery, and also to unfamiliar body scent of people of other races. It is most important when bringing up a puppy to familiarise it with all these situations and praise it for correct behaviour. Some dogs will run away from fear situations but others will attack if they feel threatened.

Leave dogs to sort themselves out — by and large

An active domination sequence between members of a dog pack is shown by the superior dog putting its muzzle alongside that of its opponent, and then leaning its body against the other's so that the aggressor dog is closer than a shadow wherever the rival dog moves. Eventually the weaker dog will be driven into a corner and attacked about the head.

This behaviour pattern is often used to keep lower ranking dogs away from food, or some trophy, or even from approaching the owner.

A further step in aggressive behaviour is made by the aggressor leaping on to another animal and gripping the back of its neck. If the victim is submissive it will assume a crouching position with head low and eyes closed, making the back of the neck

Figure 3.2 Dominance exercises. (a) method 1; (b) method 2

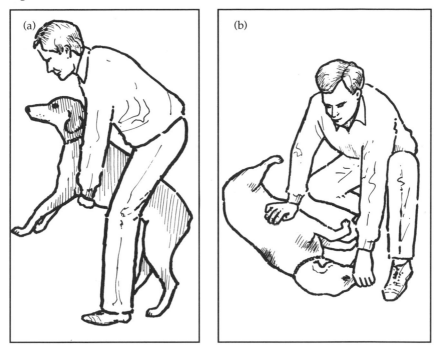

prominent for the aggressor to bite. Once complete domination is expressed in this way the aggressor usually makes no further attack.

Even greater submission is expressed by the dog which rolls over on to its back exposing its abdomen and genitals to be bitten. The aggressor normally accepts this surrender and takes the attack no further.

The balance of such a situation can easily be upset by inopportune interference by owners. See also Chapter 5, 'What If' nos 35 and 43.

Be dominant but fair

All normal dogs understand the act of submission to a superior animal or human. Training a pet dog for acceptable behaviour as a lower member of the family pack is aided by using some of the methods a canine pack leader would use to maintain discipline. Once the habit of submission to a human or dog pack leader is established, any sign of rebellion can usually be quelled by a look or a gesture from a dominant individual, but in order to do this effectively, the human pack leader must be watching for signs of rebellion as the dog pack leader would do. Once an actual bid for dominance has taken place, it is often necessary to apply more physical means to subdue the offender. (See Chapter 4.)

It should be noted that physical strength is not always necessary for a canine pack leader and **never** necessary in a human pack leader after the dog is 6 months old. Physical and mental dominance of the dog should be established very early in the dog's life. There may be subsequent attempts by the dog to assume leadership, but the owner's always superior brain power can be employed to re-establish the correct relationship.

How to reinforce your dominance

1. Stand over the dog and lift its front legs off the ground, as illustrated in Figure 3.2(a). Keep the dog's feet off the ground for at least 30 seconds. Reward the dog verbally if it remains quiet — rebuke struggling.
2. Put the dog in a submissive position on its side, as illustrated in Figure 3.2(b), and hold it there, with one hand over its mouth and the other on its chest, for at least 30 seconds. Praise or rebuke as appropriate.
3. Go through a set period, lasting for about 5 minutes, of obedience exercises, making the dog sit, stay, heel etc. Reward good behaviour with titbits and lavish praise.

The exercises noted above should normally be practised once weekly or so, but will need to be carried out once or even twice daily for dogs that have a tendency to be very dominant. As such dogs become more submissive the frequency can be reduced gradually.

Sometimes dogs and bitches, especially those with signs of false pregnancy, will become *over-submissive*. In such cases the pet can be 'built up' by giving plenty of praise for good behaviour and ignoring the dog when submissive postures are adopted. In some cases the dog can be allowed to stand on its hind legs and place its forelegs on your lap or shoulders briefly, while you adopt a squatting position — but be careful to handle this exercise carefully and not to overdo it.

If threatened by a dog

1. Stand still.
2. Avoid eye contact with the attacking dog.
3. Do not threaten and challenge the dog, for the moment.
4. Evaluate the situation, look for an escape route.
5. Keep your hands reasonably high. Moving hands tend to be the first part of your body to be bitten.
6. If you have something to hand, like a briefcase or a shopping bag, use it to block the approach of the dog. If you are a cyclist, don't cycle harder because most dogs can outrun a cyclist. Jump off your bike and position your machine between you and the dog.
7. If you are carrying food, use it to distract the dog because turning the dog to an alternative behaviour is often effective.
8. If these things are not getting the dog away from you and you cannot see the owner at hand, then shout 'sit' because most dog owners have trained their dog to sit and many dogs will obey it like an automaton. This may give you just sufficient time to reach a safer place.
9. A high priority should be to quietly look around for help or for an object, like a strong stick, with which you can defend yourself. Don't turn your back on the dog and never, ever run. Most dogs do not have the courage to confront someone who is still but they may bite the backside of someone who is running.

Table 3.1 The senses and body language

Sense	Puppies	Adults	Training aid
Sight	Puppies are born quite blind with only an indication where the eyes will be. Eyes are fully developed and open by 10-14 days after birth.	Dogs see better than humans in twilight and darkness. They are long-sighted, seeing moving objects best. They have difficulty seeing stationary figures at a distance and in focusing on small objects at close range. Dogs can see some colours; bright red and bright green are the easiest to see.	Use hand signals and move slightly when calling a dog from a long distance.
Hearing	The ears are not functional at birth but hearing is fully developed at 3-4 weeks of age. Congenital deafness sometimes occurs, often associated with white coat colouring.	Dogs can hear a wider range of sounds over longer distances than man. Hearing is most acute in dogs with open, funnel-shaped ears and in breeds that can 'prick' and swivel their ear flaps. Very loud noise and some high-pitched sounds from some household appliances may cause discomfort and even pain to dogs.	There should never be any need to shout at dogs.
Vocalisation	Puppies cry in a variety of tones from the moment of birth. Contented puppies make a soft murmur while feeding. The first bark is usually heard at about 4-6 weeks.	Barking is used in different tones and cadences, to communicate with humans, to warn off intruders etc, and as a challenge to other dogs. The howl carries over long distances and is used as a means of communication with other dogs. Some dogs will talk to their owner when content by using a low grumbling growl of varying pitch.	Dogs can be trained to bark and to stop barking on command.
Touch	For the first 2 weeks of their lives puppies can only maintain their body temperature by huddling close to each other and to their mother's mammary glands. Their very lives depend on being close to another animal or source of heat.	Most dogs enjoy being stroked on the head, down the spine and on the chest between the front legs, but some are reluctant to be touched on their feet and tail.	Body sensitivity varies. Some dogs will need strong handling while others will respond to the lightest touch on the lead.

Table 3.1 (continued)

Sense	Puppies	Adults	Training aid
Taste	From weaning time onwards puppies are introduced to a variety of tastes, and they will also investigate plants, earth and many other substances (some of which may be harmful) in order to identify edible things.	Dogs can enjoy as rewards and titbits a very wide range of sweet, salt or sharp flavours. Foods which lack a strong smell or taste are liable to be rejected.	Cherished food rewards, given **immediately** a command has been obeyed are a valuable training aid.
Body language	Puppies do not begin to use canine body language until they are about 8 weeks old.	Dogs display a variety of facial expressions, using mouth, eyes and ears, sometimes with vocalisation, to express dominant or submissive intentions. Body posture, type of walk and the angle at which the tail is held are also important indicators of a dog's feelings (see also Figure 3.1)	The observant owner will have warning of a dog's intentions by intelligent interpretation of facial expression and body posture, and so can often prevent an unhappy confrontation with an aggressive or fearful dog.

4
Training and dog behaviour

> **How dogs learn**
>
> **Training**
>
> **Behaviour modification techniques**
>
> **Behaviour problems**
>
> **Activities with dogs**
>
> **Educational opportunities**

There are three main reasons for studying dog behaviour and dog training methods. First, the owner that understands these matters will get much more pleasure from pet ownership. Second, dogs that are properly trained and do not have behaviour problems will fit into the community at large without causing friction. Third, there is no doubt that dogs appreciate leadership and like to know their status, so training and the prevention of inappropriate behaviour will make dogs happier and more contented.

It is not generally realised just how commonly behaviour problems in dogs occur. This is partly because many dog owners put up with bad behaviour either because they do not see it as a problem or regard such behaviour as simply being characteristic of dogs, but at least 50 per cent of dogs which reach rescue homes do so because of habits which annoy their owners.

Furthermore, many owners do not appreciate that something can be done to prevent or cure unacceptable behaviour. For example it was found that two-thirds of male dogs presented at veterinary surgeries had one or more undesirable hypersexual traits. Some dogs had four or five such traits and yet the owners had not complained or sought advice! (See the section on Male dogs in Chapter 1.)

There is no doubt that all dog owners need to understand how to train their dogs and how to prevent, and if necessary cure, inappropriate behaviour.

This chapter sets out the basic principles that need to be appreciated, studied and applied. But first the reader is recommended to read thoroughly Chapter 3 which deals with the motivation and intelligence of dogs, paying particular attention to the pack concept and body language.

How dogs learn

An understanding of how dogs learn is necessary before they can be encouraged to become well-mannered and properly integrated into society. Learning can be defined as 'a change in behaviour resulting from previous experience'. In technical terms dogs are said to learn by 'instrumental conditioning', which simply means that behaviour is determined by the result it brings. If a response of an animal to a command is followed by pleasure or gratification then the animal will tend to repeat the response. Conversely if the dog gains nothing from a particular behaviour, it will tend not to repeat it. This is simple enough and of course applies also to children and even ourselves.

However, in the case of dogs it is very relevant to appreciate that they can only establish whether their performance was right or wrong if it is rewarded or corrected virtually *at the same time* as the action is being carried out. It is no good rewarding a dog five minutes later for sitting on command as it will perceive the reward as applying to its very latest action which could have been wrong.

Dogs learn quickest if the reward or deterrent is given within half a second of responding to a command and this means in many cases that the situation will have to be set up. Rewards will need to be readily at hand — not wrapped up and in a tin that is hidden away — and the owner will need to pay a lot of attention to the dog.

Similarly, the methods of correction must have been thought out in advance. In many cases it pays to have an appropriate object readily available to throw, since finding one and approaching the dog will delay the administration of the deterrent.

Thrown objects can be very effective in set up situations, as the dog does not know where they have come from, and it gets an immediate deterrent while it is performing the crime.

Never pull or jerk on the dog's neck when it is wearing a choke or check collar. Pressure on the neck can cause injury to the larynx, the spine and to the eyes. This method of applying a deterrent was once advocated, but it has been shown to be extremely dangerous, as the injuries which may be caused are not immediately apparent.

The best reward is undoubtedly a very small food reward and in training sessions a ready supply will be needed. Failing that, lavish praise and petting will bring instant satisfaction to most dogs.

Essentially two forms of deterrent are used.

1.   The administration of a surprise distraction such as a thrown object or a noise such as shaking a bunch of keys or a tin full of pebbles.
2.   The withdrawal of something pleasurable — particularly sending the dog to its bed and ignoring it (social isolation), or the owner ceasing to give the dog attention.

If deterrents are used it is essential to follow these rules:

- They must be given immediately.
- They must be effective enough to disrupt the undesirable behaviour.
- The dog should be given the chance to do something else that will bring a pleasant reward.
- Deterrents should not be used on shy and nervous dogs or puppies that are between 7 and 14 weeks of age.
- Hitting and slapping will be confused with play by most big dogs and can therefore be quite counterproductive. Ignoring the dog works in most cases. In the case of a dog that jumps up, just turn aside and do not speak to it – making the behaviour unrewarding.
- Finally, if in doubt do not use deterrents or frank punishment. It is better to turn about and ignore the behaviour or to apply social isolation. Some dog trainers do not favour the use of deterrents but it can be a very quick and effective way to prevent the development of undesirable behaviour – but never, never lose your temper. It is important for the owner to apply these measures properly, consistently and fairly. It is, in fact, better to try to prevent behaviour errors by watchfulness on the part of the owners rather than trying to correct errors after they have been made.

Training

Dogs can be trained much more effectively if the following modern teaching techniques are used:

* Reward the dog very quickly for a correct response.
* Give a very small food reward *and* verbal praise.
* Early learning is quickest if the response is rewarded every time.
* To perpetuate the response reward only intermittently, but remember if rewards are never given the good behaviour pattern may be forgotten.

Behaviour modification techniques

If a behaviour is never rewarded it will be repeated less frequently and will eventually stop. Often owners do not appreciate that by 'rewarding' the dog with their attention, they are encouraging a behaviour to continue — even by, for instance, pushing, shouting or slapping their pet. Once this is pointed out the behaviour will often cease very rapidly. If you dog has an undesirable trait check first that you or a member of your family is not encouraging it in any way. The problem may be easily solved. Dogs do things they know are wrong to gain attention – just as children do.

This means teaching the dog to behave in an approved way in response to the stimulus which brought about an inappropriate behaviour previously. For example a dog should learn that it is more rewarding to sit quietly by its owner than to pull frantically on the lead, barking hysterically when another dog is met. Reward lavishly the behaviour you want. Plan your actions in advance, anticipating what the dog is likely to do so that you can take steps to avoid the dog getting into a situation where it is likely to behave badly.

Sometimes veterinary surgeons will prescribe sedatives and other drugs to facilitate the application of training methods to eliminate inappropriate behaviour.

Behaviour problems — prevention and treatment

The majority of behaviour problems encountered by dog owners fall into five major categories: aggression, destructiveness, disobedience, phobias and sexual.

Puppy owners must expect to spend some time and effort educating their puppy since there is no doubt that prevention is better and more certain than cure.

If an adult dog has been obtained there may be no alternative but to try to overcome the problem. The behavioural methods which are generally the most effective are outlined in Table 4.1 in answer to the question 'What if my dog...?' This is a format that is used elsewhere in *The Doglopaedia*, see particularly Chapters 5 and 17. These are guidelines only, and if you are in doubt or the method described does not seem to be having an effect consult your veterinary surgeon.

In relation to the prevention of behaviour problems it should be noted that puppies go through two very significant periods in respect of subsequent behaviour. If things go wrong at these times then problems that are difficult to correct can occur later.

1. *The critical period of socialisation.* This period starts at 3 weeks of age and ends at 12-13 weeks in most puppies. It is essential that they encounter as many different types of people and experience as great a variety of noises and situations as possible during this period. They are then more likely to be better adjusted later in life.

Figure 4.1. Basic training

DOWN
Give the command with a short sharp voice and insist on instant response. Do not use the word to stop dogs jumping up. It is useful to acompany the command with a downward gesture of the arm

STAY
A useful command that can help to ensure that the dog does not run across the road when separated from the owner, for example. Say in a sharp tone coupled with a hand held out palm down.

COME
This command is most useful since it can prevent accidents occurring. Training can begin on a long lead to ensure the dog's attention. Never scold a dog that has answered the command even if it was doing something very wrong when it was called. The word should be used in an encouraging way and accompanied by a beckoning gesture.

SIT
Ensure that the dog's bottom is properly on the ground and that the response is instantaneous

2. *The critical period for sensitivity.* This period lasts from 8 to 12 weeks of age. Any experience which provides acute fear during this time may make a dog anxious, shy or very fearful of similar situations for the rest of its life, especially if it already has an inherited tendency for nervousness. Harsh corrective measures *must* be avoided at this time and puppies should not be isolated from social contact for prolonged periods during this stage of their development.

Basic training

It is most important that dogs are trained to respond promptly and properly to the commands illustrated if they are to fit without friction into the community at large.

Contrary to popular belief, simple training can start from 8 weeks of age; there is no need to wait until the dog reaches adolescence.

Tips

- Set aside a few minutes, initially each day and subsequently once a week, to rehearse and reaffirm the commands you expect your dog to obey to ensure that your dog responds promptly and properly.

- Basic training classes can be fun and are of help especially if the dog has been obtained at an older age, but be selective. Always choose a kind trainer, not one of the old fashioned 'stamp, shout and yank' variety.

- Competitive obedience training and agility training can be interesting and rewarding. There is the chance not only to achieve something personally but also to make many friends with a common interest in dogs.

- Attending one of the puppy playgroups run by some veterinary practices for puppies of 8-14 weeks may help your dog to socialise properly with other people's dogs. Furthermore you will have the chance to meet other like-minded owners and exchange ideas on puppy rearing.

Activities with dogs

There are many activities which you can enjoy with your dog, and training your dog in the necessary skills will make you appreciate each other's companionship all the more.

Your stepping-stone to most activities will be to join a breed club or a local training club, or to become interested in one of the many breed or general rescue societies.

Some suggestions are given in Table 4.2-4.5

Table 4.1 Prevention and treatment of some common behaviour problems

What if my dog...	Treatment	Prevention
...is aggressive towards strange dogs	Teach the dog that it is more profitable to sit quietly rather than to attack other dogs. Regularly practise dominance exercises and give the dog planned training periods each day during which it is taught basic commands. Avoid possible confrontation situations during the training period. If a fight does break out ignore the dog and walk away—on no account pick it up as that could be construed as praise.	Ensure that puppies are 'socialised' with other dogs as they grow up. Do not play rough games or tug-of-war games with dogs, especially large breeds. From an early age praise good behaviour with other dogs. Avoid overtly aggressive dogs by crossing the road well in advance. Aggressiveness is often unintentionally reinforced by owners who stroke or pick up growling dogs.
...is aggressive towards other dogs in the same house	If its aggression is towards other dogs in the same house it is important to enhance the hierarchical system by giving support to the more dominant dog and withdrawing privileges from the underdog—this is not very British, but it often works!	Establish a proper hierarchical system from the start and immediately discourage any signs of unrest. The owners must ensure that *they* are the pack leaders.
...is aggressive when groomed	Find an area that can be groomed or touched and reward good behaviour. Gradually move to desired area step by step over a few days. Do not go too quickly and risk a set back.	Groom the dog regularly from an early age. Make it fun and reward good behaviour. Be dominant. Try to find out why a particular area is sensitive, e.g. soreness or bruising.
...has learnt to be aggressive	Stop rewarding aggression, be dominant and encourage some other acceptable behaviour. Do not play rough games with dogs that have a tendency to be aggressive. Avoid situations where the dog's aggression may come to the fore.	Do not play tug of war or rough games with big dogs especially guard dogs like Boxers and Dobermanns—they do not need to be taught their job. Be dominant. Have regular basic training sessions.
...jumps up	Be dominant and have regular basic training sessions. Do not slap dogs with rolled up newspapers as this could be construed as play. Do not use the word DOWN to discourage behaviour as that could confuse the dog. Say NO sharply, followed by SIT and if obeyed give lavish praise. Greet dogs from a crouched position and while sitting in the car with the door open rather than getting out first. Discourage the behaviour forcibly and stand away so that the dog has no support. You could give the dog something like a glove to carry off and thus distract it.	Recognise that this is undesirable behaviour and do not think that it is nice for your dog to show its pleasure at seeing you in this way. Show disapproval of the behaviour and encourage desired behaviour.
...is disobedient	Be dominant, instigate regular basic training sessions if necessary using a Flexi-lead.	Start obedience training early—as soon as puppy is obtained. Never use deterrents inappropriately. If a dog does not respond to the command COME do not use corrective measures when it does eventually come.

Table 4.1 (continued)

What if my dog...	Treatment	Prevention
... pulls on the lead	Be dominant, start regular training periods. When teaching the dog turn suddenly and frequently. In early training do not take on the lead towards its favourite walk. Persevere and reward.	Be dominant. Start training the dog to walk *properly* right from the start.
... is destructive	Do not punish bad behaviour as it is always too late. Adopt a training programme in which the dog is left for progressively longer periods starting with very short times. Reward lavishly good behaviour. Be cool with the dog before leaving; never say goodbye. Be dominant and do regular basic training exercises. Ensure that the dog is well-fed and has a comfortable place to lie when it is left. In bad cases consider using a wire crate to confine the dog. Consider 'booby trapping' the environment so that the dog is instantly deterred by falling objects if it opens a door. Tidy up before you leave to reduce temptation. You could 'set up' the situation and use a thrown object to deter the behaviour.	Do not isolate young puppies for prolonged periods. When the dog is left on its own give it a cue that you will return, ie leave a radio or small light on. Go through the same routine each time the dog is left. Make sure it has water and is warm and comfortable. Reward good behaviour but do not punish bad behaviour.
... is sick in the car	Many children and dogs suffer from motion sickness when young, but 99% of both species grow out of it in time. Accustom the puppy to the car by letting him climb in and out of it for a few minutes each day. Then cover the upholstery and take the dog for a very short ride, a few hundred yards, **before it is fed**. Drooling usually precedes actual sickness, so tie on an improvised bib to stop the fur getting soiled. Do not fuss the dog, do not sympathise and above all do not be tempted to give tranquilisers or other drugs. The results can be worse than the vomiting. Take special care driving on the early outings and make sure that queasiness is not generated by an exhaust pipe leak. It may be better to have someone ride in the back to hold the dog steady and to have a newspaper ready when vomiting happens.	During its socialisation period ensure that puppies encounter as many different situations as possible, including the car. Don't be *over*sympathetic if puppy is sick.

Table 4.1 (continued)

What if my dog...	Treatment	Prevention
... is shy	Introduce the dog to acceptable situations and people and gradually build up rewards for good behaviour. Do not use deterrent measures in shy dogs. Ignore shyness, building up the dog by giving it some privileges, but don't overdo it. Do not allow visitors to force themselves on the dog — let the dog take the initiative making friends.	Ensure proper socialisation as a puppy. Make sure that the dog meets a full range of people including children when it is young. Do not correct young puppies during the fear period.
... licks people's hands excessively	This is a sign of submission. Build the dog up by giving it some privileges and stop dominance exercises, at least temporarily. Divert the dog by throwing a toy for it to retrieve.	Do not make puppies 'mouth conscious' and discourage such behaviour from the outset. Use rewards in dogs that tend to shyness and where the parents have a history of shyness.
... shows hyper-sexual tendencies	Instant correction of inappropriate behaviour. Remove temptations. Seek veterinary advice about special medication or possibly castration.	Discourage such actions forcibly from the start. Be dominant and regularly practice dominance exercises. Give the dog an adequate amount of exercise.

For dominance exercises, see Chapter 3. If the methods described above do not seem to be having an effect consult your veterinary surgeon.

Table 4.2 General activities with dogs

Activity	Suitable dogs	Preparation	Where to get information
Competitive exhibition for beauty and breed conformation	Only pedigree dogs registered at the Kennel Club. Mongrels can compete at Exemption shows	See Table 4.3	Canine press or write to the Kennel Club, 1-5 Clarges Street, London W1Y 8AB
Obedience competition	All breeds, crossbreds and mongrels	Attend a basic training club	Ask at the veterinary surgery
Agility competition	All dogs	As above	As above
Informal tracking and drag hunting	Large hounds	Train in scent recognition	Breed clubs and canine press
Informal racing	Afghans, Salukis, Whippets, Terriers	Train tolerance of other dogs	As above
Sponsored walks	All breeds	Basic obedience	National Canine Defence League and other charity-arranged events
Water rescue	Newfoundlands	Practice swims	Breed clubs
Sled pulling and trekking	Huskies, Eskimo dogs	Lead and harness work	Breed clubs
Working Terrier shows	Small Terriers and crossbreds	Lead training	Sporting press
Lurcher shows	Hound crossbreds	Lead training	Sporting press
Collecting for charity	All breeds	Socialisation and wearing a pannier harness	Approach a charity for authorisation
Field trials	Working gundogs	Field Trial Society	List from Kennel Club
Working trials	Large guard breeds	Working Trial Society	List from Kennel Club
Advertising, stage and screen acting	All breeds and mongrels	Socialisation, immaculate obedience, extrovert personality	Animal model agencies—see Yellow Pages
Mountain rescue	Large agile breeds	Obedience, scent discrimination	Mountain rescue groups
Hospital/old people's home or school visiting	All breeds	Must be confident, responsive to strangers and absolutely reliable	Pat Dog Scheme (see section on Useful Information) or on own initiative
Picking up for a shoot	Gundogs, preferably Labradors, Flatcoats, Weimaraners	Gundog training, immaculate behaviour	Gundog clubs. Offshoot of breed clubs or sporting press

Table 4.3 Competitive exhibiting for beauty and breed conformation

Type of show	Who enters	Where to find information	Comment
Club matches	Ring craft club members	At the club	One dog randomly matched against another. An informal competition to give ring craft and judging practice
Exemption shows	Pedigree dogs and mongrels. No need to be Kennel Club registered	Local advertising	The only show you can enter on the day. Many novelty classes. *Not* a good place for your first show as classes are very large
Open shows	Dogs must be Kennel Club registered and transferred to owner's name	Canine press	Some shows restricted to club members but you can join when making the entry. Best place to get the help and opinion of other owners. Enter about 4 weeks ahead of show date.
Championship shows (breed or general)	As above	Canine press	Entries must be made 8-10 weeks ahead. These shows offer Challenge Certificates in many breeds which go towards making up a Champion. Very high competitive level, high entry fees
Crufts Dog Show	Only first prize winners in certain classes at Championship shows are eligible, or winners at Field Trials for gundogs	Canine press	The only British show which has a restricted entry

Table 4.4 Owner-related activities

Activity	Type of work	Qualifications	Where to get information
Breed rescue	Collect unwanted dogs, screen new homes. Transport dogs, house displaced dogs for assessment	Familiarity with breed	Via breed club
Club official	Organising club activities	Secretarial or organisational ability. Unpaid	Via Canine Society or breed club
Club catering	Providing food at events arranged by clubs	Cooking, serving, washing up. Unpaid	Via Canine Society or breed clubs

Table 4.5 Specialised advanced activities

Activity	Qualification	Preparation
Judging	None needed except at highest level where experience tells	Breed or exhibit for several years
Breed note-writer for canine press	Writing ability. Nose for news, attendance at many breed events	Breed and exhibit for several years
Walker of puppy for guide dogs, dogs for the disabled, hearing dogs for the deaf	Urban dweller in certain designated areas. Mixed family group preferred	Contact Puppy Walk Manager, Guide Dogs for the Blind, Tollgate House, Bishops Tachbrook nr Leamington Spa, Warks
Breed litters for guide dogs for the blind	Breeding experience needed, willing to be supervised by GDA officials. Bitch usually supplied by the Association	As above
Grooming competition	Skilled groomer in several breeds	Pet trade press

5
Mishaps and problems

> **About the house (Nos 1-27)**
>
> **Outdoors (Nos 28-43)**

This chapter provides some solutions to common problems and mishaps in the household and generally in respect of dog ownership. Each topic begins with the words 'What if my dog...?'. Hopefully the details given will help owners decide what action to take both in the short and long term to overcome and prevent the difficulty.

Homes which own dogs are never quite as immaculate as those which do not include the pleasure and companionship of pets. However, the following hints are intended to make dog ownership easier and those accidents which do occur in and around the home less serious. See also the section in Chapter 4 on the prevention and treatment of inappropriate behaviour.

About the house

What if...

1. my dog is not clean overnight?
2. my dog soils the floor with urine or faeces?
3. my dog urinates on the carpet?
4. my dog passes faeces on the carpet?
5. my dog vomits on the carpet?
6. my bitch is in season and there are male dogs in the house?
7. my bitch makes bloodstains on the carpet and furniture when she is 'on heat'?
8. my dog sheds hair over furniture, clothing or car upholstery?
9. my dog raids the kitchen rubbish bin while I am out?
10. my dog has oil or tar from the beach on its coat?
11. my dog gets tar on its feet?
12. my dog cannot be lifted into a bath?
13. my dog needs to be introduced to a new puppy?
14. my dog should need to be introduced to my first baby – should I get rid of my dog?
15. my puppy objects to wearing a collar and fights the lead?
16. my puppy chews chair legs and doors?
17. my dog needs to be introduced to a kitten?
18. my new puppy needs to be introduced into a house where there is a cat already?
19. my dog will not be groomed, or will not allow its ears, teeth or feet to be examined?
20. my dog will not take tablets?
21. my dog drools on clothing?

22. my puppy bites people's hands with its very sharp teeth?
23. my dog is tormented by a toddler?
24. my dog knocks down a valuable ornament?
25. my dog steals food?
26. my dog tracks in grass cuttings which stain the carpet?
27. my dog smells doggy?

Outdoors

What if...

28. my dog passes faeces on the pavement?
29. my bitch makes bleached circles on the lawn where she urinates?
30. my male dog kills shrubs by urinating against them?
31. my dog has trodden tar all over the car upholstery?
32. my dog will not swim?
33. my dog takes bread and fat put out for the birds?
34. my dog gets a ball stuck in its throat?
35. my dog attacks a much smaller dog?
36. my dog swallows a stone?
37. my dog digs in the garden?
38. my dog uproots plants?
39. my dog bites the heads off flowers?
40. my dog has passed faeces that need to be disposed of?
41. my dog is stolen?
42. my dog gets lost?
43. my dog gets into a fight?

The character in the box above this list is Buster. We have used him to illustrate some of the mishaps and problems which can occur. Normally Buster is a well-mannered dog, but he does go off the rails occasionally.

About the house

Early planning will help:

1. Decide collectively as a family which parts of the house are 'no go' areas for the dog; for instance it can be trained never to set foot on carpeted areas, sit on the settee, or never to go upstairs. Make sure that no member of the family encourages the dog to break these rules.
2. Never allow a young puppy the free run of the house. Restrict it to easily cleaned areas unless you can keep it under close observation.
3. Do not expect a puppy or a young dog to be 100 per cent obedient if you are not present to warn him about committing offences. Be realistic about the amount of good behaviour you can expect from an unsupervised dog.
4. Above all, avoid putting the dog into a situation where he can spoil articles you value or commit other behavioural errors. Prevention is always better than cure.

1. What if my dog is not clean overnight?

It is normal for adult dogs to have the very occasional accident but this should not occur regularly. Puppies cannot be expected to be clean for long periods until they are six months old. In an older dog consider the following:

1. Is the night too long? Eight to ten hours shut in may be as long as the dog can take.
2. Are there early morning disturbances by the milkman, etc? Once the dog is awake he may need to be let out.
3. Does the dog actually pass urine and faeces when he is let out last thing at night? You may need to accompany him in order to encourage him to concentrate on these actions until they become habits.
4. Will an alteration in diet and/or feeding times make any improvement?
5. Does the dog suffer from some condition affecting the digestive or urinary systems? A veterinary consultation will be necessary to decide.
6. Does the floor of the dog's sleeping place retain the smell or urine and faeces so that he is confused as to what is the right place? Cleaning with a strong solution of bleach, which should be left on the floor for ten minutes and then rinsed with plain water, should eliminate residue smells.

Consider providing the dog with a closed wire crate in which to sleep if all else fails, *provided* he is not left enclosed more than eight hours at night and four to five hours during the day.

2. What if my dog soils the floor with urine or faeces?

Immediate reaction: whose fault was it?
*   *Yours* for not giving the dog the opportunity to go out at the appropriate time?
*   *His* for not asking to go out or refusing to perform when taken out?
*   *Neither.* If the dog is old or ill, or has had diarrhoea, these episodes must be excused.

Immediate action
1. Pick up solid material with kitchen paper and put into newspaper for disposal.
2. Mop up pool of urine into bucket with special sponge/cloth kept for the purpose.
3. Wash floor with detergent cleaner which *does not contain ammonia.*
4. Rinse and wash over with water containing disinfectant.

Stages 3 and 4 must be separate operations, disinfectant is useless on a soiled floor.
While performing actions 1-4 express your disapproval facially and verbally if the accident has been the dog's fault. Smacking or other chastising is inappropriate, while the old-fashioned 'rubbing his nose in it' does nothing but reveal an ignorance of the dog's natural functions.
Prevention
Re-think the dog's routine and provide more opportunities for it to get out to the garden – eg dog flap in door. If the dog is to be left so long that elimination is inevitable, cover an area of the floor thickly with newspaper. If illness is suspected, consult the veterinary surgeon.

3. What if my dog urinates on the carpet?

Immediate action
1. Blot up urine with kitchen paper or, if copious amounts, by laying sheets of newspaper on the pool, weighting them down and changing them frequently as they become saturated.
2. Clean the area with carpet cleaner which does not contain ammonia.
3. Dry with iron, hair drier or hot water bottle.

Prevention
Review dog's routine as above but establish whose fault it was.

Provide exit to garden via dog flap if appropriate. If illness is suspected, consult veterinary surgeon.

4. What if my dog passes faeces on the carpet?

Immediate reaction: Whose fault was it – see 'What if...' No. 2.

Immediate action:
1. Note consistency and content in case of illness.
2. Pick up with kitchen paper, put into newspaper and dispose.
3. Wash and dry quickly as above to avoid staining.
4. Endeavour to remove all smell, as puppies in particular may return to same spot.

Comment:
Carpet tiles are ideal where dogs are kept, as individual tiles may be taken up for cleaning and airing and may be interchanged if soiling is heavy.

5. What if my dog vomits on the carpet?

Immediate action
1. Observe colour and contents of vomit and any foreign bodies therein, since veterinary attention may be required.
2. Prevent dog from re-eating vomit.
3. Pick up solid matter with kitchen paper and put into newspaper for disposal.
4. Wash area of carpet with warm water and biological washing powder, having first tested the carpet for colour-fastness to the washing powder chosen. Dry with hair drier or iron.

Subsequent action
Consult Chapter 17, 'What if my dog is vomiting?' Contact veterinary surgeon if vomiting continues.

Prevention
A dog which is vomiting frequently should be surrounded with newspaper on top of plastic sheeting. Clean the face and chest of a long-haired dog. A bib made out of towelling will prevent further soiling. Many veterinary surgeons now sell 'anti-odour' preparations which eliminate soiling stains and smells.

6. What if my bitch is in season and there are male dogs in the house?

Practically all male dogs recognise the odour of a bitch in season, as indeed nature intended them to.

It is almost a cruelty to keep a male dog in the same house as an 'in-season' bitch and they will almost certainly evade your attempts to keep them apart, as during the middle third of her season the bitch is just as eager to meet the dog as he is to find her.

The dog may refuse to eat, and become thin and poor-coated through frustration. Tempers become frayed and fights may ensue with other males.

Immediate action
Proprietary pills and lotions are generally ineffective in masking bitch odour. Either bitch or dog must be boarded elsewhere.

Subsequent action
Consult a veterinary surgeon about the prevention of heat on a temporary or permanent basis. Spaying or chemical methods are available. Castration of the male may be effective but he will still show some mating behaviour.

See the section in Chapter 1 on oestrus control and 'What if my bitch is mismated?' and 'What if my bitch is found to be pregnant unexpectedly?'

7. What if my bitch makes bloodstains on the carpet and furniture when she is 'on heat'?

The amount of bloodstained discharge when in season varies from bitch to bitch. Some bitches will lick themselves much more frequently when in season and so cause little problem, other bitches are not so meticulous.

Immediate action
1. Use salted *cold* water to soak the stains out of fabrics.
2. Wash in biological washing powder.
3. Clean floor and carpets in similar manner.

Prevention
1. Confine bitch to easily washed areas while she is in season.
2. Cover furniture with old sheets or similar cotton material.
3. Consider fitting the bitch up with sanitary pads and knickers, which can be bought at pet shops or improvised at home.
4. If the bitch is not to be bred from, consider eliminating all the nuisance of seasons. Consult your veterinary surgeon about the prevention of heat by spaying or chemical means. See the section in Chapter 1 on bitches.

8. What if my dog sheds hair over furniture, clothing or car upholstery?

Dog hair varies tremendously in the way it adheres to other fabrics. Really long hair can be easier to remove than the short hair shed by Bull Terriers, Dobermanns and similar coated dogs.

You may find any of the following aids useful:

- Stroking furniture and clothing with a rubber glove on the hand.
- Sellotape wrapped around the fingers, sticky side outermost, and stroked over fabric pile.
- Brushing with a damp nailbrush; wiping with a damp cloth.

All these methods roll the hairs together and make them easier to remove.

A special attachment for the vacuum cleaner, obtainable at pet shops, is available which can be helpful.

Prevention
Groom the dog frequently – daily when hair is being shed in quantities.

If hair is being shed excessively or throughout the whole year, have the dog checked for possible underlying skin disease or hormonal upset.

Discuss the dog's diet with your veterinary surgeon to ensure especially that it is getting sufficient B vitamins and unsaturated fatty acids.

9. What if my dog raids the kitchen rubbish bin while I am out?

Immediate action
Try to identify what has been eaten in case the dog later becomes ill.

Subsequent action
Empty or remove the rubbish bin before you go out. Train the dog, using the methods described in the behaviour section of Chapter 4, that it must *never* touch the bin.

Prevention
Reinforce the behaviour while working in the kitchen by having the rubbish bin prominently placed and standing open. Admonish the dog by saying 'No!' and/or banging a saucepan on the sink *immediately* the bin is approached.

10. What if my dog has oil or tar from the beach on its coat?

Immediate action
Be extremely careful of using any inflammable liquid, such as petrol or carbon tetrachloride, on the dog's coat. It may be preferable to cut off as much of the affected hair as possible, and then to wash the dog in mild detergent and/or canine shampoo, finishing with a plain water rinse. It can be helpful to apply suntan cream, first working

it well into the affected area and then washing it off with warm water containing a 'soft' detergent, such as washing-up liquid.

11. What if my dog gets tar on its feet?

Immediate action
Clip out the hair and lumps of tar between the pads. Soak the foot in a jug or tall tin containing vegetable oil, put butter liberally on the paws or work in some suntan cream if that is available. When tar is loosened, wash feet in warm water containing a 'soft' detergent, such as washing-up liquid, to remove grease and rinse well in plain water so that detergent does not remain on the skin.

If the tar deposit is very heavy, consult a veterinary surgeon at once, as special cleaning measures may be necessary.

12. What if my dog cannot be lifted into a bath?

Large dogs can be bathed quite successfully on the kitchen floor, or on the lawn in good weather. The following method works:

1. Take off leather collar and make the dog a collar of strong cotton or nylon material to use as an anchor.
2. Assemble two sponges, towels and as many buckets of warm water as you can muster. Dilute shampoo in a jug of warm water (always use a shampoo made for dog hair, not a human shampoo).
3. Put a ring of vaseline around the dog's eyes to keep out soapy water.
4. Soak the dog's coat with warm water using the first sponge.
5. Apply shampoo with the second sponge, lather, rinse with the first sponge and clean water, lather again.
6. Finally rinse with clean water until all shampoo has been removed from the coat. In summer, finish off with spray from garden hose.
7. Towel dry and finish with hair drier.

13. What if my dog needs to be introduced to a new puppy?

Many older dogs take on a new lease of life when a new puppy is brought into the home, provided certain precautions are taken early on.

1. Get the puppy as young as possible. At six weeks puppies are confident and unafraid, but by eight weeks the puppy may be entering a fear period (see section on socialisation period) and may become much more difficult to acclimatise.
2. Allow the older dog to become accustomed to the puppy while you are present and then allow brief periods of free socialisation, always *supervised*.
3. It may be helpful to make an enclosure for the puppy in which it can be left safely for the first few weeks in your home when you are not present. Panels sold to

enclose compost heaps can be used but a dog crate is ideal for the purpose (see Chapter 1).

4.   Protect the older dog's rights. Do not allow the puppy to make free with its toys, its bed or its food. It can be helpful to remove the most favoured canine possessions at this time to prevent problems.

5.   Make sure the older dog has a full share of attention, and always give a small titbit every time the puppy is fed – older dogs are fed less frequently than puppies.

6.   Do not leave the two alone when you are absent until they are at ease with one another – a good indication is if the pair choose to share a bed.

7.   Puppies can bite an older dog's feet and ears quite painfully. Most adults growl and snap to warn a puppy that such behaviour is not permitted, but some puppies do not heed the warning and some adults are too vigorous in their reaction, so some human intervention is sometimes needed.

8.   Consult your veterinary surgeon about not taking the older dog to canine gatherings, or to places where many dogs are exercised, until after the puppy is vaccinated to avoid the possible transmission of contagious diseases.

14. What if my dog has to be introduced to my first baby—should I get rid of my dog?

Jealousy of new babies is very uncommon, despite the fears of new parents.

A well-kept healthy dog is unlikely to be a disease risk to the baby. It is a sad thing to discard a dog which has been a good friend to you and will in the future be a good friend to the child, and it is a pity that this action is often urged on new parents by relatives and friends who are prejudiced against dogs.

Jealousy should not occur if you plan the introduction of the dog to the baby with care, assuming that you have already taught your dog good companion animal behaviour. The following tips may help.

1.   Let the dog sit beside you when the baby is attended to and talk to the dog as usual.

2.   The baby's cry may be a completely new sound to the dog and may convey a distress message to him. Teach the dog that it may look but not touch or jump up to cot or pram.

3.   If the dog is large and vigorous, make arrangements for it to have sufficient exercise, as walking with a pram may not be enough.

4.   It can be dangerous to tie a dog to a pram and leave it unsupervised.

5.   Discourage the dog from licking the baby.

6.   Do not let young babies pull the dog's ears and tail.

7.   Provide a place into which the dog can retreat away from the baby.

8.   Never leave the dog alone with the baby in the house, car or garden, especially when the baby is at the crawling stage. Remember that dogs, especially large dogs, can be very vigorous in play.

9.   Do not tempt providence by letting the baby play and crawl around the dog's feeding bowl. The dog should be fed separately and any food that is left must be picked up without delay.

10.   Take the baby or the dog with you if you have to leave a room even for a few minutes. It is better to be safe than sorry.

15. What if my puppy objects to wearing a collar and fights the lead?

Some puppies seem to object strongly to anything around their necks, but body harnesses are not a good idea.

Try the following strategy. Put the collar and lead on immediately before feeding the dog. Put the food on the far side of the room where the dog can see it. Hold the lead while the dog goes over to the food and let it trail while the dog is eating. Repeat at several meal times so that the dog is diverted from fighting the collar and associates collar and lead with something pleasant.

16. What if my puppy chews chair legs and doors?

Puppies have an in-built need to chew, which reaches its peak at 6-10 months old, although many are compulsive chewers from six weeks old. The trick is to prevent this problem arising by giving only a limited number of toys that the dog can chew. It is not a good idea to give an old slipper or a brush, since the dog will not be able to distinguish between that and new shoes or useful brushes. Chew-objects should be unrelated to household items.

This activity calls for the behavioural control methods outlined in Chapter 4 and responds to instant correction by the thrown object. Set up the situation and as soon as the dog starts to chew the item, punish it by a well-directed thrown object. Alternatively, it may help to provide the puppy with large marrow bones and direct his attention to his own chews every time you see him attack furniture. If all this fails, consider confinement in a wire crate for short periods when you cannot watch the puppy, and put temporary protection around fixed pieces of furniture, eg metal angle strip around corners of cupboards, a sheet of perspex or aluminium on the lower half of doors.

Finally, anti-chew sprays can be bought at pet shops – the most expensive ones are very effective, the cheaper varieties are not (Bitter Apple is the brand that works). However, it is much better in the long term to train the dog that chewing does not please you and that not chewing is more rewarding. Finally it is wise not to make dogs mouth-conscious by encouraging them to play tug-of-war games.

A puppy may chew in order to ease pain in the mouth caused by teething. Consider rubbing on a soothing gel made to ease teething in babies. The veterinary surgeon may be able to help in such cases.

17. What if my dog needs to be introduced to a kitten?

Dogs can become very fond of the household cat, even those that are chronic chasers of unfamiliar cats. A little strategy used at the time of introduction of the kitten makes the foundation for an easy relationship.

1. Bring the kitten into the house in a wire carrying basket so that the dog can become accustomed to the scent and look of the kitten.
2. Give the kitten an escape route so that it can sit on a high cupboard out of the dog's reach.
3. Put the kitten's sanitary tray and food where the dog cannot interfere; dogs are attracted to cat faeces.
4. Do not leave the two together until you are sure a mutual respect has developed.
5. Most kittens can take very good are of themselves against one dog, but pack action by several dogs is a greater risk.
6. Finally, praise the dog and give it delectable food rewards when it behaves properly towards the cat, but admonish it promptly if it chases the cat or objects to its presence.

.18. What if my new puppy needs to be introduced into a house where there is a cat already?

Individual adult animals take additions to the household in a variety of ways, and it is not possible to predict how the cat will react.

Many cats will be reserved and sulky at first, but most will come to accept the situation and will soon be sharing their bed with the newcomer.

Some cats resort to urine-marking indoors to express their displeasure at any change in the household. Judicious preparation of the new arrival will help.

1. Well ahead of the puppy's arrival, put the cat's sanitary tray and feeding area in a place the puppy cannot reach.
2. Provide a comfortable sitting area of the cat on a high level.
3. Make sure the cat is clear of fleas and ear mites as these are transmissible to dogs.
4. If you have a cat door, you may wish to keep it closed while the puppy is young and to train the cat to use a window instead.

19. What if my dog will not be groomed, or will not allow its ears, teeth or feet to be examined?

Puppies should be made to submit to grooming and having various parts of their anatomy examined from the first day in the new home, even if they have very little coat at that time.

Either groom the dog on the floor or put something on the table top that will not slip about and which the dog can grip. An old piece of rubber-backed carpet is ideal. Some people advocate putting the dog on a slippery table surface to make it feel insecure and so *likely* to remain quiet. If this approach is adopted, be very careful that the dog does not slip off the table and injure itself. One problem with this method is that the dog will tend to crouch low, making grooming difficult.

If grooming is done regularly it will be unnecessary to have long and painful disentangling sessions. The correct grooming tools and the use of disentangling rinses makes the process easier. Consult the dog's breeder or ask for advice at a pet shop or grooming parlour.

Remember to praise the dog for good behaviour and punish it effectively if it growls or makes a fuss. If the dog shows a tendency to misbehave or even snap in such situations, go through the dominance exercises described in Chapter 3.

20. What if my dog will not take tablets?

It is important to practice tablet-giving from the time you have the puppy. Put small vitamin/mineral supplement tablets deliberately down the throat, although they are actually palatable enough for the puppy to eat them.

Actual medicinal tablets are much more satisfactory given in the throat whole, than crushed on food or disguised in other ways.

1. Cup your finger around the puppy's muzzle, open the top jaw by pressing the lips in the gap just in front of the carnassial teeth in the upper jaw and slip your thumb, protected by the dog's lips, behind the large canine tooth on the side nearest to you.
2. With the opposite hand, open the mouth wide by pressing down on the incisors with your little or fourth finger, pop the pill on to the centre of the tongue as far back in the mouth as you can. If the tablet is put in the right place, the dog will have no option but to swallow.
3. Hold the mouth closed and stroke the throat until the dog swallows the pill, then praise the dog and release it.

21. What if my dog drools on clothing?

Some dogs with loose flews (jowls) cannot help saliva running out of their jaws. Tantalising a dog with food increases the tendency to drool.

Action
Allow the saliva to dry on clothing, then brush with a stiff brush or rub two surfaces of the cloth together.

Subsequent action
Protect unsuitably dressed visitors with a clean cloth to put across their laps or make the dog stay in its basket, bed or crate.

22. What if my puppy bites people's hands with its very sharp teeth?

Many people like to offer a puppy their finger to bite, but when the habit is established, elderly people with prominent veins and fragile skin may not enjoy the sensation.

Action
The command 'No!' accompanied by an immediate sharp tap on the muzzle should deter the puppy. Give the dog its own chew-object in exchange.

Ask other members of the family not to encourage hand-biting.

23. What if my dog is tormented by a toddler?

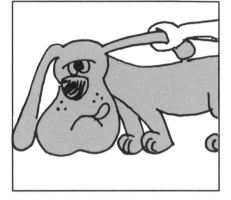

It is very difficult to impress tiny children about what is unkind, cruel or dangerous when they are at the stage of exploring and developing their own skills. Many dogs will tolerate bad treatment from children which they would not endure from anyone else.

The dog should always have some escape route so that it can remove itself if the persecution becomes too trying.

Discreet supervision is *always* necessary.

If the dog is long-haired, check the coat regularly to make sure that rubber bands have not been put around neck or legs, or other objects have not been attached to the coat.

Keep small plastic toys away from the dog – if swallowed they may cause an obstruction in the digestive system.

24. What if my dog knocks down a valuable ornament?

All dog-owning households should be covered for third party liability as a social

necessity. A dog that chases sheep or trips up an old lady may incur its owner considerable financial damage.

Similarly, damage done in someone else's house or car may be covered by this policy. Some insurance companies offer an extension to household policies to cover accidental breakages in the home.

Prevention
With puppies and small children, breakages are best avoided by removing precious objects from low or fragile tables. Do not allow the dog to become excited in a well-furnished room; put the dog into the kitchen while you get ready to go for a walk or prepare its food. Play should only be allowed in 'safe' areas.

25. What if my dog steals food?

It is a normal instinct of dogs to take anything edible which it can reach – hounds are especially good at snatching food, even the steak from under the grill!

It may be possible to train a dog to the extent that it will not approach a laden dinner table, even when all humans are out of the room, but this is a very high standard of control. It is easier to teach a dog to go to its bed and stay there until the order is given to move again. Dogs should always be sent to their own place in the kitchen while cooking is going on.

Some people advocate the folding wire crate, already described as a training aid, to be invaluable in such situations, but if training is undertaken diligently and the dog regards its owner as a true pack leader, such devices should not be required.

26. What if my dog tracks in grass cuttings which stain the carpet?

As soon as they are noticed, pick up as many of the clippings as possible using a stiff nylon brush and pan or a vacuum cleaner. Treat any stains without delay as follows. Using a weak solution of methylated spirits in cold water, make a ring larger than the stained area and gradually work in towards the stain. Then wash in the same way with a good carpet cleaner, rinse and dry thoroughly with an old towel.

27. What if my dog smells doggy?

Check the smell of your house regularly by taking a deep sniff when you come in from the fresh air. Unfortunately it is all too easy to get accustomed to animal smells which other people find very unpleasant. There should be little risk of the single or two pet house becoming smelly, but where dogs are kept in quantity and there are always puppies around, the risk can be a real one.

You will find that with even one pet, housework and laundry is increased. With more dogs, these tasks occupy even more time and may be one of the limiting factors in acquiring more dogs.

Useful tips
- The more dogs you have in your home, the greater the case for having washable furnishings and floor coverings. You may want to consider vinyl chair covers and carpet tiles which can be lifted and cleaned, rather than solid carpeting. Do not let dogs sit on upholstery which cannot be cleaned.
- Kitchen floors should be coved at the edges, if possible, to facilitate cleaning.
- Clean up urine and faeces thoroughly and immediately, and disinfect with a product containing chlorine. Special anti-odour products are available; you can obtain advice on these from your veterinary surgery. Do not use a pine disinfectant as the scent compounds badly with urine and intensifies the smell.
- Do not leave dogs shut in the house for long periods so that they cannot avoid soiling – consider having a dog door into a safe outside enclosure.
- Do not keep a male dog, or allow a male dog to visit, when entire bitches are coming into oestrus. It is almost inevitable that the male will scent mark objects in the house with a particularly odorous stream of urine.
- Consider chemical control of heat or spaying if bitches are not wanted for breeding, for they too have a distinctive scent when in oestrus.
- Air rooms frequently and wash dog bedding often. Woollen blankets and feather cushions hold dog scent while polyester fur fabric does not.

- Groom long-coated dogs right down to the skin frequently and give daily attention to the anal area where faeces may hang on the coat. The older dog does not have such a good 'cut off' by the rectal muscle and may soil the hair around the anus.
- Trim overlong hair on the male dog's sheath very carefully, as this may be a cause of drops of urine being carried on to bedding. Where there are old or sick dogs, examine the bedding twice a day in case urine is being passed in the bed.
- Some types of skin and coat emit more odour than others, particularly the dogs which were once working dogs kept outside. This is an important point to research when choosing your dog.
- All dogs smell when they are wet. The remedy is to dry them as soon as possible. You can make or buy a towelling bag fastened with Velcro which covers the dog completely from the neck down, enclosing the body, legs and feet, and the dog will dry very quickly inside it. This is a very useful aid to have in the car in case your dog gets wet on a walk and especially if you have a long-coated breed.
- When there is an unusual amount of body odour from a dog which does not normally offend in this way, examine the dog very carefully for infected ears or a putrefying wound or skin lesion, all of which can give rise to a distinct and unpleasant smell. Look carefully through the fur of a thick-coated dog to see if there is anything embedded in the fur or skin.
- If an elderly or sick dog has an untraceable body odour, consult the veterinary surgeon, taking with you a fresh urine sample in a sterilised bottle, as the condition may be indicative of a kidney or liver problem.
- Keep a particular watch on the dog for coprophagy or scavenging, as well as the habit of rolling in fox, badger or other animal excreta, or on rotting carcasses on country walks. Much of this behaviour is normal to the dog but should be prevented in the domestic pet.
- Although dogs normally do not need bathing very often, do not be afraid to bath your dog if you think it is smelly. Use a good dog shampoo and consider the advisability of using an insecticidal rinse which can be obtained from your veterinary surgeon.
- Finally, if all else fails, modern anti-odour products can be very effective. These actively eliminate the smell rather than simply mask it. Seek advice from your veterinary surgery and follow the instructions closely.

Outdoors

28. What if my dog passes faeces on the pavement?

Anti-fouling laws are here to stay and must be enforced as a social necessity. Owners must recognise the need to clear dog faeces away in parks and on pavements, and local authorities must co-operate by providing plenty of disposal bins.

Immediate action
Always carry a plastic bag or one of the

scooping gadgets available from pet shops and veterinary surgeries when exercising your dog in a public place.

Do not be too proud to pick up after your own dog!

Prevention
Give your dog the opportunity to pass faeces in an acceptable place before taking it for walks on the pavement or on beaches.

29. What if my bitch makes bleached circles on the lawn where she urinates?

Immediate action
The grass can be prevented from going yellow by pouring on two or three gallons of water immediately the urine is passed.

Prevention
With patience the bitch can be trained to use a concrete, gravel or soil area.

Prevention is not possible if the bitch is allowed to use the lawn.

30. What if my male dog kills shrubs by urinating against them?

Most male dogs, including those which are castrated, establish marking posts around their territory on which they urinate regularly. Low growing conifers, especially junipers, seem to be favourite sites, but any plant will do!

Immediate action
Douse the plant with quantities of water which may save it from urine burn.

Prevention
Leave the dead shrub in position rather than replacing with another or put a wooden post in its place. Close observation of the dog and the command 'No!' when it approaches the area may induce the dog to alter its site. This is an ideal situation for correction by a thrown object, having first set the scene and waited in hiding for the dog to offend. See Chapter 4.

31. What if my dog has trodden tar all over the car upholstery?

Immediate action
Check the dog's feet first as there may be more tar there. See 'What if my dog has tar on its feet?' (No. 11).

Subsequent action
Clean upholstery with proprietary cleaner according to instructions on the bottle. Beaucaire gives excellent results. Suntan cream can be useful in 'dissolving' the tar before it is removed with the cleaner.

Sometimes the veterinary surgeon will prescribe a medicated shampoo which has to be left on the coat for a certain length of time, or which is not rinsed out at all. The dog will have to be supervised and probably held all the time the shampoo is wet in the coat, otherwise it will try to lick itself dry, and will almost certainly vomit. It may also try to roll in the nearest flowerbed.

32. What if my dog will not swim?

All dogs can swim if they have to, but many find it difficult to climb out of pools with vertical sides, so great care must be taken with garden swimming pools, especially when they are partially covered. Tragedies have occurred. Many dogs are afraid of waves thundering on a beach and are reluctant to jump into a river from a steep bank.

Choose a lake with a gentle slope into the water and play with the dog in the shallows until it gains confidence. Teaching your dog to swim could prevent an accident later.

33. What if my dog takes bread and fat put out for the birds?

This is a common canine trait, even among dogs which are not greedy over their own food. This behaviour is not of major concern, but allowances must be made for the amount of food eaten and the dog's diet reduced accordingly, to prevent it from becoming overweight.

Prevention
Provide a bird feeding table out of the dog's reach.

Comment
Remember that if your dog is reluctant to eat its food, you could do worse than throw it out on the grass!

34. What if my dog gets a ball stuck in its throat?

This is a two person emergency.

One person should open the dog's mouth as wide as possible, being careful not to obstruct the nose, using the other hand to pull the tongue forward as far out of the mouth as possible. The other person should try to grasp the ball with fingers, pliers or cooking tongs, pulling it forward, *never* pushing it further back or it will obstruct the throat even more.

As the ball becomes coated in saliva, it may be even more difficult to dislodge. If unsuccessful after a few minutes, rush the dog to the nearest veterinary surgery, having first checked by telephone that the veterinary surgeon is available.

Prevention
Never allow a dog to play with an object which it can swallow.

35. What if my dog attacks a much smaller dog?

Large dogs will naturally sometimes seek to subdue a small dog which is not submissive enough, but such an action in today's society can cause considerable aggravation.

The normal action is for the large dog to put the small one on the ground and stand over it, possibly uttering a threatening growl.

Action
This situations can be broken up harmlessly if only the owners act in the right way. The small dog knows when it is overpowered and it will normally lie still. When the big dog feels the lesson has been learned, it will walk away, having done no harm to the smaller one other than having called its bluff.

The owner of the small dog should refrain from screaming, calling or otherwise creating artificial tension in the scene which will alter the dogs' natural resolution of the incident.

The owner of the larger dog would do well to walk away, calling the dog encouragingly to follow in a normal manner. It is best neither to admonish or praise either dog since these actions could exacerbate the situation. Having previously taught the dog to respond to the word 'Leave!' can be extremely useful in such situations and, if used when an attack is threatened, will often prevent a problem (see also Chapter 4).

36. What if my dog swallows a stone?

Many puppies are addicted to eating gravel. It may do no harm but should be prevented as far as possible.

If you see your dog swallow a large stone, take it to the veterinary surgeon at once, as it may be possible to induce the dog to vomit the stone. This will have to be done quickly; once in the intestine, the stone may cause an obstruction which can only be relieved by surgery.

It is never a good idea to throw stones for dogs. If a dog shows an inclination to eat gravel or stones on the beach it should be sharply admonished, possibly by using a suitable thrown object. Prevention is far better than cure.

37. What if my dog digs in the garden?

Digging is a natural behaviour for most dogs, but it is especially strong in Terriers and Dachshunds.

Dogs dig in order to:

* bury bones and toys – a natural instinct for secreting prizes.
* catch moles and rodents burrowing below the surface.
* create a cool hollow in which to lie during hot weather.
* create a den in which to have puppies during natural or false pregnancy.
* in imitation of human gardening behaviour.

Prevention methods

- Keep the dog with you while you are in the garden so that bad behaviour can be corrected immediately, either by a thrown object and/or verbally (see Chapter 4).
- It can help fill in the hole with large stones or slabs of concrete to deter the dog before filling it with earth.
- Put low fencing around flowerbeds until the dog has learnt garden manners.
- Bury boundary fencing at least a foot below ground, or peg down wire, to prevent Dachshunds digging their way out.

38. What if my dog uproots plants?

It is not uncommon for a puppy to retrieve and bring indoors to you things that you have recently planted.

This may be because they bear your scent strongly and the dog has misguidedly thought it necessary to return the plants to you.

It would be a pity to eradicate the retrieve instinct entirely so take some time to replace the plants and to show the dog that they must not be touched, but then allow the dog to find a dropped glove, scarf, etc and encourage him to bring it to you. An intelligent dog will soon realise what is not to be touched and what can be lifted and returned to the owner.

39. What if my dog bites the heads off flowers?

Puppies often spend their first spring and summer sampling the vegetation in the garden and it can be difficult to control this exploratory instinct.

Dogs can be trained, by constant reminders when you are outside with them, not to step on to flowerbeds but to stay on grass or path.

Preserve your choicest clumps of flowers with a circle of wire or plastic netting during the early days of puppy ownership.

Do not leave a puppy unsupervised in the garden for long periods – mischief is sure to result!

40. What if my dog has passed faeces that need to be disposed of?

Small amounts of dog faeces picked up from the garden may be put into the sewage system via the WC or by lifting a manhole cover.

Special dog WCs can be bought. They consist of a plastic dustbin-like container which is bedded into the ground and charged with a disinfectant type fluid which liquidises faeces put into it. The contents may be emptied on waste ground, dug into a pit or emptied into the sewage system.

The faeces of adult dogs may be put on to compost heaps, but if there is any chance the faeces will contain round or tape worm eggs, this disposal method is unsuitable as the compost heap will not attain enough heat to kill the eggs.

Faeces from puppies are best rolled in plenty of newspaper and burnt if possible or taken to an amenity tip to be buried with other household rubbish.

41. What if my dog is stolen?

There is an increasing risk that pedigree puppies and adult dogs will be stolen from cars, and even from their gardens or when tied up outside shops.

Most of the specialist canine insurance companies offer cover for theft of the dog, together with some of the costs of advertising and offering a reward.

First check with the police, the local veterinary surgeries and rescue kennels that the dog has not been taken in from the street. Check again every other day. In some areas a dog Helpline may be in operation.

Where it is certain that a dog has been stolen, the best tactic is to have a leaflet printed showing a photograph and description of the dog. Circulate it as widely as possible and display it in shops that offer that facility. Also contact the canine press so that breeders may be on the alert for a new dog coming into their area in possibly suspicious circumstances.

Offer a reward, but note that it is illegal to state that 'no questions will be asked if the animal is returned', as this is conniving with the thiefs.

Do not give up hope of seeing your dog again, as it may be turned loose to make its way home several days or even weeks after the theft.

But what should you do if you *find* a dog?

1. Do not be too hasty in collecting a dog which is 'lost'. It may know its way home and it may be best to leave it.
2. Examine any dog running loose for collar tag and/or tattooed numbers possibly in the ear or the inside of the thigh, which may give you some clue as to ownership. If the dog is wearing an address tag you may wish to advise the owner direct, or you may wish to ask a dog warden or the police to do so. If you contact the owner direct, be tactful as some people, possibly because they are worried or feel guilty, can be abusive even to people who have rescued the dog.
3. If you find a dog without a collar and name disc, contact a police station or rescue home as near as possible to the place where you found the dog. It is no kindness to take the dog to wherever you are going and to notify the police there. Communication on matters of this kind tends to be very poor between police stations and particularly between county forces. Taking the dog out of the area may mean it is never reunited with its owners. When a dog is caught by a dog warden it will be put into the local dog pound for 7 days, or it may be sent to a kennel which has a contract with the local authority.
4. Notify the police not only of the breed of dog, if you recognise it, but also give the description, eg brown and white with long ears, as the police are not always good at breed recognition.
5. Provided you have notified the police of your find, you may keep the dog in your home during the 7 days allowed for the owners to claim it. If you are able to do this, it is preferable to putting the dog into police kennels or a rescue home.
6. You may have first refusal of a dog you have found if it is unclaimed by the owners after 7 days, but you must keep the dog for at least a month. The original owner is not, *in law*, entitled to reclaim possession of the dog after the 7 days, from the time the finding of the dog was reported to the police.

42. What if my dog gets lost?

The dog should be wearing a name tag, so that ownership can be traced. Remember to alter the tag appropriately if you are on holiday. More and more dog owners are having their dogs tattooed, or an electronic identity chip implanted in the neck, so that they can more readily be identified.

If the dog gets lost on a walk, turn around and follow the route by which you came, back to the starting point. The dog thus has two opportunities to pick up your scent, and can also follow his own tracks.

A dog will often return to the place where you parked the car.

Many dogs tend to remain quite close to the place at which they were lost, especially when in woodland, but if the dog has become bewildered it may conceal itself from humans, even its owners.

Immediate action
Visit the place at which the dog was last seen early in the morning and at dusk each day, and be prepared to wait quietly for some time after putting bowls of food and water down. Walk about slowly as dogs see moving figures more easily than those which are standing still.

It may help to take a familiar canine companion to the scene, a bitch in season or even a blanket used by an in-season bitch, which can work wonders for attracting a male.

Report the loss separately to every police station over a wide area; to veterinary surgeons, in case the dog has been found injured; and to rescue kennels and breed rescue societies.

Alert a selection of people to look out for the dog, but beware of having too many over-enthusiastic searchers, especially children, who may frighten the dog even further away.

Subsequent action
Make sure your dog always wears a name tag on which your name and address are readable. Old medallions can become so blurred as to be useless.

For use on holiday, buy a cylinder name and address holder into which a slip of paper can be put bearing the current address and remember to keep it up to date.

In the UK Medallions obtainable from the National Canine Defence League bear the words 'If found injured, call a veterinary surgeon, the fee will be paid'. The vet's charges remain the owner's responsibility, but you are assured that no-one will be reluctant to have the dog treated. A tag with a similar message could be made by any individual.

Most canine veterinary insurance policies give ome cover towards the costs of advertising and reward for a missing dog.

43. What if my dog gets into a fight?

Fighting to establish supremacy is a natural behaviour in dogs. When a dog has this tendency, strong domination must be established by the owner. The dog should not be taken out by people who cannot control it.

Avoidance strategy is also employed – not taking the dog into public parks etc and taking it out at quiet times. It is important to train dogs to the word 'Leave!'. The dog should learn that to obey the word 'Leave!' brings rewards. If another dog approaches, start telling your dog to 'Leave!' before a situation develops.

Once a dog is into a fight, breaking up the conflict is a matter of improvisation. Fighting dogs are usually oblivious to the pain of being hit with sticks or leads, and dragging them apart is useless.

Surprise is a good friend on these occasions. Quantities of water via hose or bucket, a diversionary noise, even an *unfamiliar* voice shouting, may cause the dogs to break out of curiosity. Shouting by the owner often seems to spur a dog on to fight harder.

If one or both dogs are wearing collars, the collar may be twisted with hand or stick to momentarily cut off the air supply and allow control of the dog to be regained. But remember the risk of being bitten in the mêlée can be quite high; it may be more prudent to walk away calling the dog to follow. Dogs seldom fight to the death and usually one will surrender.

Never pull one of the participants up by the collar so that it stands on its hind legs, exposing the underbelly to the opponent.

When the dogs have parted, get control immediately and remove them at once out of range of each other, or they will resume the fight at the first opportunity.

SECTION THREE

YOUR DOG IN HEALTH AND ILLNESS

Anatomy and physiology

The major infectious diseases

Parasites

Inherited diseases

Zoonoses

Vaccination

6
Anatomy and physiology

The points of the dog

The paw

The skeletal system

The skin

The ear

The eye

The internal organs

The nervous system

The hormonal system

Introduction

In order that owners can properly look after their pets and get the most out of them, it is important to have at least a fundamental understanding of how dogs are 'made' and how they 'work'. Furthermore, owners who know the names of the various parts and organs, and their functions, can more easily describe any signs and symptoms shown by their dogs to a veterinary surgeon or breeder when seeking advice and can better understand why a specific treatment or course of action has been advised. The information given in this chapter is intended to provide this necessary information in an easily understandable and interesting way. It makes sense for all owners, and especially new ones, to read this chapter in its entirety as one would do with a manual for a new car. Thereafter, it should be necessary only to 'brush up' on specific points. The information has been provided in such a way that details can be quickly retrieved when required. Notes are made where specific structures or functions have a relation to a disease condition.

The points of the dog

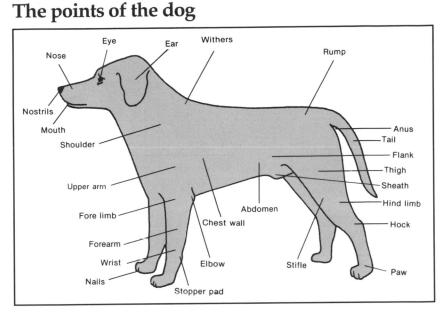

Figure 6.1 The points of the dog

NOTE
- The flank refers to the side of the dog including the chest and the abdomen.
- The ventral surface is the underneath side of any part of the dog.
- The dorsal surface is the upper side of any part of the dog.
- Recumbency is used to describe a dog that is lying down:
  Dorsal recumbency = lying on its back
  Sternal recumbency = lying on its chest
  Lateral recumbency = lying on its side.
- A dog's height is measured at the withers (the top of the shoulder blades), ie the highest part of the body.

The paw

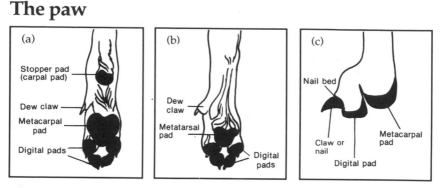

Figure 6.2 The paw (a) Right fore paw from below; (b) right hind paw from below; (c) side view

Lameness is very frequently caused by problems in the paw, eg:

- excessively cracked pads
- thorns in the pad
- cuts in the web
- interdigital cysts
- torn claws
- cut pads.

In cases of lameness it always makes sense to examine first the paw of the affected leg – especially if the leg is being carried.

The pads become very much harder, thicker and more cracked in some cases of canine distemper – so-called hard pad.

The spring clips of leads sometimes become caught in the web. Seek veterinary advice since removal can be very difficult and painful unless undertaken properly.

The skeletal system

Essentially the skeletal system is made up of bones joined by ligaments, muscles and tendons. The function of the skeleton is to support and protect the body organs and, through the muscles which are connected to the bones by tendons, to make locomotion possible.

The major bones in the skeleton

NOTE
- The long bones, eg the humerus, radius and ulna, the femur and the tibia, are most prone to fracture, particularly in road traffic accidents.
- In adult animals the bones usually break into two or more separate parts. In young animals the bone may bend and split, causing the so-called 'green-stick' fracture.
- The fore limb is not joined to the remainder of the skeleton, it is held in place simply by muscles – there is no collar bone.

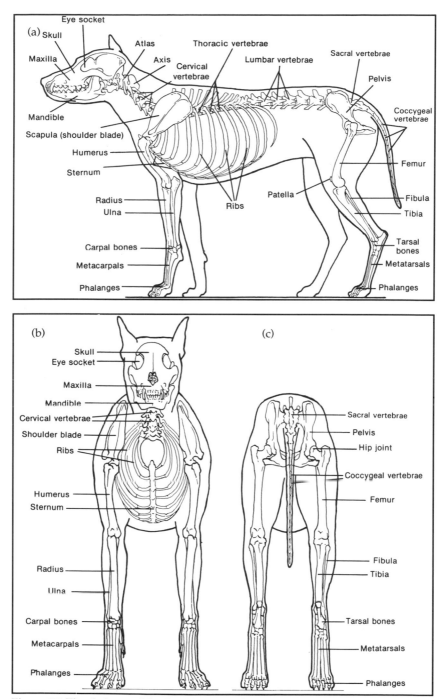

Figure 6.3 The skeleton of the dog (a) viewed from the side; (b) viewed from the front; (c) viewed from behind. (courtesy of Harold White, 1984).

The structure of long bones

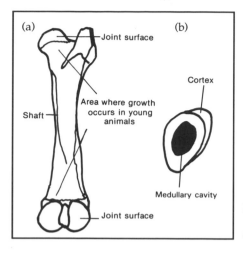

NOTE
- Fractured bones can be repaired by placing a pin in the medullary cavity or by screwing a metal plate to the cortex where appropriate.

Figure 6.4 The structure of a long bone (a) external view; (b) cross-section mid-shaft

The structure of the vertebrae

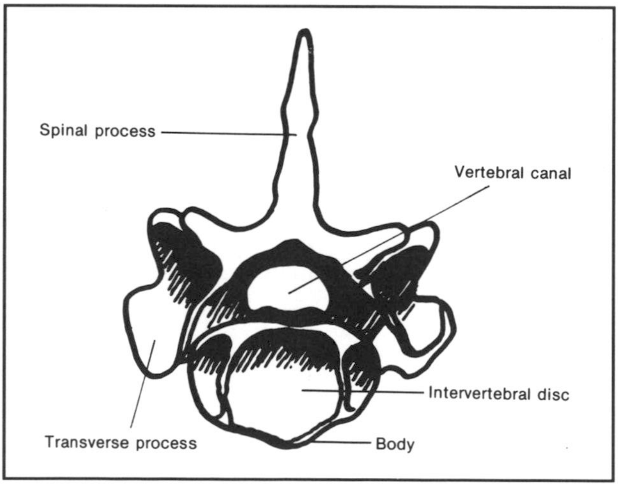

Figure 6.5 Structure of a vertebra

There is a total of 30 vertebrae plus a variable number in the tail:
  7 *cervical* vertebrae make up the neck
  13 *thoracic* vertebrae make up the spine over the chest and articulate with the ribs
  7 *lumbar* vertebrae and 3 *sacral* vertebrae form the lower back
  The number of *coccygeal* vertebrae depends on the length of the tail.

NOTE
- The spinal cord lies within the vertebral canal and is thus protected by bone.
- The vertebrae are separated by discs of cartilage which give protection against trauma and allow the spine to be more flexible. The centre of a disc may slip out of place and press on the spinal cord, causing pain and paralysis. This can be a particular problem in long backed dogs such as Dachshunds.

- The vertebrae are joined together by ligaments and muscles which are anchored to the vertebral processes. Contraction of the muscles make the spine bend vertically and from side to side.

The structure of the skull

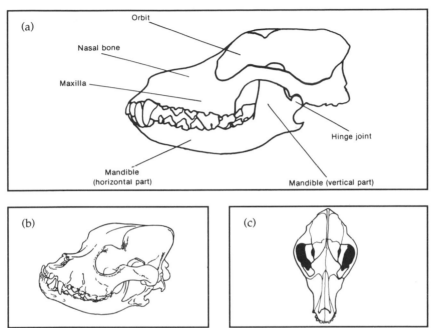

Figure 6.6 The structure of the skull (a) the skull of a normal dog; (b) the skull of a short-nosed dog; (c) the skull viewed from above

The upper jaw is made up of the maxilla bone. The lower jaw is hinged to the skull and consists of the mandible which has both horizontal and vertical parts. These can become fractured quite easily in road traffic accidents. The jaw may become dislocated by trauma but that is comparatively rare. It is quite common, however, for the left and right horizontal parts of the mandible, where they are joined in the front of the mouth, to become separated in traumatic accidents. Sometimes the bones that make up the roof of the mouth do not fuse properly giving rise to a cleft palate. Puppies with severe cleft palates cannot suck because they cannot form a vacuum in the mouth and so often die. It is sensible to check all puppies as they are born for this congenital abnormality.

In short-nosed breeds such as Boxers, the maxilla is much shorter than normal, while the lower jaw remains of normal length, giving the typical undershot mouth formation (see Figure 6.6(b)).

The bony plates that make up the top of the skull are fused together in the middle of the forehead. In some small very dome-headed (apple headed) breeds such as Chihuahuas, this fusion fails to occur, leaving a gap or fontanelle, which is also called by breeders a molera. Such animals are, of course, very vulnerable to brain injury.

The teeth

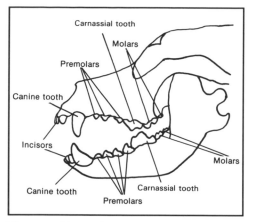

Figure 6.7 The teeth

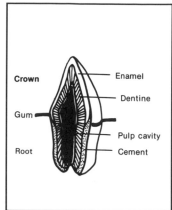

Figure 6.8 Structure of the tooth

Adult dogs have a total of 42 teeth. These are made up as shown in Table 6.1

Table 6.1 Adult dentition

Tooth type	Upper jaw	Lower jaw
Incisors	6	6
Canine	2	2
Premolars	8	8
Molars	4	6

Puppies begin to cut their milk teeth at about 14 days after birth. There are no molars in this set.

Milk teeth are shed and replaced by adult teeth at 4-6 months of age. If any milk teeth persist which threaten to obstruct the correct growth of the permanent teeth, they can easily be removed by a veterinary surgeon.

Dogs' teeth are shaped for tearing and cutting rather than grinding, thus particles of food do not tend to become lodged in the teeth and dental decay is, therefore, relatively rare. Two of the molars are exceptions to this rule.

Dogs frequently accumulate tartar (a hard deposit) on their tooth surfaces, particularly if they only have access to soft food. This scale can be fairly easily removed by veterinary surgeons and should not be allowed to accumulate as it can lead to gingivitis (inflammation of the gums) associated with smelly breath and premature loss of teeth.

Two molars in the upper and lower jaws are much larger than the rest of the teeth. They are called the carnassial teeth. They have more than one root which can make them difficult to extract.

Tartar starts to accumulate at tooth/gum junction. Infection can also enter at this point. Both can lead to inflammation of the gum.

The joints

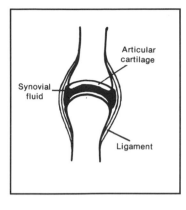

Figure 6.9 The structure of a simple joint

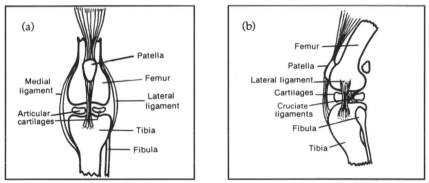

Figure 6.10 The structure of the stifle joint (a) front view; (b) side view

A joint is the region where two or more bones come together to form a hinge. Simple joints allow movement in one plane only, whereas ball and socket joints, eg the hip, allow rotation to occur. The ends of the bones which form joints are covered with smooth cartilage to facilitate movement and the joint itself is lubricated with an oily liquid called synovial fluid. The bones are bound together with ligaments which may become damaged if the joint is sprained by being bent or straightened beyond its normal limits. If the ligaments break or are so stretched that the bones become separated, a dislocation occurs. The stifle and hip joints are particularly prone to problems in dogs. Their structure is shown in Figures 6.9, 6.10 and 6.11.

- In arthritis the articular cartilage becomes inflamed and makes movement painful.
- The upper part of the patella is joined by a tendon to the muscles which straighten the leg.
- The lower part of the patella is joined by a ligament to the tibia.
- The patella runs in a groove in the femur and moved up and down as the leg is straightened and bent.
- The patella may be dislocated to either side if the joint is subjected to trauma. This can occur quite easily if the animal is born with a groove which is abnormally shallow.

117

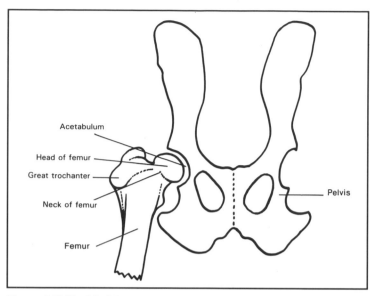

Figure 6.11 The hip joint

- Within the joint lie two cartilages which cushion the joint against trauma, and two ligaments – the cruciate ligaments. These latter structures may become ruptured so allowing excessive, sometimes painful, movement of the joint.
- The hip joint is a typical ball and socket joint.
- In cases of hip dysplasia changes occur in the acetabulum (socket) and/or to the head of the femur so that the joint cannot function properly. In severe cases the joint may be dislocated. This condition can be painful and cause affected animals to limp severely. Hip dysplasia often affects both hips since it is partly an inherited condition. It is commonly seen in the larger breeds of dog, ie those weighing over 45 lb (20 kg).

The skeletal muscles

Muscles are made up of fibres which contract when stimulated by a nerve impulse. Some muscles, for example those making up the stomach wall, are flat and relatively thin, others are cylindrical and when contracted are quite fat (eg the biceps muscle which flexes the elbow, and the quadriceps muscle which lies in front of the femur and straightens the hind leg). Since the ends of the muscles are attached to bone by tendons, contraction and relaxation causes movement in the joints, making them bend (flex), extend, move inwards (adduct), move outwards (abduct) or rotate. In principle each muscle is opposed by another which exerts the opposite effect, thus the animal can adjust the position of any joint very precisely.

Apart from their obvious actions in causing locomotion, the muscles also serve to generate body heat by shivering. The muscles over the chest contract and relax to bring about respiratory movements. The abdominal muscles come into play when a dog passes motions or gives birth, as well as helping to flex the spine when the dog is galloping. The shoulder muscles hold the fore leg to the dog's trunk.

Over-extension of muscles can cause damage and this is called muscle strain. Myositis is the word used to describe inflammation of muscles, often accompanied by acute pain.

The skin

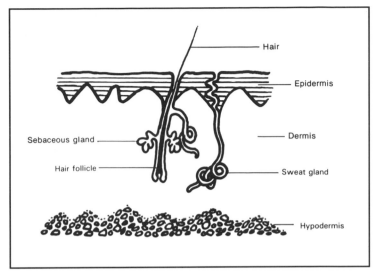

Figure 6.12 The structure of the skin

The overall purpose of the skin is to cover the body and protect the underlying tissues and organs, but it is also responsible for carrying information about objects that come in contact with the animal, and the environmental temperature. The skin is also, of course, sensitive to pain and will warn the animal of danger from sharp objects, etc. The skin consists of two main layers – the *epidermis* and the *dermis*.

The epidermis

This layer is made up of hardened plate-like cells which are formed continuously from the bottom layer and are shed or worn away from the top. The layer contains no blood vessels. The epidermis may become thickened and cause callouses on the hocks and elbows of heavy dogs through pressure on contact points when lying down (see also 'What if...' No. 18, Chapter 17).

In places, the epidermis extends down into the underlying layer to form a hair follicle which produces a single hair by growth from the bottom. When this growth stops that hair is shed and usually another begins to grow in its place. In dogs a number of hairs group together to emerge through a common opening. One hair in such a group is often thicker and longer than the others and is called a guard hair. The rest of the coat is formed by the smaller, softer hairs in the bunch. The size of these hair bunches will vary according to the coat type. Sebaceous glands feed into the hair follicle producing a thick fluid that lubricates the skin and keeps it pliable.

Sweat glands also open up to the surface through the epidermis. In man, the evaporation of fluid produced by these glands is a major cooling mechanism. However, dogs lose heat principally by panting over their tongues.

The dermis

This layer contains blood vessels that nourish the lower layer of the epidermis, and connective tissue which supports the hair follicles and sweat glands. It also contains nerve ends which are sensitive to pain and touch. Small muscle fibres in the dermis, which can lengthen and contract, alter the shape of the skin and erect or lower the hairs. This effect is noticeable particularly in the centre back area and neck when the dog is mentally aroused, aggressive or fearful.

Modified skin structures

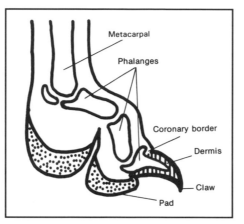

Figure 6.13 The claws

- **The mammary glands** are skin glands that have become specially modified to produce milk.
- **The anal sacs** (or so-called scent glands) are inversions of the skin where it joins the end of the digestive tract. The cavity formed is, in most dogs, big enough to take a broad bean. There are two sacs which lie on either side of the anus, producing a sickly smelling fluid of varying consistency. Occasionally the opening of these cavities becomes blocked and, unless expressed, the fluid may become infected and a painful anal abscess will form and possibly burst to the outside. (See also 'What if...' No. 22, Chapter 17.)
- **The claws** originate from the coronary border, the circular junction between the base of the claw and the skin. The claw grows down over the dermis that lies over the underlying phalanx. The dermis contains a lot of blood vessels and will bleed profusely if cut.

NOTE

In *subcutaneous injections* the needle passes through the epidermis and dermis and the medicament is deposited in the hypodermis. *Intramuscular injections* are given into the muscles (usually in the hind leg) underlying the skin; *intravenous injections* are given straight into the blood stream (usually the vein running down the front of one of the forelegs is used). *Intraperitoneal injections* are given into the cavity between the abdominal wall and the abdominal organs.

The ear

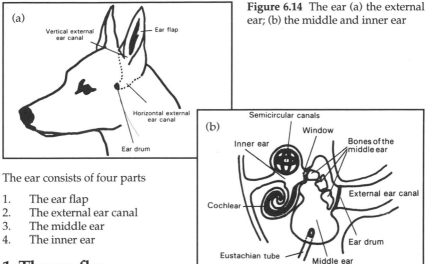

Figure 6.14 The ear (a) the external ear; (b) the middle and inner ear

The ear consists of four parts

1. The ear flap
2. The external ear canal
3. The middle ear
4. The inner ear

1. The ear flap

The ear flap is made up of a sheet of cartilage covered with skin. It varies in size between breeds and may be held erect, as in Terriers, or folded over as in Spaniels and Basset Hounds.

2. The external ear canal

This is composed of tubular cartilage and is lined with a specially developed skin called the integument, which produces a waxy material. In some breeds the canal is hairy. The canal has a sharp bend at its lower end where the vertical part joins the horizontal part. The end of the horizontal part of the canal is sealed by the ear drum.

It is important that the external ear canal be kept clear of excessive amounts of wax and debris, otherwise infection may occur, resulting in *otitis externa* (ear canker). It may be necessary to pluck or remove some of the hair in dogs with very hairy ears, such as Poodles, to allow proper ventilation and prevent the accumulation of wax. This should be done, however, with great care (see also 'What if...' No. 14, Chapter 17). In chronic cases of *otitis externa* the lining of the ear becomes very thickened so that the canal is blocked and the ridges often rub together to form ulcers. By the time that has happened, the only sure cure is to open the canal to the outside by carrying out an operation called an aural resection.

3. The middle ear

The middle ear is housed in a cavity in one of the bones which make up the skull. It consists of a chamber that contains three small bones which connect the ear drum to a window at the opposite side. These bones transmit sound vibrations to the inner ear. Pressure differences between the middle and external ear are equalised by means of the eustachian tube, which leads to the back of the mouth and which is also situated in a cavity in a bone of the skull.

4. The inner ear

The inner ear consists of a number of sealed tubes which contain fluid. The cochlea picks up vibrations from the middle ear and is concerned with hearing. The semicircular canals contain nerve ends which sense the fluid movement in the tubes which are set at right angles to each other. By monitoring the fluid movement the animal is able to keep its balance and orientate itself in space.

While disease of the external ear is common, middle and inner ear disease is rare, but is usually very serious when it does occur.

If external ear disease is not treated promptly and properly, it can lead to a serious problem that may need a surgical operation to correct (see also 'What if...' No. 14, Chapter 17.)

The eye

Essentially the eye is a fluid-filled globe that is housed in the orbit in the skull. Attached to the outside of the globe ear a number of muscles which are able to move the eye upwards, downwards and from side to side.

The lens, iris and the ciliary body divide the eye into two parts:

(i)   the anterior chamber, which is filled with fluid called the aqueous humour;
(ii)   the posterior chamber, which is filled with a thick fluid called the vitreous humour.

The correct pressure within the eye is maintained by fluid being continually produced and drained away. If this mechanism goes wrong, the pressure in the eye will rise, resulting in the eye increasing in size and the cornea becoming opaque – this is called glaucoma, (see also 'What if...' No. 13, Chapter 17.)

The outermost layer of the eye is tough and thick and is called the sclera. Over the front of the eye this layer takes the form of a transparent window called the cornea.

The lens is attached by the suspensory ligament to the ciliary body, which is muscular. Contraction of this muscle alters the shape of the lens so that the animal can focus on objects at different distances. The iris arises from the ciliary body and projects in front of the lens. It has a central orifice called the pupil. The pupil becomes smaller when the iris contracts in response to bright light, and bigger when the iris relaxes in the dark. The size of the pupil can be controlled by some medicines applied as drops to the eye. They may be used by veterinary surgeons to help examination of the eye or to treat or alleviate certain eye conditions.

The back of the eye is lined with the retina. Nerves which have light-sensitive endings in this layer transmit messages through the optic nerve to the brain, where they are decoded into a 'picture' of what is being seen. The back of the eye of dogs and cats also contains a separate area called the tapetum which reflects light. The glowing effect of dogs' and cats' eyes at night is produced when a beam of light falls on to the tapetum in surrounding darkness and is reflected.

The front of the eye is protected by the upper and lower eyelids which, when closed, completely cover the eye in most dogs. The place where the eyelids join is known as the corner of the eye. Dogs have a third eyelid which lies close to the surface of the eye in the inner corner of the eyelids. When the eye recedes into the skull, as can occur when the dog is out of condition and the fat behind the eye decreases in amount, or when the

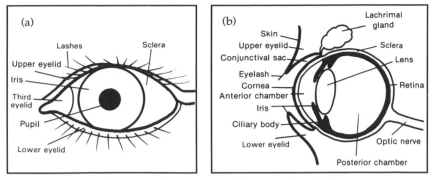

Figure 6.15 The eye (a) external appearance; (b) section through the eye

eye is pushed backwards into the head, the third eyelid will come across to protect the eye from possible damage. A gland which produces lubricating fluid (the Harderian gland) lies under the third eyelid. It may occasionally become enlarged and protrude from behind the third eyelid and cause a problem.

The skin on the outside of the eyelid is continued on the inside of the eyelid and over the cornea as a thin layer called the conjunctiva. Because the lids protrude over the eye the conjunctiva is bent back on itself to form a sac as it continues over the eye. The surface of the eye is lubricated by fluid (tears) produced by the lachrymal glands that have their outlet into the conjunctival sac. Any excess tears are carried away in small ducts that are situated in the inner corner of the eye and which lead to the nose. If more tears than normal are produced, or if this duct becomes blocked, fluid will run down the side of the animal's face and may cause staining or inflammation of the skin. The upper and lower eyelashes protrude from the point where the skin on the outer side of the eyelids and the conjunctiva join. Sometimes there is an extra layer of lashes, distichiasis, which rub on the surface of the eye and cause a problem. In other cases the eyelids may turn inwards, making the lashes rub on the surface of the eye causing inflammation – this is called entropion. The reverse of this situation, when the eyelids turn outwards exposing the conjunctiva as occurs quite commonly in breeds such as Bloodhounds where it is known as the haw, is called ectropion. Both these conditions require veterinary attention and in some situations surgery may be needed (see also 'What if...' No. 11, Chapter 17).

- If the cornea is damaged or the pressure in the eye increases it will become opaque.
- In young animals the lens is elastic. This elasticity decreases as animals age, so focusing becomes more difficult.
- Sometimes the lens will become detached from its ligaments and fall either forward or backward. This is a lens luxation (dislocation) and can lead to glaucoma.
- Opacity of the lens is known as a cataract which may be partial or complete.
- Hereditary defects in the retina can affect vision, viz. Collie eye anomaly (CEA) and progressive retinal atrophy (PRA) (see 'What if...' Nos 12 and 13, Chapter 17).
- Bacterial infection of the conjunctival sac leads to inflammation – conjunctivitis.

The internal organs

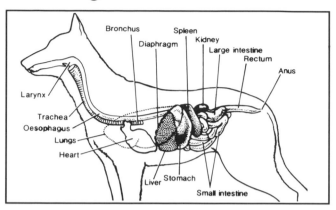

Figure 6.16 The internal organs

The inside of the body is divided into two parts by the diaphragm:

1. the thoracic cavity – the chest (thorax)
2. the abdominal cavity – the abdomen.

1. The circulatory system

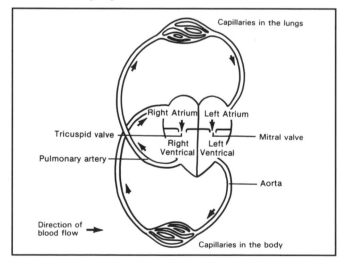

Figure 6.17 A schematic illustration of the circulatory system

All the organs which make up the body need oxygen in order to function normally. This essential requirement is brought about by the red cells in the blood, which in turn are carried around the body in a continuous tube called the circulatory system. The blood is propelled around the system by the action of the heart, which is in fact a muscular pump fitted with valves to ensure that the blood travels in the right direction. Problems can occur if the heart valves leak (incompetence) or do not open properly (stenosis).

Sometimes drugs need to be given to strengthen the beat of the heart if the muscle becomes weakened by age or inactivity.

Essentially, blood which has circulated round the body and become exhausted of oxygen returns to the right atrium. It is pumped through the tricuspid valve into the right ventricle which pumps it through the pulmonary artery to the lungs. As the blood passes through the small tubes in the lungs (the capillaries) it picks up oxygen. Oxygen-enriched blood returns from the lungs to the left atrium, is pumped through to the left ventricle and then via the aorta to be distributed to the capillaries throughout the body.

A small amount of the fluid from the blood and some cells leak out into the tissues to be gathered up in another series of channels called the lymphatic system, which in turn drains back into the blood system. This lymphatic system has a number of glands or nodes situated throughout its length. These glands, which sometimes become swollen in the case of infection in a tissue, act as filters to remove bacteria and other debris from the blood and they are also responsible for the production of some types of white blood cells and antibodies that protect the body against infection.

The spleen – lies near the stomach in the abdomen. It is responsible for producing some of the elements that make up blood and also for removing old worn out red blood cells. It also acts as a storage area for blood and thus varies considerably in size according to the amount of blood required in the circulatory system at any particular time.

The bone marrow – the cavity of the long bones is filled with marrow which produces red blood cells and some types of white blood cells.

Blood contains:

- red blood cells – which carry oxygen
- white blood cells – which can engulf bacteria and other foreign matter within the body
- blood platelets – cell fragments.

These components are carried in a fluid called plasma.

Clotting – if blood leaks from the system, fibrin filaments formed from one of the constituents in the plasma link together to form a web or net which traps the cells in the blood to form a clot. The clear fluid that remains is called serum.

Blood tests – veterinary surgeons will sometimes take a blood sample to test for:

- the number of cells of each type in a standard volume of blood.
  the packed cell volume (PCV) – the amount of space taken up by the cells, when they are allowed to settle, in comparison with the plasma.
- the erythrocyte sedimentation rate (ESR) – the speed with which the red blood cells settle out when the blood is left to stand.
- the levels of various enzymes and other constituents normally found in blood.
- the levels of protective antibodies to various diseases for diagnostic purposes, to identify the best time for vaccination or to check that vaccination has been effective.

Such tests help in the diagnosis of diseases and can also give a guide to the prognosis of a case.

2. The digestive system

In order to work, the body needs food to provide a source of energy to allow organs to grow and to replace worn out tissues. Food needs to be processed by the digestive system in order to provide materials in a form that can be utilised. Essentially, the digestive system is a muscular tube or tract, with openings at one end where food goes in and at the other end where waste material (excreta) comes out. A number of glands associated with the digestive system discharge the fluids they produce into the tube to facilitate the breakdown of food into essential elements.

The digestive process

1. If the food is presented in chunks, it is torn into small pieces and crushed briefly by the teeth in the mouth. Otherwise it is swallowed whole.
2. Saliva, produced by the salivary glands, helps to lubricate the food as it passes through the oesophagus into the stomach. The salivary juices also begin the digestive process.
3. The oesophagus is a simple tube which passes down the neck and enters the chest, passes over the heart and through the diaphragm into the stomach. Inadvertently swallowed large objects may become stuck in the oesophagus at the entrance to the chest, over the heart and where the oesophagus goes through the diaphragm, and may require surgical removal.

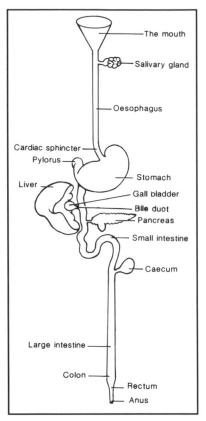

Figure 6.18 A schematic representation of the digestive tract

4. The entrance and exit to the stomach are guarded by a ring of muscle, the cardiac sphincter and the pyloric sphincter. The pyloric sphincter is responsible for regulating the passage of food from the stomach. The stomach wall produces juices (hydrochloric acid and enzymes) which help to break down the food, particularly proteins, so that it can be absorbed from the intestines into the blood. Inflammation of the stomach is called gastritis.
5. Digestion continues in the small intestine aided by the bile and enzymes in the pancreatic juice. The useful products are absorbed through the intestinal wall into the blood stream and lymphatic system.
6. The digestive process, aided by bacteria, and absorption of useful material continues in the large intestine. The main function of the large intestine is the resorption of excess fluids.
7. The caecum is equivalent to the appendix in man. It seldom causes a problem in dogs.
8. The faeces (the motions, or stools) are made up of waste material and are 'stored' in the rectum to be passed, usually twice a day.

3. The pancreas

The pancreas produces juices which help digestion, but it also manufactures the hormones insulin and glucagon which are responsible for regulating the amount of available glucose (sugar) in the bloodstream. In diabetic dogs, this system malfunctions.

4. The liver

Besides producing bile, which helps digestion, the liver is also responsible for regulating the storage and usage of carbohydrate, the mobilisation of body fat, the detoxification and excretion of toxic substances, the synthesis of proteins that occur in the blood and to help stabilise the body temperature.

NOTE
- The collective word 'viscera' is used to describe all the abdominal organs together.
- Sometimes the rectum will protrude through the anus – this is called a rectal prolapse. It is nearly always a sequel to a severe and protracted attack of diarrhoea and requires veterinary attention and possibly surgical correction.

The urinary system

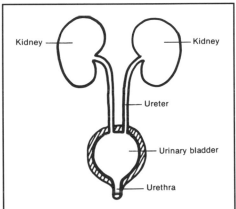

Figure 6.19 The urinary system

The urinary system is responsible for removing much of the excess water and many waste products that accumulate in the body. The kidneys, which lie one on each side of the body near the spine, high up in the abdomen, filter these materials from their blood supply. Fluid leaves the kidney by the ureter which leads to the bladder. The urethra leads from the bladder, either though the vulva in the female or the penis in the male. In the female the urethra is short, whereas in the male it is long and arches over the pelvis.

- Stones (uroliths) made up of various waste materials may accumulate in the bladder and need surgical removal. Special diets are available from vets which can help dissolve bladder stones and help prevent them reforming afterwards.
- In male dogs small stones may become stuck in the urethra as it passes over the pelvis or in the penis itself, behind the bone that is present in the penis.
- Nephritis is the word used to describe inflammation of the kidneys.

The respiratory system

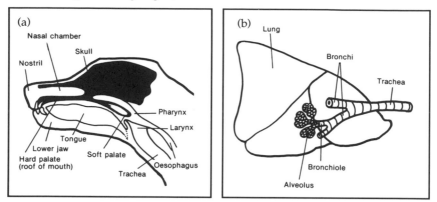

Figure 6.20 The respiratory system (a) section through the head to show the larynx and pharynx; (b) the lungs

It has already been said that in order to function the body needs oxygen. The main function of the respiratory system is to bring about effective oxygenation of the blood, but it also plays a role in heat regulation and the loss of excess water. Expansion of the chest, brought about by the movement of muscles in the chest wall and a downward movement of the diaphragm, creates a negative pressure in the thorax which inflates the lungs and causes air to be drawn in through the nose and, during exercise, through the mouth. Air passes through the pharynx, which is common to the respiratory and the digestive tracts, into the larynx and reaches the lungs via the trachea. Within the lungs the trachea divides into two bronchi and these divide again like the branches of a tree, to form bronchioles, which end in air sacs, the alveoli. Blood circulating in the walls of the air sacs picks up oxygen as it passes through. The lungs are made up of a mass of grape-like air sacs supported in connective tissue.

- **The nasal chamber** is lined by scrolls of delicate bone covered with a sensitive lining. Its main function is to warm and filter air and to aid the sense of smell. The chamber is linked to sinuses which are cavities in the bones that make up the skull.
- **The pharynx** is common to the respiratory and digestive tracts. When the dog is eating, the trachea is closed by the epiglottis and the nasal cavity is sealed by the soft palate.
- **The larynx** consists of a tube made up of cartilage. Its function is to prevent food entering the trachea and to produce sound (vocalisation) by vibration of the vocal chords it contains.
- **The trachea** is a straight tube held permanently open by ringed cartilages. The trachea branches in the chest to form the two bronchi. In kennel cough the trachea and bronchi become inflamed and this results in a persistent, retching cough.
- **The respiratory rate** in a normal resting dog is 10-30 breaths per minute.

The genital system

The male

Like all male animals, dogs have two testicles in a pouch (the scrotum) between the hind legs. The testicles produce spermatozoa which pass down tubules to a duct called the epididymis where they are stored. During mating the spermatozoa pass from the epididymis to another duct which joins the urethra (see also The urinary system). On the way the spermatozoa are mixed with fluid from the prostate and other glands to form the semen which is ejaculated from the erect penis through the urethra during mating.

The testicles also produce the male sex hormone, testosterone, which is responsible for producing the secondary male characteristics. The testicles descend into the scrotum from the abdomen during puppyhood in normal dogs. In some animals, one or both testicles are permanently retained in the abdomen. A dog with only one testicle descended is known as a unilateral cryptorchid (monorchid) and where neither is descended, a cryptorchid. Retained testicles are a hereditary problem, and although a monorchid dog is fertile, it should never be used for breeding as the fault may be transmitted to its offspring. Monorchidism is regarded as a major fault in the show ring.

A castrated dog is one in which the testicles have been completely removed surgically, usually to curb excessive inter-male aggression and objectionable sexual behaviour. Such dogs are, of course, infertile, although they may continue to be interested in bitches and may even mount bitches that are in season. The castrated male tends to put on weight and the calorie content of the diet should be reduced accordingly.

The female

Bitches have two ovaries which are situated in the abdomen near the kidneys. When the bitch is in season, the ovaries produce eggs which are caught by the fimbriae and pass down the oviducts into the uterus where they develop into foetuses, if the bitch has been successfully mated. The bitch's uterus is made up of two long horns and the uterine body. It opens into the vagina by the cervix which is kept shut, except during oestrus and when giving birth. The female genital tract opens to the exterior through two lips which make up the vulva.

Between heats the uterine horns are no thicker than a piece of string, but when the bitch is in season they increase in size to become rather thicker than a pencil. The pregnant uterus has a diameter of 2-4 inches according to the breed and may contain, in the case of the large breeds, as many as 12 or 14 puppies.

Besides producing eggs, the ovaries manufacture the female sex hormones, oestrogen and progesterone. These are responsible for bringing about the secondary female sex characteristics and the development of the mammary glands (see also The hormonal system).

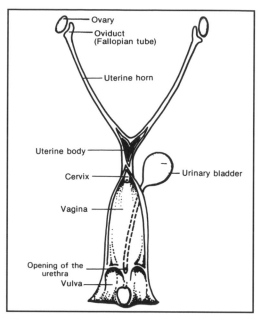

Figure 6.21 The genital organs of the bitch

- During coitus, spermatozoa ejaculated from the male penis are deposited around the cervix. They pass through into the uterus and up the fallopian tubes where the eggs are fertilised.
- Spaying (ovarohysterectomy) involves the complete removal of the uterus and the ovaries of the bitch. this is, of course, done under general anaesthesia and is a major operation.
- Very occasionally the lining of the vagina will protrude through the vulva after whelping. This is called a vaginal prolapse and requires veterinary attention.
- Vaginal hyperplasia is the term used to describe the swelling and protuberance of the lining of the vagina that occurs during heat, particularly in Boxers and Bulldogs.

The nervous system

The function of the nervous system is to receive messages from outside the body and, after analysing them, to cause the animal to respond in an appropriate way.

The nervous system is essentially divided into two parts:

1. The central nervous system

This consists of the brain and spinal cord, both of which are protected by bone – the skull in the case of the brain and the bony canal through the vertebrae in the case of the spinal cord.

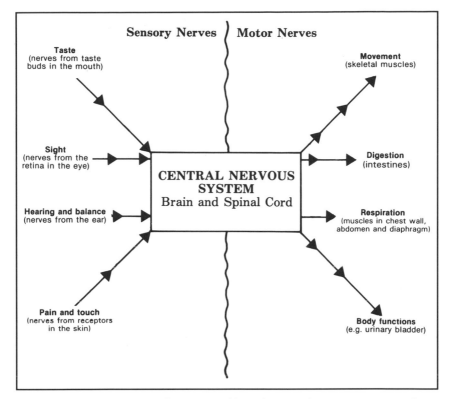

Figure 6.22 A diagrammatic illustration of how the central nervous system works

2. The peripheral nervous system

This consists of nerves which connect the central nervous system to the rest of the body.

If a ball is thrown for a dog to catch, messages are sent through the sensory nerves from the light-sensitive nerve endings in the eye to the brain. This in turn sends messages via the motor nerves to the muscles which move the dog into the right place and open its mouth at the correct time. All this, of course, takes place in a split second of time.

Some nerve impulses are sent automatically from an organ, for example the stomach, when it is full, and the central nervous system responds, also automatically, to send a nerve impulse to the muscles in the organ to make them contract and empty it. In some cases, eg the urinary bladder, the brain can override the automatic response, as occurs in house-trained animals. In other cases, for example the filling and emptying of the stomach, the nervous impulses which cause contraction of the muscles and dilation of the sphincters are purely automatic and cannot be overridden consciously.

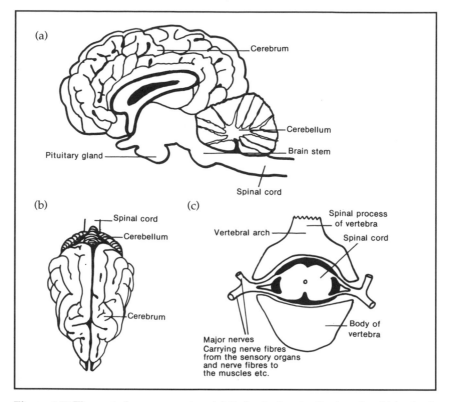

Figure 6.23 The central nervous system (a) the brain, longitudinal section (side view); (b) the brain, from above; (c) the spinal cord (section through vertebral canal)

The hormonal system

A number of glands, the endocrine glands, situated in various parts of the body, produce hormones which are spread by the bloodstream throughout the body. They instruct the organ or body system they control to perform a specific function. Many organs which are under hormonal control receive messages from one hormone which makes them work more quickly and from another which makes them work more slowly or stop. Thus the hormones act rather like the accelerator and brakes on a car and control very precisely the body's activity.

Besides their effect on specific parts of the body, the hormones work together rather like the players in an orchestra, the whole being conducted by the hormones produced by the pituitary gland which is situated at the base of the brain. The amount of hormones present in the blood is being continually monitored by the body and adjusted to meet the animal's need at any particular time. See Table 6.2.

Table 6.2 The endocrine glands and the hormones they produce

Gland	Situation	Hormone(s) produced	Action
Thyroid	The gland lies alongside the trachea at the end nearest the mouth	Thyroid hormone	Controls the activity of the body tissues. Deficiency (hypothyroidism) results in poor growth in young animals. Older animals, lacking in the hormone, become sluggish, overweight and have poor hair growth. Excess amounts of the hormone cause hyperactivity.
Parathyroid	Two small glands alongside the thyroid	Parathyroid hormone	Controls the calcium stores in the body and is therefore important in the development of the skeleton.
Adrenal	Two small glands near the kidneys	Adrenaline – produced by the centre of the gland (medulla)	Prepares the animal for action and is excreted in quantity if the animal is frightened, needs to fight or run away.
		Corticosteroids – produced by the outer layer of the gland (the cortex)	One group of these hormones controls the salt and water content of the body. The other hormones produced by the adrenal cortex enhance the animal's resistance to stress and infection. Excessive production of corticosteroids causes Cushing's syndrome. Addison's disease is caused when too little hormone is produced.
Pancreas	Lies in a loop in the small intestine	Insulin and glucagon	These hormones control the amount of glucose in the blood. Animals with diabetes lack the hormone insulin or it is ineffective.
Testes	The two testes are situated in the scrotal sac	Testosterone	Responsible for the male characteristics of dogs, particularly aggression.
Ovaries	Contained in the abdomen near the kidneys	Oestrogen	Responsible for the female characteristics of bitches. Stimulates the genital tract and causes bleeding when the bitch is 'on heat'. Also brings about development of the mammary glands.
		Progesterone	Progesterone is responsible for preparing the uterus so that it can support the foetuses. It maintains pregnancy. It causes the mammary glands to develop so that they can eventually produce milk.

Table 6.2 (continued)

Gland	Situation	Hormone(s) produced	Action
Pituitary	Situated at the base of the brain. The gland is divided into two parts, the anterior and the posterior.	*Anterior part* Thyrotropic hormone Corticotropic hormone Growth hormone	Controls the action of the thyroid Controls action of the adrenal cortex Controls the animal's growth particularly up to puberty
		Gonadotropins Follicle-stimulating hormone Luteinizing hormone Prolactin	Promotes the ripening of eggs in the ovaries Causes ovulation Stimulates the mammary glands so that they are ready to produce milk
		Posterior part Anti-diuretic hormone Oxytocin	Acts on the kidneys to prevent excessive excretion of water Makes the pregnant uterus conract at whelping and stimulates the release of milk from the mammary glands.

7
The major infectious diseases

> **Canine distemper**
>
> **Infectious canine hepatitis**
>
> **Leptospirosis**
>
> **Canine parvovirus infection**
>
> **Kennel cough**
>
> **Rabies**

The most important infectious diseases of dogs are:

- Canine distemper
- Infectious canine hepatitis
- Leptospirosis (two forms)
- Canine parvovirus infection
- Infectious canine tracheobronchitis (kennel cough)
- Rabies

Dogs can be protected against all these diseases and a vaccination programme should be discussed with the veterinary surgeon, ideally before a puppy is bought. Prevention is far better than cure. If an adult dog or older puppy is being acquired, and its vaccination status is not available on a certificate signed by a veterinary surgeon, it will be wise to consider with the vet the protection which should be given.

Reputable boarding kennels will require to see up-to-date vaccination certificates given (within the previous 12 months) for the first four diseases mentioned above and probably for *kennel cough* too. *Rabies* vaccine is currently used in the UK only in newly imported dogs and in dogs for export.

Canine distemper

Cause:
A virus infection, usually complicated by secondary bacterial invasion.
Incubation period:
Usually 7-21 days.
Transmission:
The virus is transmitted from dog to dog, usually by inhalation of particles in the air which have become contaminated by discharges from dogs suffering from the disease.
Major signs:
Initially, a cough accompanied by high temperature, lethargy, lack of appetite, reddened eyes, runny nose, noisy breathing and, possibly, also diarrhoea and vomiting. Subsequently, usually after some weeks, nervous signs – a nervous twitch *(chorea)*, fits

or paralysis – may develop, often accompanied by thickening of the pads and the nose (*hyperkeratosis*).

Action:

Veterinary consultation immediately. If distemper is suspected do not take the dog into the waiting room but ask the receptionist where the veterinary surgeon would like to see the case.

Prevention:

Primary vaccination with modified live vaccines when puppies are 6-12 weeks of age and subsequent annual booster doses are usually advised.

Disinfection:

Thorough cleaning of the house or kennel is required, first with detergents to remove grease, followed by disinfection using chlorine derivatives particularly. Subsequently the affected areas should be opened to the air and, where possible, sunlight, and left unoccupied by dogs for as long as possible.

Comment:

- *Canine distemper* used to be rife nationwide before effective vaccines were introduced more than 35 years ago. Now the disease is mostly confined to unvaccinated populations in large cities. Thus dogs in more rural surroundings do not receive a natural boost to their immunity by exposure to infected animals and therefore booster vaccinations are most important.
- Good nursing is an essential part of treatment.
- Dogs that develop nervous signs are most unlikely to make a full recovery.
- In some cases the primary signs may be so mild as to go unnoticed. In others treatment may appear to bring about a recovery, but there is always the possibility that nervous signs may develop later, sometimes much later, often accompanied by *hyperkeratosis*. The latter signs earned this stage the name 'hard pad', once thought to be a separate disease but now known to be simply a sequel to distemper.

Infectious canine hepatitis

Also known as Rubarth's disease or canine viral hepatitis.

Cause:

This highly contagious disease is caused by a canine adenovirus (CAV-1). It has no connection with hepatitis in man.

Incubation period:

Five to 7 days, but it may strike suddenly and the dog may pass from apparent health to acute illness within 24 hours.

Transmission:

Dogs catch the disease by swallowing material contaminated with faeces, saliva or urine from infected dogs.

Major signs:

Puppies in their first year of life are most commonly affected, but all ages of dog are susceptible. The major early signs are generalised illness and lack of appetite with pale conjunctivae and gums, greatly raised temperature, vomiting, diarrhoea, abdominal pain. Yellowing of the whites of the eyes (*jaundice*) may occur. Some 20 per cent of dogs which are recovering from *hepatitis* show a blue clouding over the whole of the cornea of one or both eyes (*blue eye*). In most cases this clouding will disappear within a few days without additional treatment but, if it persists, veterinary advice should be sought. A similar clouding of the eye may be seen in some puppies after vaccination against *infectious canine hepatitis* when live CAV-1 vaccines are used. Most modern vaccines contain live CAV-2 antigens and do not cause blue eye.

Action:
Urgent veterinary consultation, taking precautions not to transmit the disease to other dogs.
Prevention:
Have puppies vaccinated early. A number of different types of vaccine are available – your veterinary surgeon will advise which is the most suitable for your dog in your area. Booster doses may be needed.
Disinfection:
Normal cleaning routine. Segregation of sick dogs. **Note:** Dogs suffering from this disease will shed the virus in their urine during the progress of the disease and possibly for several months afterwards. Some may become permanent carriers of the disease.
Comment:
* If a kennel has continual problems with ICH, blood testing of older stock will help identify carriers.
* This infection has been linked with puppy mortality in breeding kennels.

Leptospirosis

This is a disease caused by a group of bacteria called Leptospires. Dogs can be infected by two of these: *Leptospira icterohaemorrhagiae* and *Leptospira canicola*. Both these organisms can be passed to children and adults.

Leptospira icterohaemorrhagiae

Incubation period:
Five to 15 days.
Transmission:
This bacteria is carried by rats and is transmitted to dogs which kill rats or play with dead vermin. Dogs may also be infected by rat urine on the ground, in ponds or water bowls, or on fallen fruit, etc. The disease is particularly prevalent amongst dogs on farms, at ports and in mining areas.
Major signs:
High temperature, severe thirst, increased frequency of urination, abdominal pain, depression, possibly ulceration of the mouth, coated tongue, diarrhoea containing blood, jaundice and persistent vomiting.
Action:
Urgent accurate veterinary diagnosis, probably assisted by laboratory tests. This is a very serious disease.

> Does the dog take exercise around barns or junk yards or play in rural streams where rats may be found?

Prevention:
Keep dogs away from rat-infested water and do not leave drinking bowls outdoors over-night. Take steps to rid your premises of rats, but put the poison where dogs cannot get at it. Do not neglect vaccination against *leptospirosis* and the annual boosters.
Comment:
* Leptospires excreted in the urine of the dog during this illness, and possibly for months after apparent recovery, can infect other dogs and also humans; where the illness is known as *Weil's disease*. Particular attention should be paid to hygiene when attending to a sick dog, and especially when clearing up urine.

Leptospira canicola

Also known as Lamppost disease and Stuttgart disease
Incubation period:
Five to 15 days.
Transmission:
Dog to dog via sniffing at urine (hence lamppost connection).
Major signs:
Similar to those described under *Leptospira icterohaemorrhagiae* except that jaundice is much less frequently seen and less marked. Mild cases with few signs occur quite frequently. This infection can cause damage to the kidneys which may become critical later in life.
Action:
Immediate veterinary consultation, especially in puppies. Segregate patient from other dogs.
Prevention:
Most of the dogs which recover will excrete bacteria in their urine for up to a year. It must be a matter for consideration whether should dogs should be kept on the same premises as young puppies. Prompt vaccination of puppies at 8-12 weeks of age, and annual boosters are necessary.
Disinfection:
Recovered patients should be kept in the same kennelling/living space for at least 6 months, as eradication of the disease by disinfection may be difficult.
Comment:
• **It should be remembered that this infection can be passed on to man. Great care must be taken when nursing dogs with this disease.**

Canine parvovirus infection (CPV)

Cause:
A small, but very tough and persistent virus. This disease has only been recognised in dogs since 1978.
Incubation period:
Five days.
Transmission:
Dog to dog, via virus excreted in faeces, and also via virus carried on human clothing, footwear and objects which may have been contaminated by an infected dog. Infection occurs through ingestion of virus particles. The virus may remain viable for up to one year in a house where there has been a case, and may be almost permanently present in kennels where there have been successive outbreaks. Disinfection is exceptionally difficult.
Major signs:
Two forms of canine parvovirus are recognised:

Canine parvovirus myocarditis

Where the dam of a litter has not been vaccinated and has not been infected by the disease, she will have no protection to pass on to her puppies. Canine parvovirus, which always seeks out the cells of the body which are multiplying most rapidly, will concentrate in the heart muscle of newly born puppies exposed to the virus. The heart muscle is weakened or completely destroyed. The effect is not usually seen until the puppies become active at 4-10 weeks, when seemingly healthy pups will suddenly collapse and die after play or feeding. The whole litter is usually affected, although some individuals may survive longer than others; none of them should be sold as sound puppies.

This form of CPV is now becoming rare, as most breeding bitches will have some antibody to the infection either through previous exposure to the disease or through vaccination.

Intestinal form of canine parvovirus infection

This is the most common form of CPV. It affects dogs from 4 weeks of age into old age, but most severely in their first year, when the disease can be quickly fatal. The signs seen in this form of the disease are: depression, severe protracted vomiting, abdominal pain, refusal of food and water and very profuse diarrhoea, often with considerable blood content. Mostly CPV infection is rapid in resolution, and if the dog is going to survive it will be noticeably better within 4-5 days of the start of the illness. When puppies are badly affected by CPV, growth may be stunted and the puppy may be bald for up to a year.

Action:
Immediate consultation with the veterinary surgeon, initially by telephone, if possible, in order to avoid transmission to other dogs.

Prevention:
Consult your veterinary surgeon as soon as you get your puppy about a course of vaccinations to protect against CPV and do not neglect annual boosters. When a dog is suspected of having CPV, not only should it be kept in isolation, but all members of the owner's household should avoid dogs also, as the virus can be carried on shoes and clothing.

Disinfection:
It is very difficult to eradicate CPV from a home or a kennel. Sodium hypochlorite (domestic bleach) and formalin are active against CPV; many disinfectants will not kill the virus. Where a single puppy has died of CPV on domestic premises, it is wise to wait at least 6 months before introducing another puppy.

> It is important to know if the puppy has been hand reared from birth, as then it will have received no protective antibodies at all. If it is known that the disease is endemic in the kennel where the puppy was born, tell your veterinary surgeon.

Comment:
- CPV destroys the cell lining of much of the intestine, so that the badly infected dog has no means of absorbing fluid and nourishment. Fatalities are often due to dehydration, and intravenous drip therapy, to replace fluid loss, as an in-patient may be necessary. Consequently treatment can be expensive.

Kennel cough

Also known as infectious canine tracheobronchitis.

Cause:
A complex package of bacteria (particularly *Bordetella bronchiseptica*) and viruses which may vary in content at each outbreak, so making it possible for susceptible dogs to have kennel cough more than once during the boarding season, or to have kennel cough every year.

Transmission:
While this disease is mainly transmitted from dog to dog where a number of animals are gathered under one roof, eg at a dog show or in boarding kennels, it is possible for the singly owned pet to suffer from kennel cough too. Dogs become infected by breathing in infected airborne particles. The infective agents are carried in the air in a manner similar to the way human colds or influenza are spread. Peak time for infection is the summer, when dogs which do not normally mix with others are gathered in boarding kennels.

Major signs:
The most important sign is a protracted harsh cough which sounds as though the dog has a bone stuck in its throat. Affected adult dogs usually remain relatively cheerful and continue eating. In puppies, however, the disease may be complicated by a secondary pneumonia which can cause death.

Action:
Consult the veterinary surgeon, but do not take the dog into the waiting room, or allow it to approach other dogs. Cancel attendance at any gathering of dogs (shows, training classes) for 6 weeks.

Prevention:
Keep your dog away from any dog which is heard to be coughing during the summer season – do not believe the common excuses of 'He has just been pulling on the lead' or 'just ate some grass', etc.

A vaccine, which is put straight into the nasal passage where the disease enters, protects against infection with the bacterium *Bordetella bronchiseptica* which is considered to be the major cause of *kennel cough*. Protection will last for about 6-9 months. In relation to this disease, primary and booster vaccination against canine distemper and adenovirus infection is most important. In some situations veterinary surgeons may advise the use of a combined vaccine that not only stimulates immunity to those infections but also gives some protection against infection with canine para influenza virus, one of the viruses which is involved in causing *kennel cough*.

Consult your veterinary surgeon about the use of vaccine, particularly if the dog is going into boarding kennels or to dog shows, and especially if you are also planning a litter during the summer. Remember immunity takes some time to become established so consult your veterinary surgeon at least 2-3 weeks before you are due to go on holiday.

Comment:
* While this disease is trying and can be long lasting, it is seldom life-threatening except possibly in the case of very young puppies.
* Even after the cough seems to be cured, it may be reactivated by excessive exercise or stress.
* Problems arise because dogs may be infectious to others before they show signs and after they have apparently recovered. Chronic carrier dogs may also exist.

Rabies

Rabies is a fatal infection transmitted through the saliva of many animals. Foxes are the most important carriers of infection in Europe, followed by dogs and cats and small rodents.

Incubation period:
The time between infection and positive signs being shown may be very long (several months) but since most animals bite other animals around the head and mouth, the virus usually reaches the brain quite quickly and the incubation may be as short as 2-3 weeks.

Transmission:
The virus is present in the saliva of affected dogs and is transmitted through the bite of an infected animal, or through saliva entering a wound already present in the skin. The virus travels via the nerves to the brain, where it sets up inflammation (*encephalitis*) causing the typical nervous signs. It then returns via the nerves to enter the salivary glands and other organs.

Major signs:
Rabies in animals takes two forms – dumb or furious rabies. Both are demonstrated in obvious personality changes, wild or ferocious animals may become affectionate and seek human company, while normally quiet animals in the furious form will become exceedingly savage and make unpredictable attacks on humans and animals. The facial expression changes, the eyes become staring and the jaws fixed and paralysed, drooling copious saliva. Dogs tend to hide away from light and are extremely dangerous to approach. Death is usually preceded by paralysis and coma and dogs seldom survive for more than 15 days once the signs have been noted. Although affected dogs may develop difficulty in swallowing, they do not go into spasms at the signs of water, so the term 'hydrophobia' does not apply to the dog as it does to man.

Prevention:
In most countries of the world, rabies control is mandated by local regulations and involves owners securing veterinary vaccinations for pet animals to prevent the occurrence of the disease. While rabies is comparatively rare, it can be transmitted to a pet dog by the bite of infected dogs, cats or any warm-blooded wild animal.

In the UK six months quarantine has been the law for over 100 years, and this has been most effective for keeping the country rabies-free. At the time of writing, the future of the quarantine law is in question, in part due to the opening of the Channel Tunnel. Time will write the final chapter on this longstanding legislation.

Given the serious nature of rabies, any suspicion of the incidence of rabies should be reported to the local animal control officials.

Action:
If a dog is suspected of having rabies, avoid touching it, barricade it by some means in a small room or some other confined space, and report the situation to the police, animal control officer or a veterinary surgeon immediately – day or night.

There is no treatment for rabies, and the disease is always fatal. Dogs suspected of having contacted rabies are kept under observation in an official facility until their deaths. Positive proof of the disease is ascertained by post-mortem laboratory tests on the dog's brain.

Precautions:

As mentioned above British quarantine laws have protected animals in the UK for well over a century. Other countries such as Australia and New Zealand also use quarantine to combat rabies. In the United States and Canada, by contrast, protection is by effective vaccination programmes. Wherever you live, your veterinary surgeon, local animal control or public health officials can tell you all you need to know to be a responsible dog owner in this regard.

8
Parasites

Endoparasites

Ectoparasites

Endoparasites

Endoparasites are parasites which live inside the body, as opposed to on its surface. A great variety of such parasites infect dogs, but four are particularly common to all breeds of dogs in the UK, however kept. They are:

1. *Toxocara canis* – a roundworm
2. *Toxascaris leonina* – another type of roundworm
3. *Dipylidium caninum* – a tapeworm
4. *Toxoplasma gondii* – a protozoan parasite

Toxocara canis

Description:
A round, white worm 7.5-15cm long and pointed at both ends, which infects, most frequently, pregnant nursing bitches and young puppies. Adult worms are passed by puppies with or without accompanying faeces. Often several worms are passed at one time, coiled like a spring or in a loose hank.
Life cycle:
The release of hormones during pregnancy activates roundworm larvae which may be lying dormant in the tissues of the bitch. Some will migrate to the uterus, mammary glands and into the developing puppies, while others will continue their lifestyle in the intestine of the bitch.

Larvae already within the puppy at birth develop into adult worms by the time the puppy is 2 weeks old. The puppy will also receive more toxocara larvae via the bitch's milk, from being licked by the bitch and from her coat, where traces of faeces may remain. Additionally, the bitch will take into her body eggs, larvae and adult worms when she cleans up the faeces of her puppies. Within the puppy, ingested toxocara eggs hatch into larvae which burrow through the gut wall and migrate via the liver to the lungs, where they undergo further development. As they pass through they may cause respiratory problems. Some of these larvae are distributed by the blood to other tissues where they remain dormant. Other maturing larvae are coughed up, swallowed and pass down into the digestive system where they mature into adult worms which lay thousands of eggs within the intestine. These eggs, with or without adult worms, pass out in the faeces to lie on plants, grass or soil, sometimes for many months, until ingested by another susceptible dog. Then they start the toxocara lifecycle all over again.
Signs:
It may be taken that all young puppies and nursing bitches have a roundworm burden, whether you see any live adult worms or not. A very heavy worm burden in puppies will cause breathing problems, coughing and possibly pneumonia, while the larvae are

migrating through the lungs. Abdominal pain, diarrhoea, retarded growth, a pot-bellied, poor appearance and harsh coat will be seen when the stomach and intestines are full of worms, which may eventually form a complete blockage of the digestive system. Badly affected puppies whine and adopt a characteristic straddle-legged position.

Action:

In puppies a heavy toxocara burden can be very debilitating, even life threatening, and because of the added risk that puppies are most likely to be handled by children, it is very important indeed that they are wormed early, at 2-3 weeks old, again at 2 week intervals until 3 months of age, and at 6 and 12 months old. There is generally no need to dose adult dogs subsequently, but bitches should be dosed 6-7 weeks after mating, 2 weeks after whelping and during lactation when the puppies are wormed. It may also be helpful to worm entire adult bitches 2-4 weeks after they have been 'on heat'.

If you have just purchased a puppy, find out whether it has been wormed and if so with what. Discuss with your veterinary surgeon the need for further dosing.

If you have a litter of puppies, weigh the bitch and each of her puppies and obtain from the veterinary surgeon an effective wormer (vermifuge) at the right strength for each animal, including, very importantly, the bitch.

When you have carried out a worming or if you see worms in the faeces, be sure to pick up and dispose of the faeces properly. Worm infected faeces should not be put on to a compost heap, nor should they be dug into the garden, as many worm eggs can survive for years in soil. Burning, or putting into the WC is the best disposal method. In kennels the numbers of eggs can be reduced by vigorous scrubbing with large quantities of hot water and detergent and, if practical, the use of a flame gun – the eggs are resistant to disinfectant.

Comment:

- Recent research has produced a vermifuge which acts on the encysted larvae in the bitch's tissues during late pregnancy and soon after whelping. This remedy is only available through veterinary surgeons, but if you mean to breed your bitch it is well worth making enquiries about this development. Daily dosing of the bitch towards the end of pregnancy and at the beginning of lactation is needed with this compound, but puppies free from toxocara infection or with a greatly reduced worm burden will be produced. Such puppies will thrive more effectively and command a premium price from discerning purchasers.
- Wormers purchased over the counter are not likely to be so effective and the old-fashioned remedies may cause purging and abdominal discomfort.
- With many modern wormers, you are unlikely to see any live worms passed, as they are digested within the animal and pass out unnoticed in the faeces. **Do not discontinue worming because you see no worms passed.**

Risk to humans:

The sticky eggs of *Toxocara canis,* too small to be visible to the eye, may be picked up from soil, grass or from an animal's coat or bedding, and may be subsequently swallowed – children run the greatest risk. Eggs that have been eaten in this way can hatch into larvae in the human gut but will not develop into adult worms. Instead, the larvae, which are very small, will travel around the body and become embedded in the body tissues, usually causing no problems at all. Very rarely, however, these migrating larvae may settle by chance, in a particularly sensitive tissue such as the retina at the back of the eye. In some cases where this has happened, there has been impairment of vision. Sensible precautions, such as those listed below, will reduce any such risks.

Precautions:
- Insist that any puppy you buy has been wormed at least twice, with an effective wormer, before it is 8 weeks old.
- Continue with a worming programme as described earlier and train it to defecate in a specific fenced off area in the garden before it is taken for walks.
- Pick up promptly and dispose properly of post-worming faeces and faeces passed by dogs less than 6 months of age. Dogs under 6 months of age must not be exercised in public places where children play or where families picnic.
- Do not allow small children to handle very young puppies and nursing bitches, and do not allow dogs to lick children's faces or to share biscuits or ice-creams. Teach children to avoid areas where dogs defecate.
- Do not allow dogs to eat of crockery used by humans.
- Keep long-haired pups well groomed especially around the hindquarters.
- Insist that children wash their hands and faces after handling a puppy. There is no need to stop children playing with clean puppies since freshly passed faeces are not infective.

Comment:
Freshly passed dog faeces are not a hazard to people, as the eggs of *toxocara canis* need some time to mature outside the host before they are infective, so that while stepping in a pile of faeces is unpleasant, it is not dangerous.

The already low risk of damage to sight associated with this infection in children can be reduced still further and possibly eliminated if the advice given above is followed.

Toxocara canis cannot cause threadworm infection in children since that condition is due to another species of worm.

Toxascaris leonina

Description:
A round, white worm very similar in appearance to *Toxocara canis*.

Life cycle:
The life cycle of this worm is much more simple. Infection occurs by the ingestion of infective eggs. The eggs hatch in the stomach of dogs and the larvae develop in the wall of the stomach and intestine. They do not migrate as is the case with *Toxocara canis*. Thus infection of puppies in the womb or via the milk does not occur.

Action:
Worming methods indicated for the elimination of *Toxocara canis* will be effective. Similar precautions should be taken in respect of the disposal of faeces, etc.

Dipylidium caninum

Description:
This worm is a segmented tapeworm which occurs in the small intestine of dogs. It can measure up to 50 cm in length. The worm has a small head which attaches to the wall of the intestine and a long, segmented body which contains maturing eggs in each segment. It is rare to see a complete tapeworm in faeces but individual segments loaded with ripe eggs, which resemble cucumber seeds, may be noticed around the anus or on the dog's coat or bedding.

Life cycle:
Fleas are a necessary part of the life cycle of *Dipylidium caninum*. Flea larvae swallow eggs shed by dogs and these mature as the flea develops so that adult fleas are infectious for dogs. When a dog kills and eats a flea, the worm larvae are released in the intestine, where they will mature into adult worms.

Signs:
Severe tapeworm infestation causes diarrhoea and poor growth in puppies.
Action:
Your veterinary surgeon will prescribe a specific remedy for this tapeworm – be prepared to quote the weight of the dog or puppy.
Precaution:
Maintain a regular campaign against fleas on the dog and around the home, see Table 8.2, and worm adult dogs regularly as directed by a veterinary surgeon.
Transmission to man:
This worm can infect humans, mainly young children, who accidentally eat a flea containing infective larvae, but such cases are rare.

Toxoplasma gondii

Description:
A very small parasite of cats which uses most mammals, including dogs and humans, as an intermediate host.
Life cycle:
During a relatively short period of infection (because the cat develops an immunity) mature parasites in cats' intestines shed a large number of eggs. If these eggs are eaten by an intermediate host, such as a dog, the eggs mature and the parasite invades the tissues and forms cysts, mainly in muscles but sometimes in the brain. At this stage the intermediate hosts become immune and the cysts lie dormant. They may become active, however, if the dog is stressed by some other disease. If this occurs in pregnant bitches, or if bitches encounter the infection for the first time during pregnancy, puppies may become infected in the womb and be aborted or 'fade' soon after birth. Dogs may also acquire infection by eating muscles of prey animals that contain cysts. Cats become infected by eating animals such as mice which have cysts in their muscles and so the cycle starts again.
Signs:
Most toxoplasma infections in dogs do not produce clinical signs or they are so mild as to go unnoticed. More severe infections may be associated with diarrhoea, muscle weakness and respiratory difficulty.
Action:
None, since the infection can only be diagnosed by a veterinary surgeon.
Prevention:
It is not really possible to prevent the disease since dogs can become infected in so many different ways which are not controllable. However, in homes where there are also cats, it makes sense to remove all cat faeces from litter trays daily, so that they do not have time to mature and become infective.
Comment:
This infection can occur in man. If pregnant women become infected, there is a possibility that the infection can reach the baby in the uterus causing abortion or pre-natal damage. It is most important therefore that pregnant women are extremely cautious about feeding raw meat to animals. They should avoid contact with cat faeces and certainly should not clean out cat litter boxes.

Heartworms

Incidence:
Heartworms are a concern for dogs and their owners in much of North America. They are not a serious problem in the UK except with infected dogs which have been

146

imported from other countries.
Life cycle:
The infection is spread by a mosquito. The dog, bitten by a mosquito, has larvae deposited on its skin which eventually burrow into a vein. From there they travel to the right side of the heart where they can live for several years, blocking the flow of blood and eventually causing heart failure.
Signs:
May be none for several months or years after the dog has been imported. Most frequent signs are a soft cough, fainting after exercise, listlessness and bloodstained sputum.
Action:
Blood test by veterinary surgeon, medication, possibly surgery if heartworm is identified.
Precautions:
In areas where mosquitoes present a threat, dog owners have several options. Usually dogs are blood-tested in early Spring and if found negative for the presence of microfilariae, they are put on a regimen of oral medication, administered either daily or monthly. The dosage depends on a dog's weight. This regimen is continued until after the first frost when mosquitoes are dormant. Some owners prefer to keep their dogs on heartworm preventative all year round, and have blood tests performed only occasionally. Others may opt not to use preventative drugs, but test at regular intervals to be sure their dogs are not showing any signs of the parasite.

Other endoparasites

A number of other types of worms can infect dogs in the UK. Details are contained in Table 8.2.

Prevention of endoparasite infections

Where meticulous care is necessary, for example in households with young children, a small sample of faeces can be taken to your veterinary surgeon for screening for the presence of worm eggs. This process is not costly and is worth having done periodically as many dogs can tolerate a light worm burden (less than 10 worms in the gut), without showing any signs of ill health.

Giving worming medication

Using modern vermiguges it is not usually necessary to starve the dog before worming. The instructions given by the veterinary surgeon should be followed to the letter and, if the vermifuge has been given in bulk to cover several wormings, the dog should be weighed on each occasion to ensure the dose given is adequate but not excessive.

Not infrequently, puppies vomit soon after the worming dose has been given but, in general, if the vermifuge has remained in the stomach for 20 minutes it will have served its purpose, and the puppy should not be re-wormed for at least 7 days. Contact the veterinary surgery if you are at all doubtful about what you should do.

Ectoparasites

Ectoparasites are parasites that live on or in the skin. The major ectoparasites of dogs are:

- Fleas
- Lice
- Ticks
- Harvest mites

- Mange mites
  Sarcoptes scabei
  Demodex folliculorum
  Otodectes cynotis
  Cheyletiella specie

Details relating to these parasites are given in Table 8.3.

In general terms it can be said that ectoparasite infection is probably the major cause of skin disease in dogs. Unfortunately the signs of skin disease are not usually specific for any one infection and thus diagnosis and the correct selection of medication is far from easy. Unless the cause of a problem is very obvious, or it is a recrudescence of a previous infection, it makes sense to consult a veterinary surgeon about any skin lesion or signs of skin irritation in dogs.

Very often diagnosis will entail the taking of samples for microscopic examination and the careful noting of the history of the case. With skin conditions particularly, owners should go to the surgery with the ability to give a full account of the signs that are being shown, when they started and whether their intensity varies daily, monthly or not at all. It is also important to have noted whether or not the signs are aggravated by particular events or certain surroundings. It is also relevant to tell the veterinary surgeon any details that are known about other related and in-contact animals. Be prepared to tell the veterinary surgeon about the dog's diet, the conditions under which it is kept (eg does it have its own bed; is it allowed over the whole house; etc) and particularly whether it has access to other dogs, cats or any other animals. The more information the veterinary surgeon gets in these respects the easier it is for him to select the most appropriate medication so that the animal makes a quicker and more complete recovery. Finally, don't forget to tell the veterinary surgeon if you or any of your family also have a rash or some skin problem, since some parasites can cause problems in both man and dogs.

Table 8.1 Roundworm infection in dogs – the essential facts

- The roundworm, *toxocara canis*, is a round, white worm 7.5-15 cm in length

- Currently, virtually all puppies are born infected. Puppies will have adult worms capable of laying eggs by the time they are 21-30 days old.

- Puppies under 3 months old can be infected by worm eggs on grass or plants in the garden, or on the bitch's coat. These hatch in the puppy's stomach, moving through the body and back to the intestine where they become adult. Puppies can also be infected by immature worms in their mother's milk.

- In puppies over 3 months of age, the larvae make only a limited migration and lie dormant in the bitch's tissues, particularly the muscles, the diaphragm and kidneys.

- When bitches become pregnant, the larvae lying dormant are stimulated to migrate again. They reach the womb and the mammary glands, infecting the puppies and completing the cycle.

- Thirty to 40% of puppies under 3 months old have adult worms in their intestines which are able to pass eggs into the environment.

- Eggs in freshly voided faeces are not infective to dogs or people. Eggs take 2-3 weeks to become infective.

Table 8.2 Other endoparasites that occur in dogs

Type of parasite	Scientific name	Life cycle/description	Signs in dogs	Comment
Hookworm	*Uncinaria stenocephala*	A thick, round worm only 2 cm long which lives in the small intestine. Hookworm larvae may invade the skin causing a dermatitis between the toes. The main cause of infection is ingestion of larvae which hatch in the open from shed eggs.	Usually none but may cause diarrhoea and possibly anaemia as the adult worms live on blood.	Infection with this parasite is very common in Greyhounds especially those kept in grass runs. The infection can be cured by strict hygiene measures and regular worming with an appropriate product.
Whipworm	*Trichuris vulpis*	Worms 7 cm in length with a thin front end and a bulbous rear end. They are found in the caecum. Infection is by ingestion of larvae which develop within the eggshell.	Mostly none but may cause intermittent diarrhoea with dark faeces.	The infection is common in Greyhound kennels. Treatment is difficult. Eggs shed on the ground can stay viable for several years, making control difficult. Treatment is not easily accomplished.
Lungworm	*Oslerus (filaroides) osleri*	Adult worms are found in nodules, about 2 mm in size, in the trachea and bronchi. The method of transfer is not fully understood. The tails of the worms can be seen on bronchoscopy, protruding from the nodules.	Many infections go unnoticed but severely affected dogs have a protracted harsh cough, particularly when exercised, and may lose weight.	Mostly young animals are affected. The infection is more commonly found in dogs housed in groups, eg breeding kennels. Treatment is very difficult and surgical removal of the nodules may be required.
Tapeworm	*Echinococcus granulosus*	A tapeworm, only 9 mm in length, that lives in the small intestine of dogs. Eggs shed by dogs are eaten by a great variety of intermediate hosts including man, but particularly sheep in which the parasite develops into a hydatid cyst. Dogs become infected by eating carcasses of sheep or deer which contain cysts in their tissues, particularly the lungs and liver. Most commonly affected are working dogs which find dead animals on mountainous grazing land.	Few signs are seen in dogs except possibly loss of condition and occasional diarrhoea.	Dogs may harbour more than a thousand worms in their intestine. Hydatid disease in man is of consequence particularly in some areas in Wales. A national control scheme involving supervised worming of dogs, as is practised in New Zealand, is in force in some areas of the country. Regular worming of dogs is important. The feeding of raw offal should be avoided.

Table 8.2 (continued)

Type of parasite	Scientific name	Life cycle/description	Signs in dogs	Comment
Tapeworm	*Taenia species*	Large tapeworms measuring up to 3 m in length that live in the small intestine of dogs. A number of different intermediate hosts are infected by eating eggs shed by dogs. In the intermediate hosts, cysts develop in various areas depending on the species involved. Dogs become infected by eating the tissues of the intermediate host that contain cysts.	Most infections go undetected.	Tapeworms have little public health risk. Control is by regular worming and avoiding feeding raw offal to dogs.

Table 8.3 Ectoparasite infections of dogs

Parasite	Life cycle	Signs shown by dog	Comment
Fleas Scientific name: Ctenocephalides species (dog and cat fleas) most commonly but also *Pulex irritans* (human flea) and Ceratophylus species (hedgehog fleas)	The life cycle of the flea is completed off the dog. Eggs are laid on the dog's bed, around the edge of carpets and in upholstered chairs. Dependent on the environmental conditions they hatch, within 2-16 days, into larvae which take 7-10 days to reach maturity and pupate. The adult fleas emerge after a variable period dependent on temperature, moisture, etc. Sometimes hatching is stimulated by vibrations, for example moving furniture. Fleas act as intermediate hosts for the dog tapeworm *Dipylidium caninum* — see page 145.	Thin, elongated, brown, wingless insects with long legs which run rapidly over the skin and which jump off the animal. They occur particularly around the neck and on the abdomen. The movement of the fleas causes irritation such that affected dogs will scratch frequently and bite at their coats with nipping movements of the incisor teeth. The majority of dogs show few signs even though they are harbouring a lot of fleas — others, however, become sensitive to the fleas themselves or their excreta and will develop a severe allergic dermatitis even though only a few fleas are present.	Flea droppings (dirts) are black, hard and the size of grains of sand. If placed on wet blotting paper the blood they contain will leach out and stain the paper red. Regular treatment at intervals of 7-10 days with baths, powders and sprays is required to overcome a severe infection and to prevent immediate re-infection. It is also necessary to vacuum carefully all the places where eggs may have been laid, to treat the environment with a suitable insecticide and to apply an insecticide to the dog every 3-4 weeks to prevent re-infection. Flea collars can be helpful in some cases where re-infection occurs regularly but they need using with care to avoid possible hazards.

Table 8.3. (continued)

Parasite	Life cycle	Signs shown by dog	Comment
Lice Scientific name: *Trichodectes canis*	Adult lice feed on the skin and lay eggs on the hair. These hatch into young lice which resemble the adults. Lice cannot exist off their host for more than a few days — infection is spread therefore by close contact between animals.	Light brown, flat, wingless insects with short legs that move slowly on the skin and which lay eggs (nits) that are stuck to the animal's hair, particularly around the neck and ears. Dogs with lice will scratch frequently at the area where the insects are to be found. Severe infections may cause anaemia in young puppies.	Regular treatment of infected dogs with an insecticide is required and it makes sense to comb and wash away the nits. Since lice breed on an animal there is less need to pay attention to the environment than is the case with a flea infection.
Ticks Scientic name: Ixodes species	Dogs become infected by coming in contact with larvae which have hatched from eggs laid by adult ticks that have left their natural hosts (sheep and hedgehogs) which climb on to blades of grass and shrubs.	Brownish-white, rounded insects which may, when engorged, be the size of a bean or pea. The insects lie attached to the skin by their heads which are firmly buried in the epidermis. The larval forms of some ticks may cause irritation to some dogs. Most dogs will, however, tolerate an adult tick or two without showing any signs. Indeed it is common for these parasites to be noticed only curing routine grooming.	Adult ticks can be removed by soaking them with a swab soaked in ether or surgical spirit. This has the effect of making the tick loosen its hold on the skin so that its mouthparts and head can be removed intact. If the head is not removed a local skin infection may result. If in doubt seek veterinary help. Dogs in close contact with sheep and which have ticks regularly, can be bathed in a suitable dip. Regular dipping is necessary to prevent re-infection.
Harvest mites (Chiggers) Scientic name: *Trombicula autumnalis*	Both the adults and immature forms are free-living but the larvae are parasitic. The larval mites occur most frequently in the autumn and attack animals and people working in low-lying fields. The natural hosts are field mice.	Small, red larval mites, just visible to the naked eye, mostly seen in the inter-digital spaces and in a small pocket that is present on the edge of the ear flap near the head. Infected dogs lick their feet continually since mites cause irritation.	The incidence of mites in different areas of the country is very variable. Seek veterinary advice to obtain a suitable parasiticide.

Parasite	Life cycle	Signs shown by dog	Comment
Mange mites Scientific names: 1. *Sarcoptes scabei* 2. *Demodex folliculorum* 3. *Otodectes cynotis* 4. Cheyletiella species	The lifecycle of all mange mites occurs on the host. The adults lay eggs which hatch into larvae in 3-7 days, these mature into nymphs which develop into adult mites. Mange mites do not survive long off the host.	1. *Sarcoptes scabei* causes sarcoptic mange. The mite is invisible to the naked eye and burrows superficially into the skin. The irritation is intense, causing frequent and frantic scratching. The most commonly affected areas are under the thighs and forelegs and the edges of the ears in dogs of all breeds and ages. 2. *Demodex folliculorum*. A microscopic mite normal in small numbers in canine hair follicles. In circumstances not fully understood the mites multiply causing severe dermatitis with hair loss. Common in short-haired breeds, there may be an inherited tendency to the infection. Often localised, it may erupt over the whole body; secondary bacterial infection may occur. Demodectic mange is common in young dogs. Surprisingly the condition does not cause itching. 3. *Otodectes cynotis* is a white mange mite just visible with a magnifying glass, found in the ears. It occurs naturally without usually causing much problem in cats; in dogs a small infection can cause severe otitis externa (ear canker). 4. Cheyletiella species. A small parasite just visible to the naked eye. Mostly few signs in dogs but heavy infection can cause skin scaling. The mites, their eggs and the scurf they produce, have been called 'walking dandruff' most frequently seen on the back.	1. Treat 3-4 times at weekly intervals to kill new generations. Destroy the dog's bedding and spray the environment with an insecticide, since the mites can persist long enough off the host to infect another animal. Sarcoptic mange is readily transmissible from dog to dog and the mites can exist on people for a short while causing irritating spots. 2. Dogs with skin lesions like pustules on the skin of the head, hocks and elbows should be taken to a veterinary surgeon without delay, since treatment is more difficult after general eruption. Proper diagnosis and meticulous treatment is important to bring the disease under control. Occasional courses of treatment will often be required throughout the dog's life as patches recur. *Demodex folliculorum* does not affect people. 3. Ear preparations against this mite are available through veterinary surgeons. It is prudent to treat both ears even though one may appear normal. Cats and other animals living with infected dogs should also be treated to help prevent re-infection. 4. Cheyletiella mites can cause an irritating rash in people. Treatment of the dog is relatively simple but should be under veterinary supervision. Medication is prolonged because of the mite's long lifecycle.

9
Inherited diseases

> **General hereditary problems**
>
> **Hip dysplasia**
>
> **Eye conditions**
>
> **Ear conditions**

The employment of increasingly sophisticated diagnostic methods in veterinary medicine has led to the identification of a number of diseases and deformities in dogs as being inherited, from immediate parents or from ancestors further back in the pedigree.

The mode of inheritance in many cases has yet to be determined and many breed clubs are co-operating with research projects aimed at eventually eliminating these conditions from the breed. Frequently it is not until dogs have been bred from, and the disease recognised in their offspring, that it is realised that one or both parents are capable of passing on traits which are not apparent in themselves.

The passing on of genetic or congenital defects is to some extent the breeder's responsibility, but often not the breeder's fault, especially if this is the first time the defect has occurred in their strain of dogs. The ethical breeder will be aware of the particular problems which are common in their breed and will do as much as possible to identify them and to breed away from such problems.

There is no breed which can be said to be totally free from hereditary defects. Mongrels and crossbreds suffer from the same conditions, but in these dogs eradication in the future is impossible because their ancestry is not recorded.

General hereditary problems

These include defects of the skeleton, malformations of the eye and the facial construction, and a tendency to conditions leading to blindness, heart disease, deafness, bleeding disorders and epilepsy, although some of these conditions may also arise from injury.

It is as well to remember that some inherited conditions are quite common and may cause trouble, suffering and expense later. It makes sense, therefore, to take newly purchased puppies to a veterinary surgeon to have them checked in this respect. Such problems as in-turning eyelids (entropion), umbilical or inguinal hernias, weak knee joints (slipping patellas), incorrect undershot or twisted (wry) jaws or cryptorchidism (one or no testicle descended into the scrotum), may not have been noticeable to you but will be readily picked up on a routine full examination. The vet will tell you whether the condition is likely to cause an immediate or long-term problem and give advice about what can be done, usually surgically, to correct the fault. On occasion he may even advise you to contact the breeder, or even to return the puppy. Some breeds may be more likely to develop certain inherited conditions than others. It is as well to bear this in mind when choosing a dog. Your veterinary surgeon or a knowledgeable breeder will be able to advise you in this respect.

Hip dysplasia

The British Veterinary Association and the Kennel Club (BVA/KC) jointly administer a scheme to evaluate hip dysplasia in dogs (see Chapter 6), a condition of deformed hip joints which can lead to chronic pain and lameness. Hip dysplasia is especially important in German Shepherd Dogs (Alsatians), Briards, Golden Retrievers, Great Danes, Labradors, Old English Sheepdogs, Pyreneans, Rottweilers and Rough Collies, but other breeds of medium to large size are also affected.

The dog's hips are X-rayed by your own veterinary surgeon, once only, after the age of 12 months. Your veterinary surgeon will give you all the necessary information. The X-ray is then sent to the British Veterinary Association where it is examined and evaluated for normality by members of an appointed panel who have a special interest in orthopaedics.

The X-ray is assessed on nine different aspects of the hip joint, each leg being calculated separately. Each aspect of the hip is scored up to a maximum of 6 points – 6 being indicative of a high level of deformity, 9 x 6 points equals a maximum of 54 scored for a really bad hip, or 108 for both. Low scores, eg 2 right and 4 left equalling 6 in total are very good hip dysplasia scores. 0 : 0 is absolutely normal.

In some breeds normality has not been reached and may be difficult to achieve, so what may be a poor score in one breed may be acceptable in another. The breeder or breed club should be able to tell you the target score for your breed.

In all the breeds mentioned earlier, puppy buyers should insist on seeing a BVA hip score for both sire and dam, and should in due course have their own pet X-rayed in order to contribute information on the progeny those dogs are producing. Dogs and bitches are capable of producing puppies with hip joints better or worse than their own, and correct rearing plays some part in determining the final state of the hips. However, breeding from the best is slowly improving the state of the hip joint in those breeds where the BVA/KC scheme has been used for some time.

It is important that every hip X-ray should be sent to the BVA for scoring so that hips are evaluated on a nationwide standard. Local evaluation by individual veterinary surgeons may not be acceptable to stud dog or bitch owners and does nothing to improve the standard within the breed. The extra expense of scoring by the official panel is always worthwhile.

Eye conditions

BVA and the Kennel Club also operate an official eye examination scheme to detect several eye conditions, among them those leading to painful blindness. The recommendation is that dogs and bitches should be examined annually for the whole of their lives, as many eye conditions can be late in onset, often after the dogs concerned have been used for breeding. This applies of course to those breeds which are principally affected by such problems and particularly the animals intended for breeding.

When a fault is found in the eyes of a dog which may have produced one or two generations of descendants, ethical breeders will want to withdraw that dog from their breeding programme, but obviously all those who have related animals will also be affected. It is only by this means that we can hope to eradicate the many eye diseases from which dogs suffer.

The official eye examinations are conducted by a panel of veterinary surgeons with post-graduate qualifications in ophthalmology. Examinations are either held privately (your veterinary surgeon will refer you) or at examination sessions arranged, often in conjunction with shows, by breed clubs. Where numbers of dogs are examined at one time, the fee for each is reduced and, by special permission of the Kennel Club, dogs not entered at the show may attend for eye examination. No anaesthetic is required. The examination takes only a few moments and a report is given immediately.

Breeds most susceptible to eye problems include Smooth and Rough Collies, Border Collies and Shetland Sheepdogs. Puppies from these breeds should be screened at 8 weeks old for a defect peculiar to Collies – Collie eye anomaly. Do not buy a puppy in these breeds with a view to using it for breeding until you have the examination verdict. Other eye diseases affect primarily American Cocker Spaniels, Bassets, Bloodhounds, Briards, Cavaliers, Cockers, English Springers, Golden Retrievers, Irish Setters, Labradors, Miniature and Toy Poodles, as well as other breeds.

Ear conditions

Some white coated dogs, Dalmatians, white Boxers and Bull Terriers, may be deaf in one or both ears. A deaf dog is extremely handicapped and needs very special care. Puppies may be tested for hearing at 8 weeks of age at the Animal Health Trust at Newmarket in Suffolk.

> Some breed clubs operate their own screening schemes for particular diseases which affect that breed, eg heart defects in Cavaliers and Boxers. Ask the breeder *and* your veterinary surgeon about breed-related diseases.

10
Zoonoses

> **Definition**
>
> **Simple preventive measures**
>
> **Signs, treatment and prevention**

Zoonoses is the term applied to diseases which are transmissible from animals to humans. Most domestic animals, including dogs, cats, birds, horses and rabbits are capable of transmitting some disease, but the risk is minimal in respect of dogs if the simple hygienic precautions listed below are taken.

1. Keep pet animals healthy, have any signs of illness diagnosed and treated promptly by a veterinary surgeon. *Regular worming with tablets obtained from the veterinary surgeon is especially important.*
2. Groom your pet regularly and thoroughly.
3. Do not allow pets to lick children's faces.
4. Insist that adults and, particularly, children wash their hands after handling pets and especially so if sick dogs are being nursed.
5. Do not feed pets from household crockery.
6. Store pet food separately from human food; sterilise knives and chopping boards after handling pet quality raw meat.
7. Wash pet bedding frequently.
8. Treat dogs and the environment regularly for fleas.
9. Pick up excreta passed in the garden and dispose of it properly.
10. Wear gloves when gardening.

These rules, which should become a way of life in pet-owning households, go most of the way towards ensuring that your pet will never be a health risk to you or your children. Most human disease is caught from other humans, so do not be too ready to blame your pet until you have positive laboratory-investigated evidence that the pet is the vector.

Sore throats, tuberculosis and fleas can be transmitted from humans to dogs, as can the diarrhoea-causing bacteria salmonella and campylobacta and in the fungal skin disease known as ringworm. Again, hygienic precautions will prevent you infecting your dog.

Rabies is the most serious zoonosis. This disease is transmitted by the saliva of an infected animal. Rabies is kept out of Britain by a strong and continuing campaign by government, by the vigilance of customs officials, by the general public and by our sensible quarantine laws. We must hope that we never have to concern ourselves with the possibility of rabies either in wildlife or in our pets.

Details relating to some other zoonoses are given in Table 10.1.

Table 10.1 The signs, treatment and prevention of some zoonoses which occur in the UK

Disease in animals	Transmitted by	Symptoms in humans	Action – in dogs	Action – humans	Prevention
Toxocariasis	Mature worms in the canine intestine. See Chapter 8.	Usually none, but migrating larvae may cause problems if, for example, they end up in the eye.	Regular worming especially of puppies but also adults with remedy prescribed by veterinary surgeon.	None. Condition usually undiagnosed.	Regular worming of dogs. Prompt disposal of animal faeces. Wear gloves when gardening.
Echinococcosis	See Chapter 8.	Hydatid cysts.	Regular worming with specific remedy in those areas where the disease is endemic.	Medical, possibly surgical, treatment when disease is diagnosed.	Do not allow dogs to eat carcasses of sheep or cattle.
Leptospirosis	Via urine of dog suffering the disease. See Chapter 7.	Hepatitis. Jaundice.	Veterinary treatment.	Medical treatment.	Dogs—regular vaccination and boosters. Humans—strict hygiene when attending sick dogs.
Brucellosis	The causal bacterium may be excreted by bitches at whelping. The condition is very rare in the UK among the public although veterinary surgeons in large animal practice are at risk. The most likely source of brucellosis is unpasteurised milk.	Intermittent bouts of fever, headache, joint pain.	Positive identification by laboratory tests.	Medical treatment.	Avoid possible sources of infection. Always drink heat-treated milk.
Sarcoptic mange	Transfer of mange mite from infected dog.	Irritating rash as mite burrows below the skin on hands, wrists, etc. Can also be caught by human/human contact.	Treatment by veterinary surgeon. Clean dog's bedding and the environment.	Clean environment. Apply an anti-mite lotion to affected skin.	Early professional diagnosis of any skin disease on dog.

Table 10.1 (continued)

Disease in animals	Transmitted by	Symptoms in humans	Action – in dogs	Action – humans	Prevention
Cheyletiella infection (rabbit fur mite)	Transfer of mite from rabbit to spinal and neck fur of dog, thence to owner – smooth-coated dogs most affected.	Very irritating rash often on chest and waist area where dog/puppy is held. Mite can penetrate clothing.	Identification of mite and bath with shampoo provided by veterinary surgeon.	None necessary. Rash usually clears when mite is eliminated from dog.	Prompt attention to scurf-like deposits on dog skin.
Ringworm	The infection can be caught by direct contact with cats, horses and cattle.	Non-irritating eroded patches on skin, probably the wrists – not necessarily circular.	Positive identification as ringworm by laboratory tests, followed by specific treatments.	Treatment by doctor.	Avoid contact with animals which may be infected.
Salmonellosis	Salmonella organisms are shed in the faeces.	Food poisoning – diarrhoea and vomiting.	Laboratory tests to identify bacteria and likely source.	Laboratory tests to identify source of bacteria, ie human or animal carrier.	Strict hygiene precautions when handling animals and food.
Tetanus	A wound such as a dog bite may become infected with the causal organisms.	Fever, lock-jaw.	None.	Medical treatment of bites.	Keep anti-tetanus injections up to date.
Fleas	From environment where dog/cat fleas are breeding.	Typical irritating bite. Possibly a full blown allergic reaction in susceptible individuals.	Anti-flea treatment of dog and environment.	None necessary, but possibly the application of antihistamine creams.	Regular de-fleaing of all animals and environment.
Toxoplasmosis	For details see Chapter 8.				

11
Vaccination

> The immune system
>
> Types of vaccine
>
> Booster vaccination
>
> Methods of administration
>
> When to vaccinate
>
> Vaccination vs socialisation

Immunity

We are all under constant attack from the millions of micro-organisms which inhabit our world, so some means of protection is essential for survival. Healthy bodies are equipped with several defence mechanisms which are in operation all the time. The skin is a barrier to invasion by microbes; the mucous membranes in the nose trap foreign substances which are breathed in and the cough reflex comes into play when throat and larynx are irritated and to prevent 'germs' getting into the lungs. The acidity of the stomach will kill invaders which get that far and the quantities of mucus produced by the small bowel acts as a barrier to infection. Other invaders will pass from the body in faeces and urine, while the liver will destroy toxins produced by bacteria. These defence mechanisms are similar in man and animals and they work very well when health is good, but are not so effective when the body is in a run-down state, underfed or weakened, or when there is a state of mental or physical stress.

When an organism succeeds in passing these primary barriers, the body still has resources to use against the invader. *The immune system* comes into action to manufacture special and specific weapons – antibodies – to use against the organism making the attack.

Puppies

Puppies do have an immune system of their own at birth, but it is not fully developed. Thus nature has arranged for them to acquire some protective antibodies from their mothers. These are called passive antibodies since they have not been produced by the puppy itself. A modicum of passive maternal antibody passes to the puppy while it is still in the uterus, but most comes via the colostrum, the first milk from the dam. Antibodies to disease in the colostrum can only be absorbed by puppies for the first day or so after birth and that time can be much shorter. It is obvious therefore that when the litter is very large or the whelping prolonged, the early puppies are going to have more opportunity to get colostrum than those born later, so the ability to resist disease may vary between the members of the litter.

The antibodies which the dam passes to her puppies will be against those diseases which she herself has encountered or been vaccinated against. If she has lived a very isolated or protected existence, rarely met other dogs, and has never been vaccinated, she will have no protection to pass on and her puppies will be vulnerable to all the infectious canine diseases from their earliest days.

Although the normal dam will pass on protective immunity through the colostrum, this type of protection will fade quite soon – in fact the amount in the blood roughly halves each week, so the puppy must develop its own active antibodies either by encounter with disease or by vaccination if it is to be protected for the rest of its life.

Adult dogs

Most disease-causing organisms consist mainly of proteins. A healthy body is quick to detect proteins foreign to itself and to set about rejecting them by the production of specific antibodies to the invader. These active antibodies (ie they are created by the animal itself) are produced by specialised white blood cells found mainly in the lymph nodes and spleen.

The first time the body encounters a specific disease, or a vaccine, active antibodies may take as long as 10 days to be produced, but the next time that disease presents itself, memory cells come into action and antibodies are 'manufactured' very quickly, so that the disease does not have the chance to become established. This is why some diseases of man and animals occur only once in a lifetime. For example, measles in man is usually a once-only disease and once an attack has been survived there will be lifelong protection.

Antibodies tend to be very specific and destroy only the microbe (the antigen) which stimulated their production. A blood sample taken from the dog and processed at a laboratory will show if the dog has antibodies to a particular disease circulating in the blood, and sophisticated techniques can often reveal whether the antibody has been made in response to a recent infection or has been present for some time. Antibody levels wane with time, but another encounter with the right antigen will cause a quick resurgence of production.

Vaccines

Since we do not want dogs to have to endure an episode of disease to develop their own protection, we turn to the creation of active immunity by vaccination. This is the deliberate triggering of the immune response by the giving of a small, weak dose of the disease in order to stimulate the production of antibodies.

Essentially modern vaccines fall into four main classes:

1. *Attenuated living vaccines.* Fortunately bacteria and viruses can be modified to reduce their ability to cause disease yet maintain their ability to stimulate the formation of active antibodies. This is achieved by a process called attenuation and is usually brought about by growing the organism in an unnatural host, eg in eggs, a different species of animal or in tissue culture. The amount of attenuation depends on how long the germ is maintained in the 'artificial' system. The trick is to get the right balance to achieve maximum antibody production in the animal given the vaccine and yet not cause disease. The big advantage of live vaccines is that usually only one dose is required in adult dogs to stimulate immunity. Dogs injected with the ideal live vaccine will not shed organisms to other dogs – indeed that is the case with modern canine distemper vaccines. If this is not so then organisms shed from vaccinated dogs may infect in-contact animals and if this

happens on several occasions there is always a risk that the organism's ability to cause disease may return. Such vaccinations are better not used where a good alternative dead vaccine, or a live vaccine that is not shed, is available.

2. *Killed vaccines.* These are made from 'germs' which have been killed by heat or chemical agents such as formalin. Although the organisms are incapable of multiplying in the vaccinated animal, they nevertheless stimulate the formation of antibodies. However, two doses are normally required and an additive, or adjuvant as it is called, may be needed to enhance the effect. By and large, the immunity produced is not so long-lasting but obviously the safety factors in vaccines of this type are greater.

3. *Toxoids.* The lethal effect of some organisms is brought about by the fact that they produce poisonous substances called toxins. The body reacts to these by producing specific antibodies called anti-toxins which are capable of neutralising toxins. This can be done artificially by injecting a toxoid which is a detoxified toxin. Toxoids are generally made by inactivating toxins either by heat or by chemical means and on injection they stimulate anti-toxin to be formed in the body. Two doses are normally required to stimulate immunity and booster doses may be needed over 1, 2 or 3 years. Probably the most familiar example is tetanus toxoid.

4. *Mixed vaccines.* It is possible to make mixed vaccines provided that care is taken to ensure the compatibility of the antigens. Mixed vaccines may contain, for example, two live antigens, several dead antigens or even a combination of live and dead antigens. Such vaccines make it possible to establish an effective degree of protection against diseases with a minimal number of injections.

Booster vaccination

Protection created by vaccines is generally not as long-lasting as natural immunity, so boosters are needed periodically, different intervals being advised for the different diseases and different products. Dogs which are kept in isolated conditions, exercised only on their owner's land and never taken to shows or training classes, are *more* in need of booster protection than those dogs which live in towns and mix frequently with other dogs and hence get a degree of natural 'boosting' from the low level of infection present in the environment.

Methods of administration

Vaccines are generally given by subcutaneous or intramuscular injection, but in certain circumstances, where there is a need to stimulate local protection, they are given by other routes. For example, the vaccine used to protect dogs against kennel cough caused by the bacterium *Bordetella bronchiseptica* is given by the intranasal route. Administration by this route stimulates the production of local antibodies in the upper part of the respiratory tract within only a few days, just where they are needed. This is followed later by the production of antibodies in the bloodstream.

When to vaccinate

Obviously the aim is to stimulate the production of active antibodies, by vaccination, as early as possible in a puppy's life. Unfortunately this is not easily achieved, since not only does maternally-derived antibody protect against disease, but it also prevents a proper response to vaccination. There is, incidentally, an immunity gap during which puppies will not have enough maternal antibodies to protect them against infection, but sufficient to prevent effective vaccination. Much effort has gone into devising vaccine strains and vaccination regimes to keep this time of vulnerability to a minimum.

Canine maternally derived antibody declines at a fixed rate, halving every 7-8 days or so, thus its duration in a particular puppy will depend on the quantity it received from its mother, which in turn depends on *her* antibody level. In fact, puppies, on average, acquire levels that are about 77 per cent of their mother's, provided they suck properly in the first 24 hours of life. Clearly then, the earliest age at which puppies can be successfully vaccinated will vary considerably although it will be roughly the same for animals from one litter. Orphan puppies which have had no colostrum can theoretically be vaccinated at birth, but it is wiser to wait until 3-6 weeks of age to allow the immune system to develop properly.

The optimum times for vaccination against distemper have been plotted most carefully by scientific sampling, and this work provided a standard formula for vaccination times, *until* the advent of canine parvovirus.

In the case of canine distemper it was shown that:

- at 6 weeks old, 30 per cent of puppies have no maternal antibody left;
- at 8 weeks old, 65 per cent of puppies have none; and
- at 12 weeks old, 98 per cent of puppies have none.

Thus, if puppies are vaccinated against distemper at 6 weeks of age, only a third of them will be able to respond. From these figures the optimum timing for distemper vaccination was evolved. One injection at 6-8 weeks, when about half the puppies will be ready for it, another at 12 weeks to take in the rest, and a booster injection when the puppy is a year old. It is more than probable that either the 8-week or the 12-week injection will be wasted, because the puppy is still protected by maternally-derived antibody or the early dose has already stimulated an active immunity, but this formula serves to protect the majority of puppies by the time they are being taken out. It is as well to remember however that there will still be an immunity gap during which puppies will not be protected. However, the regimen referred to above ensures that this period of susceptibility is minimal.

In the case of canine parvovirus infection the situation can be more complex because bitches which have been exposed to this disease may have very high antibody levels. Puppies born to such bitches are likely, in turn, to have high levels of maternally-derived antibodies and they may have to wait a long time before they are ready for vaccination with conventional vaccines, perhaps up to 20 weeks. If the bitch has not much antibody to pass on, the pups may be ready for their own vaccination at 6 weeks. This wide variation has in the past caused a considerable dilemma and is the reason why several doses of vaccine have been recommended.

However, since 1986 live canine parvovirus vaccines which can immunise puppies in the face of low levels of maternally-derived antibody have been available and are now widely used. This has simplified the protection of young puppies and means that vaccination can be completed by 12 weeks of age. Your veterinary surgeon will advise.

Veterinary surgeons need to calculate the optimum time for vaccination in the light of local disease conditions and the history of the kennel in which the puppy was born, possibly in conjunction with blood sampling. In the case of canine parvovirus infection, the most recent studies have indicated that exposure to natural infection, as can occur in kennels where the disease is endemic, may lead to a more rapid decline in maternally-derived antibody than anticipated. This could crucially affect control programmes based on the separation and isolation of puppies that are waiting to be vaccinated.

Finally in this connection, it has to be remembered that there will always be a proportion of dogs (and humans) whose bodies fail to make any response to vaccine given to them.

Vaccination does not usually affect behaviour or appetite. Some dogs may feel off colour for a day or two, a few days after vaccination and a few may show mild local reaction at the site of injection. If such signs are severe or prolonged the veterinary surgeon who gave the injection should be consulted. A common side effect in the past that affected Afghans in particular was blue eye. If the front of one or possibly both the dog's eyes becomes cloudy soon after vaccination, consult the veterinary surgeon who gave the dose without delay. Since the introduction of newer infectious canine hepatitis vaccines based on CAV-2 virus, such side effects are only rarely seen.

A multiplicity of safe, effective vaccines are available these days to protect dogs against the five major infectious diseases from which they suffer – canine distemper, infectious canine hepatitis, leptospirosis, canine parvovirus infection and kennel cough. As explained in this chapter the situation is complex and veterinary surgeons have to consider a great number of factors before selecting which vaccine to use and recommending when it should be administered. There is considerably more to vaccination that simply 'giving a puppy a jab'.

- Don't forget booster vaccinations – they are required for continuing immunity.
- Most kennels insist that boarders are protected against the major infectious diseases. Consult your veterinary surgeon a month before you intend to board your dog if you do not have a current vaccination certificate signed by a veterinary surgeon.

Vaccination vs socialisation

Increases in dog and human population density have brought new pressures on dogs and their owners. There is a greater need for dogs to fit into society with minimal irritation to those who do not like dogs.

All puppy owners should discuss the vaccination/behaviour dilemma with their veterinary surgeon, preferably before they obtain their pet. Deciding whether to keep the puppy isolated until it is protected by vaccination or to start its integration into society before it has gained immunity to the major infectious diseases will depend on several factors which should be considered in depth:

- The general temperament of the breed, of the puppy and its parents
- The family circumstances, the place for the dog and how dogs kept previously by the owner have behaved
- The disease situation in the area and where the puppy came from; the vaccination history and likely immune status of the puppy's mother, if known
- The risk of infection, bearing in mind how the dog will be kept and how the major diseases are passed on.

With guard dogs such as Dobermanns, Boxers and Rottweilers, most vets agree that early socialisation is paramount. With the more biddable breeds like Cavalier King Charles Spaniels, especially those living in urban areas, the establishment of immunity will be of greater importance. In many cases a compromise will be recommended: to get the puppy out and about as soon as possible but to avoid places where the risk of disease is likely to be higher—parks used by large numbers of dogs, training classes and doggy events. You can be sure that advice from your vet will be based on his knowledge of dogs. Don't just ask for advice, take it!

SECTION FOUR

TAKING CARE OF YOUR DOG

Veterinary services

First aid and home nursing

Accidental poisoning

Dog maintenance

12
Veterinary services (UK)

> **Veterinary surgeons**
>
> **Veterinary nurses**
>
> **Pet Health Counsellors**
>
> **Fees**
>
> **Insurance**
>
> **Consulting the veterinary surgeon**
>
> **Second opinions**
>
> **Changing practices**
>
> **Veterinary hospitals**

Veterinary surgeons

Animals may only be treated by a qualified veterinary surgeon, except that an owner may diagnose and treat illness in his own animals, and anyone may give first aid to an animal in distress. Boarding kennel owners, trainers and people working in grooming businesses are acting illegally if they diagnose a condition and prescribe or apply medication – including homoeopathic and herbal remedies – to a dog that is not owned by them.

A student applying for a place at one of the six British veterinary colleges requires the very highest scholastic qualifications. Very few drop out during the 5-year course, and even fewer fail to qualify. Just over 300 new veterinary surgeons emerge every year to join the 6,000 or so already working in the various types of veterinary practice.

On graduation, the new graduate becomes a Member of the Royal College of Veterinary Surgeons (MRCVS). These initials will follow those which denote the university attended, eg London University Veterinary School, also known as the Royal Veterinary College, grants the degree of Bachelor of Veterinary Medicine (BVetMed). Fellowship of the Royal College of Veterinary Surgeons (FRCVS) is granted for service to the profession or by thesis. British veterinary surgeons are addressed as Mr or Ms unless they have earned the higher Doctor of Philosophy degree, denoted by the initials PhD after their names, when they are entitled to the prefix of Dr. In many other countries all veterinary surgeons are called 'Doctor' regardless of whether or not they have a PhD. Some veterinary surgeons are now earning post-graduate qualifications: CertSAD denotes a specialist in dermatology, DipSAD is the ultimate qualification in this specialty. Similarly, there are post-graduate qualifications in orthopaedics, ophthalmology and anaesthesia.

The Royal College of Veterinary Surgeons is the governing body of the veterinary profession and one of its important roles is acting as mediator and investigator in response to complaints from the public. The vast majority of these complaints stem from poor communication between the client and the veterinary surgeon, and it is hoped that some aspects of this situation may be eased after a study of this book.

Every veterinary practice, whether it is run single-handed by one person, or whether it is owned by several partners employing a number of assistants and lay staff, is a small business which must pay its overheads, allow a reasonable profit for its principals and a return on the capital invested in equipment. Veterinary fees are worked out on this basis; there is no nationally agreed scale of fees. Most practices now display a list of their basic fees.

While wide differences in charges are found, this may reflect the amount and standard of the equipment provided and the additional services offered, as well as the amount of skilled lay help available for the care of animals. Of course, the area of the country will affect the fees charged. It is usually much more expensive to have dogs treated in the London area, the south of England and the Home Counties.

Veterinary nurses

The Royal College of Veterinary Surgeons supervises the training and examinations for veterinary nurses who become, after qualification, members of the British Veterinary Nursing Association entitled to use the initials VN after their names. Full details of the course of tuition can be obtained from RCVS, 32 Belgrave Square, London SW1X 8QP.

However, many veterinary surgeons train lay assistants to their own needs and do not require them to be formally qualified. The number of people looking for this type of work always greatly exceeds the number of posts available.

Pet health counsellors

This is an exciting initiative for the veterinary profession, sponsored by Pedigree Petfoods. The programme is designed to help promote veterinary practices as 'Pet Health Centres' rather than simply emergency wards where sick pets are treated. The aim is to advise clients on all matters affecting their pets in a friendly and relaxed environment.

The programme is operating successfully in many practices around the UK.

A pet health counsellor can be a qualified veterinary nurse or a practice-trained person with at least 3 years' experience who is already working in the practice. Pedigree Petfoods supply in kit form the essential information and equipment needed to ensure that the programme runs efficiently and professionally.

The pet health counsellor's role is to:

- Listen to clients' problems and questions.
- Give simple practical advice on a variety of subjects, eg preventive medicine, pet selection, nutrition, insurance, pet accessories.
- Organise clinics on subjects such as obesity, ageing, training and behaviour, oral hygiene.
- Run puppy parties and open evenings.
- Make appointments for clients to see a veterinary surgeon if necessary.
- Supply veterinary approved foods, books and pet accessories.

Fees

If you feel that you have been charged too much for veterinary services, remember:

- You can always ask about the cost of treatment in advance. To be cautious about what you may be required to pay will not be taken as lack of concern for your dog.
- You can ask for an itemised bill to see how the total accumulated.
- Veterinary medication is often expensive to manufacture because in comparison with human needs, demand is low.
- Unlike private medical consultations and drug prescriptions, VAT is charged on all veterinary services.
- If the treatment advised is really more than you can afford, your veterinary surgeon may agree to payment by instalment. The animal charities can now only help those who are receiving social security benefits.

Insurance

In order not to have the risk of embarrassment you may wish to take out an annual insurance policy which covers veterinary fees for illness and accident, as well as other benefits. Your veterinary surgeon will have proposal forms from several companies offering different levels of cover. All the companies exclude preventative vaccinations and elective spaying and neutering.

Most companies have an upper age limit beyond which they no longer accept dogs for enrolment, but it is important to choose a company which will insure your dog for life if it is enrolled when young. It is often the early years, and again old age, which prove to be the most expensive in terms of veterinary fees.

One company will also insure your bitch for veterinary fees which may occur during pregnancy and whelping, so it is worthwhile reviewing all the policies on offer and also asking your veterinary surgeon which company is found to be the most satisfactory to deal with.

Third party insurance cover is a social necessity which may also become a legal requirement in the future. Even the smallest, most friendly dog can cause an accident which may result in considerable sums in compensation having to be paid to the victim.

Specialist pet insurance companies provide cover for the owner's legal liability to others in respect of damage or injury caused by their dog. Household insurance policies sometimes provide third party cover for the *owner* and not the dog. The pet is therefore only covered when in the care and control of the insured householder or his family.

A dog owner is not automatically liable to pay compensation to a claimant simply because their dog caused damage. It has to be proved that the accident was the owner's fault, that is, that they could have done something to prevent it or that they knew the dog was likely to do whatever caused the damage.

Veterinary Services (USA)

Animals may only be treated for an illness or injury by a qualified veterinary surgeon, except that an owner may diagnose and treat illnesses in his or her own animals, and anyone may administer first aid to an animal in distress. Boarding kennel owners and operators, professional trainers and groomers and others professionally connected to animal care are not technically qualified to make diagnoses and prescribe or administer any form of medication - including homeopathic or herbal remedies - to any dog not owned by them.

Anyone interested in pursuing a career as a veterinary surgeon must have truly superior qualifications including very high grades - especially in math and science courses. In the United States an aspiring veterinary student faces four years of study to earn a Bachelor's Degree plus another four years to qualify as a veterinary surgeon. Most American schools confer the degree DVM (Doctor or Veterinary Medicine) although some earn a VMD (Veterinary Medical Doctor). Most notable among the schools granting this latter degree is the School of Veterinary Medicine of the University of Pennsylvania.

It has been observed that getting into veterinary school in America can be more difficult than getting into medical school. This is due in part to the small number of schools for the former as compared to the latter and the great numbers of prospective students applying at any given time.

Upon graduation from veterinary school, it is routine for the new doctor interested in small animal work to serve an internship before launching a career in private practice. This internship is often served in a large practice or in a veterinary hospital attached to a school or located in a major population centre.

In America a veterinary surgeon is routinely known as a veterinarian and all are addressed as 'Doctor'.

Increasingly, as in other parts of the world, American veterinary surgeons are embracing a host of specialties: neomatal medicine, cardiology, oncology, dematology, and many others. This enhanced climate of knowledge can only benefit dogs and their owners as we move into the future.

As in every service-oriented endeavour, there will always be complaints from dissatisfied clients. Anyone finding themselves in a disagreement with their veterinary surgeons should seek out the local professional organization for a resolution to their specific problems. The vast majority of these complaints stem from poor communication between the client and the doctor, and it is hoped that some aspects of this situation may be eased after a study of this book and a greater understanding of the veterinary surgeon's role in the health of the client's dog.

Every veterinary practice, whether it is run singlehandedly, or whether it is owned by several partners employing a number of assistants and lay staff, is a small business which must meet its operating expenses, pay its overheads, allow a reasonable profit for the principals and a return on the capital invested in equipment. Veterinary fees are worked out on this basis; there is no nationally agreed-upon scale of fees for the services available. Some practices display a list of their basic fees; others will advise on an individual basis in the course of a consultation. Giving quotations for all but the most basic services on the phone is not fair to client or doctor and is not usually done.

It is uncommon for there to be wide differences in the fees charged for the same services or supplies. This may be a reflection of the amount of equipment owned by the practice and the extent of the services it offers as well as the amount of skilled lay help available for the care of the animals and the running of the office. Geography also comes into the pricing picture. The same service may be considerably more expensive in a large, urban practice than it would be in a small practice located in a rural community.

Support staff

Regardless of the practice the veterinary surgeon cannot possibly do it all. In the UK the Royal College of Veterinary Surgeons supervises the training and examination of veterinary nurses who become, after qualification, members of the British Veterinary Nurse Association. In America the closest thing to a veterinary nurse is a veterinary technician. A 'tech' assists the doctor in a host of important ways to help make the veterinary surgeon more effective and efficient. Many of the speciality publications for those interested in pets feature large advertisements which provide full details on how to become qualified as a veterinary technician.

However, many veterinary surgeons train lay assistants to their own needs and do not require formal qualification for their staff members. There is always strong competition for work in veterinary practices and the number of interested applicants routinely exceeds the supply of available positions.

13
First aid and home nursing

> Dog care and first aid kit
>
> A first aid kit for the car
>
> Emergency muzzling
>
> Finding a veterinary surgeon in an emergency
>
> Dealing with a road traffic accident
>
> Table of common emergencies
>
> Care of dogs before and after a surgical operations
>
> Vital signs
>
> Household measures

First aid

There will inevitably be times when your dog will need some first aid before being taken to a veterinary surgeon for treatment. First check the 'What if...' section of Chapter 17. If you are in doubt about what to do, telephone the veterinary surgery and ask the nurse or receptionist for advice if you are unable to speak to the veterinary surgeon at the time.

The following list of equipment, kept in a box labelled 'Dog first aid kit', will be invaluable both for you and for anyone who may be taking care of the dog for you. Your veterinary surgery can provide you with most of these items.

The prudent owner will also carry a few first aid items in the car, in order to be able to help his own dog or another which may be in distress (Table 13.2).

When a dog travels in the car, *always* carry a bottle of water and a drinking bowl. In summer a flask of ice can be invaluable. A strong blanket on which an injured dog can be carried is a necessity.

Putting on an emergency muzzle

An important action when trying to cope with an injured dog is to put on an emergency muzzle so that helpers do not get bitten (Figure 13.1). However, do not muzzle dogs that are having difficulty with breathing. Even the sweetest tempered dog may bite when shocked, bewildered and in pain. Practice putting the muzzle on your own dog in a non-emergency situation.

171

Procedure:

1. Stand behind the dog, holding a length of material in both hands.
2. Centre the bandage/material on top of the muzzle, in front of the eyes.
3. Pass the bandage under the chin from both sides and cross over, bringing the bandage round to the back of the neck and tie behind the ears. In dogs with strong jaws it will be necessary to have a simple knot under the jaw rather than just crossing the ends under the jaw as described above. The real experts use a clove hitch on the muzzle (see Figure 13.2).
4. For short-nosed dogs, a second length of bandage may be looped over the first and brought up between the eyes to anchor the restrainer to the mouth.

Figure 13.2 Clove hitch

Figure 13.1 Emergency tape muzzle

Finding a veterinary surgeon in an emergency

Try: Police, Post Office, Yellow Pages or a local breeder, kennel or pet owner. In some cases a pet helpline is available – check in advance.

Always plan to take the dog to a veterinary surgery. A vet is restricted in what he can do to help a dog in the road or at a private house. Telephone first to be sure of locating a vet on duty.

It is as well to be aware that if you are helping an unknown, unowned animal, you may be required to pay some or all of the cost.

If an animal has been killed in an accident, call the police rather than a veterinary surgeon. It is a misuse of veterinary time for them to be asked to act as undertakers.

Dealing with a road traffic accident involving a dog

- Hold up the traffic.
- Restrain the dog, perhaps by throwing a coat over its head, while you assemble your thoughts and collect what you need for first aid treatment.
  Comment: Even a badly injured dog may run away from the scene, complicating your efforts to help.
- Loop a restraining lead over the dog's head. Protect yourself with whatever means possible, eg thick gloves. Put on an emergency muzzle *unless* the dog is having trouble with breathing.
- Gently move the dog to the roadside if necessary by lifting it onto a blanket and sliding it along.
  Comment: Many drivers will not take kindly to being held up for too long.

- If blood is being lost, inspect the wound to see if it contains any obvious large pieces of glass, stone etc which can be easily removed; do not probe for smaller pieces. Apply a large pad to the wound with firm pressure, adding more pads if the blood seeps through. If there is debris in the wound which cannot be removed, bandage lightly to avoid driving it in; only use a tourniquet if blood is actually spouting from the wound. If that is not the case pressure bandages usually work and are safer.
- Locate a veterinary surgery to which the dog is to be taken. If fractures are suspected, transport the dog on a board, keeping the spine as straight as possible.
- Keep the dog lightly covered and warm during transport to the surgery.

Common emergencies

Wounds, cuts and abrasions

(i) *Minor wounds and grazes.* Allow the dog to lick and cleanse but be careful that it, or any companion animals, does not lick the wound excessively. This can be prevented by distracting the dog and teaching it not to lick (see Chapter 4) or by bandaging. For certain wounds, and where bandaging is difficult, it may be necessary to apply a wide collar (an Elizabethan collar) around the dog's neck to prevent it getting at the wound – your veterinary surgeon will advise.

If the dog cannot reach the wound or is not licking itself, cleanse the wound with soap and water, or salt water (1 tablespoonful/15 ml in half a pint/275ml) and dilute antiseptic, eg TCP. Subsequently apply a small amount of antiseptic ointment. This treatment should be repeated 2-3 times daily until healing has occurred.

(ii) *Severe wounds.* Seeping dark blood indicates that a vein has been cut. Clean the wound as above and apply a pad of lint (woven side to the wound) or a strip of bandage, cover with a layer of damp cotton wool and bandage lightly with a woven cotton bandage or a crepe bandage. Be careful not to apply the bandage too tightly. Check at regular intervals that swelling is not occurring below the bandage. Remove the bandage daily, dress the wound and re-bandage until healing takes place or is well on the way. A piece of Tubigauze (woven tubular bandage) may be used to help keep bandages in place.

Foot bandages may be kept clean by putting the dog's paw in an old sock which can be covered with a polythene bag when the dog goes outside. It is best to tape the sock and bag in place with Elastoplast rather than use an elastic band, since the latter can cause severe problems if left in place for too long and can be picked up and swallowed only too easily.

Bright red, spurting blood from a wound indicates that an artery has been severed. Provided that a large vessel is not involved, a pressure bandage, applied as described above, will usually suffice to control the haemorrhage. A second layer of cotton wool and bandage may be required if blood seeps through first. Once the bleeding has stopped, treatment can continue the next day as described previously. If such methods fail to stop the bleeding then a tourniquet will need to be applied at a suitable point between the heart and the wound. Do not leave tourniquets on for excessive periods; check by feeling the skin below the tournique – if it is cold and blue, the pressure must be released slightly. If it is necessary to apply a tourniquet, veterinary help must be sought since ligation of the artery may be required so that bleeding is controlled without adversely affecting the blood supply to the rest of the limb.

Cuts more than 1 in/2.5 cm in length may need suturing (stitches). It is wise to seek veterinary help without delay in such cases since if the wound is repaired early, the chances of it healing quickly are greatly increased.

Wounds in the pads or the ear flaps present special problems in that walking or head shaking may well make the wound start to bleed again. Foot wounds may need suturing if deep and professional bandaging can save a lot of mess in the house. A length of Tubigauze, or a tube improvised from the leg of a pair of tights can be placed over the dog's head for 12-24 hours to prevent the ear flapping when the head is shaken; the ears should be folded over the top of the head. It is unwise for owners to attempt to bandage a dog's head since such bandages slip only too easily and obstruction to breathing can occur if the bandage is not correctly applied, especially in the case of the short-nosed breeds.

Comment
* It is important to ensure that hair is not getting into the wound – this may necessitate clipping around the edge with blunt-edged, curved scissors.
* Deep puncture wounds can lead to abscess formation since they often heal too quickly on the surface, leaving infection to brew under the skin. If your dog has been in a fight with a cat it is wise to visit the surgery since a course of antibiotic medication may be needed to prevent abscesses forming.
* If you have any doubts about the severity of a wound, or if during healing the edges are very inflamed and sore and the surrounding area feels hot to the touch, seek veterinary advice without delay.

Table 13.3 provides hints to help you deal with some other common emergencies.

Home nursing

Since most owner nursing is carried out in relation to surgical operations, the information in this chapter is given with that in mind. However, much of the detail such as the giving of tablets, will of course apply in other situations too. Some information on nursing is given in the 'What if...' section of Chapter 17 and reference should also be made to the relevant section there. *If in doubt consult your veterinary surgeon.* A short telephone call to the surgery will ensure that mistakes are not made and will help set your mind at rest.

Care of the dog before and after a surgical operation

Many dogs will need surgery under a full anaesthetic at some time in their lives. The care that you give the dog before and after the operation will contribute greatly to the successful outcome.

Dogs make much better surgical patients than humans, possibly because they are not apprehensive before the event. Many breeds have a high pain threshold and will behave entirely normally two or three days after surgery.

Small animal veterinary surgery has now reached a high degree of sophistication, but there is always some risk involved in a full anaesthetic.

Before surgery
If the operation is non-urgent ('elective' or 'cold' are words used in this context), plan to have a few days free when you have plenty of time to devote to your dog after the operation.

If you are unable to keep close observation on the dog in the post-operative days, it may be wise to ask the veterinary surgeon to keep it as an in-patient. It is not unknown for dogs to burst their sutures or to remove them if they are left to their own devices.

Pre-operative starvation
- Your veterinary surgeon or the veterinary nurse will give precise instructions on withholding food and drink, usually for 12 hours but possibly longer, before the operation.
- *It is very important that these instructions are carried out, as otherwise the dog may choke on vomit during the anaesthetic.*
- Tell the veterinary surgeon if a mistake has been made as it may be better to postpone the operation.
- Tell the veterinary surgeon if your dog has ever had special problems in recovering from an anaesthetic, or if there is a known tendency in the breed to take anaesthetics badly.
- If the dog is on medication, ask the veterinary surgeon whether it should be withdrawn.

On the operation day
- Arrive at the surgery at the time requested.
- Provide a telephone number where you can be contacted all day.
- Be aware that the hair will have to be shaved from around the operation site. If you hope to show the dog again soon, ask if as little hair as possible can be removed.
- The dog will probably be given a 'pre-med' tranquillising injection and you may be asked to sit with the dog while this takes effect.
- You will probably be given a time at which you may telephone to enquire about your dog.

After surgery

Collection of the dog

Dogs vary in the time they take to recover from an anaesthetic. They should remain under skilled supervision until they are fully conscious and able to walk.

Before your dog is handed over to you, make sure you have all the information you will need. Never be afraid to ask!

1. Ask about food and fluid – what should be given and when.
2. Ask about medication – when should you start giving what is prescribed.
3. Ask about contacting a veterinary surgeon should the dog develop problems after it reaches home.
4. Ask about exercise.
5. Ask when you are to report progress and when the sutures are to be removed. The costs of suture removal and post-operative checking are often included in the operation fee. You may wish to ask if this is so.

The journey home

1. Keep the car warm but well-ventilated, or you may pick up the anaesthetic the dog is breathing out. Fat dogs can give out anaesthetic gases for 48 hours or more.
2. Prevent the dog from rolling off the seat, possibly having someone to hold it upright.
3. Prevent post-operative shock with hot water bottle and blanket.
4. Be aware that the dog may relapse into a deeper sleep when in familiar surroundings. If you cannot remove the dog from the car at the journey's end, let it recover where it is under close supervision.

Post-operative care

1. The dog's first need will be to pass urine. Support may be needed to enable it to reach its usual spot and while it 'performs'.

2. Make up a comfortable bed on the floor so the dog cannot roll off. Use plastic protection as the dog may pass urine while in a deep post-operative sleep.
3. Unless instructed otherwise by the veterinary surgeon, after major operations offer small quantities of water/glucose solution one tablespoonful/15 ml of glucose to one pint/550 ml of boiled water) or an electrolyte solution provided by the veterinary surgeon, every hour.
4. Give small amounts of easily digested food every 3-4 hours, unless instructed to the contrary.
5. Be prepared to support the dog to pass urine and faeces for 24-48 hours after surgery. If balance has not been regained by that time, tell the veterinary surgeon.
6. Be aware that the dog may have a slight cough, caused by intubation for the anaesthetic, for two or three days after surgery, and the throat may be sore making eating difficult.

Post-operative nursing
Veterinary surgeons often say: 'Give me a ring if you are worried!' The following conditions will give reason for post-operative concern and should be reported to the veterinary surgeon.

1. Sinking deeper into unconsciousness.
2. Cold, clammy feel to the paws, pale gums and lips.
3. Still not fully conscious and only cautiously active within 48 hours post-operation.
4. Persistent retching and vomiting, dog not retaining even small quantities of water.
5. Failure to regain limb control in 48 hours.
6. Passing faeces with blood content – estimate how much.
7. Acute swelling and redness around wound site or unpleasant smell from wound.
8. Convulsions or seizure.
9. Allergic reactions, such as bumps or weals appearing on skin, or acute swelling of face, mouth or throat.
10. Removal of the sutures by the dog.

Medication
Before you leave the surgery, make sure that the name of each drug is written on the container, together with its use, eg to stop vomiting, antibiotic, etc. Enter the names of the medication in your dog's records: it may be invaluable to you later on.

Make a chart for the dosage, marking off each time you give a dose.

If you have more than one pet, make sure the invalid is alone when you give the tablets, so that another dog does not snatch the tablet up if it should be dropped.

Control of water intake
Dogs which have become dehydrated during surgery will be very thirsty, but water in large quantities may make them vomit.

Remove all water bowls, flower pots and vases, and prevent access to puddles, ponds, water butts, etc.

Give fluid in appropriate quantity, one teaspoonful to one tablespoonful/ 5–15 ml every hour by the clock. After 2 hours, if the dog is not vomiting, the quantity may be doubled and thereafter increased cautiously until the dog is able to drink freely.

Fluid may be given in a hypodermic syringe (without a needle in place) if the dog finds it difficult to raise its head.

Dressings
If the dog has a dressing on leg or foot it may be kept clean when the dog goes outside by putting the foot into a plastic bag secured loosely by an elastic band. Remove the bag

and the elastic band immediately on return to the house and put them in a safe place. Elastic bands are bad news for dogs! If the dressings are becoming soiled but are still in place, another layer of conforming bandage may be put on top. It is important not to allow dressings to become wet.

Sutures
If the sutures are well positioned and not too tight, most dogs tolerate them well. The leg of a pair of tights makes a useful body stocking to keep dressings in place.

If the dog is inclined to worry about the sutures, try putting a bandage on a front paw to offer a distraction. An Elizabethan collar is another solution. Take a plastic bowl or bucket big enough to contain the dog's head; cut the bottom out of the bucket and discard it. Make a row of holes around the edge which remains, and thread through with string to lash the bucket to a leather collar. When this device is in place the dog will not be able to reach any part of its body, but these collars are tolerated surprisingly well.

Giving tablets
It is better not to crush tablets or to hide them in food. Once you have the knack of giving them, the procedure will be quite simple.

1. Open the dog's mouth with the left hand by tilting the head upwards with the thumb and index finger pushed in from outside the lips behind the dog's upper canine teeth. The jaw can then be easily opened by pressing on the lower incisors with the middle two fingers of the right hand. Keep the mouth open by pressing the dog's lips over its molar teeth.
2. Holding the tablet between the thumb and index finger of the right hand, push it as far back as possible over the back of the tongue.
3. Close the mouth and hold it closed while stroking the throat to make the dog swallow.

Some tablets (eg antibiotics) are designed by veterinary pharmaceutical companies to be palatable so that the dog will take them readily from the hand. If your dog is difficult about taking tablets, ask your veterinary surgeon if a palatable form of medication is available instead. Sometimes it can be helpful to hide the tablet in a chocolate or soft dog treat and hope that the dog will swallow it whole. Your vet will be able to advise.

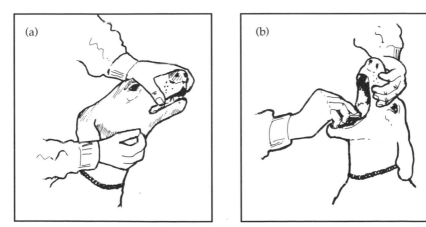

Figure 13.3 Giving tablets (a) opening the dog's mouth; (b) administering the tablet

Giving liquids
To give liquids to dogs easily, hold its jaws closed with one hand and tilt the head backwards. Pull out one corner of the closed mouth to form a pouch. Pour the liquid into this pouch alongside the molar teeth.

Puppies and very small dogs are probably dosed with greater safety if a medicine dropper is used, being inserted just inside the lips or cheek.

Vital signs

Body temperature	°F	100.9-101.7
	°C	38.3-38.7
Pulse rate		70-100 beats per minute
Respiration rate		15-30 breaths per minute

Approximate household measures

1 large teaspoonful	=	$^1/_6$	fl oz	=	5 ml
1 tablespoonful	=	$^1/_2$	fl oz	=	15 ml
1 wineglassful	=	2	fl oz	=	60 ml
1 cupful	=	7	fl oz	=	200 ml
1 pint	=	20	fl oz	=	550 ml

Table 13.1 Dog care and first aid kit

- Tweezers, curved and straight scissors, nail clippers
- Strip of soft strong tape for emergency muzzle
- Conforming bandage which sticks to itself as layers are put on
- Hydrogen peroxide to cleanse cuts/wounds
- Cotton wool
- Antacid emulsion for indigestion and flatulence
- Children's soluble aspirin as analgesic
- Liquid paraffin for constipation
- Meat tenderiser, soothes both wasp and bee stings
- Expectorant or emetic, prescribed by a veterinary surgeon
- Tube of antiseptic cream
- Roll of 2 in/5 cm or 3 in/7.5 cm wide adhesive plaster
- 2 in/5 cm and 4 in/10 cm open weave cotton bandage
- 2 in/5 cm crepe bandage
- Small sterile container for urine sample
- Small jar or plastic bag
- Small empty bottle for giving liquid medicine
- Anti-flea spray, as advised by veterinary surgeon
- Environmental flea spray
- Shampoo specifically made for dogs
- Glucose powder
- Ear drops, as advised by veterinary surgeon
- Eye drops, as advised by veterinary surgeon
- Antihistamine tablets, as advised by veterinary surgeon for use after insect stings
- A small notebook in which to record the dog's weight and details of previous illness and treatments given. Most importantly the book should contain a note of the veterinary surgeon's telephone number together with two alternative numbers for emergency use and the telephone number of a taxi company.

Table 13.2 First aid kit for the car

- Strong washable nylon braid slip collar and lead
- Length of soft tape for an emergency muzzle
- Curved scissors, tweezers
- Small bottle of diluted antiseptic
- Large pad of cotton wool
- 2 in/5 cm crepe bandage
- 3 in/7.5 cm wide adhesive plaster
- Leg from a pair of tights to put over head if ears are bleeding
- Bottle of meat tenderiser to put on stings
- Roll of kitchen paper for blotting, cleaning, etc.

Table 13.3 Coping with common emergencies

Emergency	Immediate action	Subsequent action
Bloat (stomach full of gas and greatly expanded in size)	One of the true great emergencies. **Get to the veterinary surgery immediately**	See 'What if' No. 33
Corrosive or irritant liquid splashed in eye	Bathe quickly with plenty of water at body heat. Restrain dog from rubbing eye	Veterinary surgery at once. See 'What if' Nos. 11 and 12
Caught in wire or thorn hedge	Pause long enough to *protect yourself* with strong gloves or by throwing a coat over the dog's head. Lift dog up to cut free. Don't forget to talk to the dog to pacify and reassure it.	Clean wounds as soon as possible and apply antiseptic ointment. Most wounds of this nature heal quickly but veterinary attention will be needed if lacerations are extensive.
Dog fight	A stick thrust through the collar and twisted to momentarily cut off the airway will give the opportunity to part two dogs. Be ready to remove them from each other immediately. Cold water via hose or bucket is effective, so is a sudden loud noise, a ringing door bell or a shout by an unfamiliar voice. Screaming by owner only encourages fighting between guard dogs.	Fights may reoccur between protagonists. They may have to be parted for life. If your dog is habitually aggressive to other dogs refer to Chapter 4.
Drinking seawater	Dogs have to find out that seawater is not good to drink. Carry fresh water for the dog.	Frequent and copious urination often follows drinking salt water
Drowning	Check airway, remove mud or debris from mouth. Hold dog up by hind legs to drain water out of lungs. If it is not breathing, lay it on its side and press intermittently on its chest or, having closed its mouth, blow gently up its nose until it starts to gasp.	Take the dog to surgery. *On the way* start to dry the dog and keep it warm
Electrocution	*Switch off electricity.* If this is not possible do not touch the dog with your hands but move it away with a wooden handled broom.	Pull the tongue forward in the mouth to allow the dog to breathe. Push down rythmically on the ribs at about 5 second intervals to induce breathing. If this fails then mouth to nose resuscitation, as described under drowning, may be tried. Keep up the artificial respiration while transporting dog to veterinary surgery
Fainting	Pull the dog's tongue forward to make a clear airway. Wait quietly with the dog while it recovers, applying ice or cold water if available to forehead and mouth	A relatively unimportant and quite common occurrence in Boxers, Boston Terriers, etc. Report to vet if fainting occurs frequently. See 'What if' No. 43

Table 13.3 (continued)

Emergency	Immediate action	Subsequent action
Falls	Dogs fall over cliffs when chasing seagulls and also slip down gullies in rocky country. Leave one person to identify the place where the accident took place	Contact Royal National Lifeboat Institution, Mountain Rescue or police
Fits	Protect dog from injury, eg falling down stairs. Turn off radio and TV, darken room. Do not touch dog but observe behaviour and duration of fit	Report to vet when dog has recovered and make an appointment for a full examination. A single fit is not a true emergency, dog is likely to be perfectly normal once active phase of fit is over. See 'What if' No. 38
Foreign body in eye, injury to eye	Apply a cold wet pad as described under prolapse of eyeball if the dog seems to be in great pain. In any case prevent the dog from scratching the eye and rubbing its face on the ground.	Veterinary surgery without delay. See 'What if' No. 12
Fractures, sprains, torn muscles	Restrain dog, make it lie down, restrict movement, confine in box or small space. Arrest any bleeding. Cover dog lightly and keep warm.	Contact veterinary surgery. See 'What if' No. 34
Heat stroke	Cool the dog's body temperature by any means possible – cold water, ice, dunking in a stream, even surrounding it with packs of frozen food. *Note:* the commonest cause of heat stroke is leaving dogs in cars into which the sun shines, but it can also occur when driving, even in cold weather through sun shining on a hatchback car	Beware of cooling the dog too much and lowering the body temperature too far. Ten minutes application of cold should be enough. Take the dog for veterinary check even if it appears fully recovered.
Picking up stones and sand	A dog can consume large quantities of sand while playing with a ball on the beach and diarrhoea may result. If you see your dog eating sand or something unidentified on the beach, a dose of liquid paraffin that night and the next morning can help prevent problems	Veterinary treatment to control diarrhoea
Poisoning	Take as much evidence as possible to the veterinary surgery, eg vomit, and packs, tins or plants which the dog has been chewing	Take the dog to the veterinary surgery at once, being prepared to give the full history of the incident. See Chapter 14

Table 13.3 (continued)

Prolapse of eyeball	Do not attempt to replace eyeball. Soak a cloth pad in cold water, apply to cover the eyeball and socket. keep cool and wet dressing gently in place	Veterinary surgery immediately
Emergency	**Immediate action**	**Subsequent action**
Scalds, burns (serious)	If caused by hot fat, wipe as much as possible off the coat with paper. Douse burn with cold water, do not apply ointments, etc.	Get to veterinary surgery quickly
Scalds, burns (minor)	Clip off hair around the place as the burn may be more extensive than you think. Apply cold water to ease the pain, then antiseptic ointment. Keep all burns and scalds scrupulously clean	Observe area closely, especially for the next 5-7 days. If inflammation persists seek veterinary help
Snake bite	Britain's only poisonous snake is the adder, found in heathland in summer. The marks of two fangs may be seen at the site of bite, on head or legs. Gross swelling begins immediately. Carry the dog if possible rather than let it walk, to avoid spreading the poison. If bite is on leg, put on a tourniquet above the bite, release it every 15-20 mins. Heroic treatment is useless, but the wound may be cleaned with soap and water	Veterinary surgery at once
Trapped underground	In sandy country dogs pursuing rabbits can become trapped in the burrows. Another dog is your best assistant, using its superb sense of hearing and smell. Carry a spade to dig the dog out and water as it will be dehydrated. Keep searching; the dog may survive for as long as 7 days underground	Rest and care should be enough for complete recovery but the dog may do the same thing again
Wasp and bee stings	If sting is visible pull it out with tweezers. Apply meat tenderiser to area. Observe amount of swelling. Keep dog indoors and quiet	Veterinary attention needed if swelling is acute in mouth and throat. If the dog seems in great pain your veterinary surgeon may be able to give you extra advice over the phone

14
Accidental poisoning

> **Risks**
>
> **Signs**
>
> **Common poisons**
>
> **Dangers in the house and garden**

All our houses, gardens and garages contain substances which can be poisonous to dogs, and the risk is particularly high in puppies during the 'chewing stage'.

Potentially poisonous material should be stored where the puppy cannot possibly reach it, and were it cannot be knocked down to the puppy's level by a cat or other animal. Some substances, especially mouse/rat bait, are cumulative poisons, although they may be declared safe on the container. Beware of rat poisons laid by local authority rodent eradicators, as they may be more dangerous than those sold to the general public. Do not allow your dog to nuzzle or play with carcasses of rabbits, birds etc found in woodland, as they may have been baited with deadly poison in order to destroy foxes or other vermin.

Be safe rather than sorry. Never shut a dog, even temporarily, into a garden shed or garage where poisonous substances are kept.

Signs of poisoning

Among the signs of poisoning will be sudden, violent vomiting and/or diarrhoea, fits, foaming at the mouth, staggering gait, collapse and coma, but all these signs may relate to other conditions not caused by poisoning. All will require immediate veterinary help.

> If the dog's illness can be associated with access to a dangerous substance, or if the dog is found with a container or packet, take all the associated material, packaging and any vomit with you to the veterinary surgeon to help in identifying the cause of illness and the finding of a possible antidote.

Table 14.1 indicates some common poisons, their sources and how to prevent accidental poisoning.

Table 14.1 Poison risks

Situation	Poison	Source	Prevention
Garage	Engine oil Antifreeze (ethylene glycol) Old lead paint Paint remover Wood preserver fumes Glue Tar and creosote (phenol) Putty	Spillage on the floor and old containers Spillage on the floor and old containers Flaking paint, old paint tins improperly stored Improperly stored containers Improperly stored containers Old pots and tubes of glue Spillage and old containers Old putty containers, old window frames	Keep the garage clean and tidy with possible poison sources on high shelves. Keep dogs out of garages as puppies will sample almost any fluid and older dogs may walk in poisonous substances and then ingest them by licking their feet.
Kitchen	Acrolein	Vapour from overheated oil or cooking fat	Ventilate kitchens properly when cooking and keep young puppies in another room.
	Detergents	Bottles containing concentrated detergents	Make sure that kitchen cupboards can be firmly shut and that containers are properly closed
	Disinfectants	Disinfectant containers and areas where disinfectants are used undiluted	Such substances may be swallowed and sometimes absorbed through the skin.
	Carbon monoxide	Leaking coal/gas appliances. Stoves burning Calor gas, oil or solid fuel without adequate ventilation.	Have such appliances checked regularly and only use them when ventilation is adequate. Do not provide dogs with beds close to stoves and allow proper ventilation of sleeping quarters.
Bathroom	Various medicines intended for human or animal use	Old medicine containers	Keep part-used medicines in containers that can be properly closed, not packets. Throw out unused medicines. Keep all medicines in cabinets that can be closed and locked.
Garden shed	Herbicides (arsenicals and bypyridyl), diquat and paraquat insecticides/fungicides	Old containers that are not properly closed. Material spilt on floor. Many of the older insecticides are quite safe but products containing organochlorines, organophosphorus compounds or carbamates can be very toxic for dogs	Ensure that all such products are in properly sealed containers kept well out of reach of dogs. Sweep the floor regularly. Do not leave diluted products ready for use in places where they can be reached by dogs. Keep dogs away from plants that have been recently sprayed; they may eat them or even absorb the poison through the skin. Do not use herbicides and insecticides near where the dog's food is kept.

Location	Substance	Source/Description	Precautions
	Molluscicides (slug killers) (metaldehyde)	The pellets are very attractive to dogs.	Make sure that slug pellets are not used where dogs can reach them, or that they are accidentally spilt on the floor.
	Antu, calciferol, alpha-chloralose, crimidine phosphorus, thallium, warfarin, arsenic	Rat and mouse poisons based on these compounds.	Take great care with the use and storage of such products. If in doubt seek professional advice. Be careful of spillage and ensure that proper containers are used. Dispose of old material with proper care.
Other rooms in the house, conservatory	Plant poisons	Some house plants, eg oleanders	Make certain that houseplants are kept out of reach of puppies. Train dogs not to go near house plants
	Nicotine	Cigarettes or cigar ends	Empty ashtrays regularly – do not leave full ashtrays within reach of dogs overnight
	Detergents	Dry powder carpet cleaners may cause inflammation of the skin	Ensure such cleaners are properly vacuumed up as directed and keep dogs out of the room while they are being applied. It is probably better not to use such products where there are dogs in the house
	Lead	Old toys, old paintwork, other lead objects	Replace old paintwork with non-lead based paint
Garden	Fungi/toadstools	Hedgerows	Keep hedgerows clear
	Berries	Berries eg mistletoe	Keep dogs away from trees where mistletoe is growing and be careful if the berries are brought indoors
	Laburnum	Laburnum trees	It is probably better to forego having such trees in the garden, especially if a number of dogs are kept. Keep puppies away from such trees and branches which have been pruned.
	Bulbs – daffodils and snowdrops	Garden beds	Train dogs not to dig in the garden and take care when planting. Keep stored bulbs out of reach.
	Various herbicides, eg malathion, paraquat, sodium chlorate	Garden spray and weedkillers	Keep dogs away while spraying and do not allow dogs access to sprayed plants until the spray has dried on the leaves. Cover or take water bowls indoors while spraying. Take special precautions if farm land or road verges are being sprayed
	Cyanide	Products used to destroy wasp nests	Be careful with use and storage of such products

15
Dog maintenance

Record keeping

Regular health checks

Your dog's personal data

It is my no means unusual for owners not to be able to remember the incidents in their dog's life, and very often they have not had the opportunity to know what medication has been given, etc.

It is of great help to the veterinary surgeon if you can contribute a full history without irrelevant detail, and it may save you money in terms of consultation time if you are able to supply the information needed. Furthermore it can be of great interest both to you and your family to keep a full record of the dog's life and history, perhaps in great detail during the first year, and then later noting down illnesses, accidents, when the dog was boarded and the start of new behaviour patterns, etc.

A record of the way a puppy was fed, weight gains and achievements in the way of house-training and obedience will be invaluable as a reference point for other new puppies which may be acquired by family and friends.

Keep a note of vaccinations given and when boosters are due.

Always ask the nurse or receptionist at the veterinary practice to write on any container the name of the product, the strength (especially for tablets) and the dosage regime and add this to your records, together with a brief description of any surgical procedures carried out.

It can be particularly useful to have information on any adverse reaction to medication, skin dressing or anaesthetic.

Record cards can go astray in the veterinary surgeon's office, so your back-up file can be of vital importance, and especially if you are obliged to change veterinary practices or if, for some unforeseen reason, your dog has to be cared for by someone else.

Don't be afraid to go into the veterinary surgery with written notes to remind you about the current illness and your dog's past history. It is better to do that than forget something important. The more relevant details the veterinary surgeon has to hand, the easier it will be for him to diagnose the cause of the problem and select the most appropriate treatment so that your dog will make a more rapid and complete recovery.

Finally you should not necessarily feel guilty if you have delayed taking your dog to the surgery. Almost the first question a veterinary surgeon asks in the consulting room is, 'How long has this condition been present?' This is not meant to be an accusation of neglect, but it is of vital importance to the veterinary surgeon when making his diagnosis to know whether a sign of illness has been present for hours, days or weeks. Even if you know you should have consulted the veterinary surgeon sooner, it is best to be frank about the time the signs were first apparent, as it will help the dog more now that treatment is to be given.

Regular checks for your dog

It makes good sense to give your dog a formal checkover for signs of illness at regular intervals. Tables 15.1 and 15.2 are provided as a guide.

Record of illness and medication*

Date	Signs shown/ diagnosis	Medication given/ surgical procedure	Comments

Ask your veterinary surgeon to write down the name of the injections or tablets prescribed.

* To include medication given for treatment and prevention of disease, ie antibiotic injections, chemical control of heat, worm doses etc.

Table 15.1 Health checks for all dogs

Daily	Eyes	Look for the presence of excessive discharge or pus in the conjunctival sac. Check that the cornea is clear and not cloudy, that the dog can see clearly. Sight can be checked readily by throwing a titbit for the dog to catch.
	Faeces	Note consistency, colour. Check frequently. Look for undigested food, foreign bodies (plastic bags, cardboard etc)
Weekly	Ears	Check that there is no discharge or odour coming from the ear canal. Examine ear flaps for presence of wounds or swelling.
	Paws	Examine for wounds, cracks, cysts between the toes and nail-bed infections.
Monthly	Skin/coat	Look for areas of thickened skin and baldness, particularly on elbows and hocks. Check for evidence of excessive scratching and the presence of abrasions. Test the skin's mobility. Look for worm segments around the anus. Check the whole body for new warts, lumps under the skin, etc. It is a good idea to chart these on a sketch of the dog's outline so that you can monitor their rate of growth.
	Claws	Check nail-beds for signs of inflammation. Examine claws for length and presence of splits. Don't forget the dew-claws.
	Teeth	Check the teeth and mouth for dental decay, accumulation of tartar and inflammation of the gums.
Annually		Visit veterinary surgeon for annual booster vaccination and ask for a full health check to be carried out.

Table 15.2 Additional health checks for bitches

Daily	Urination	Note the frequency of urination and if possible the colour of urine passed. More frequent squatting may indicate that your bitch is about to come on heat or that there is an impending infection of the urogenital tract.
	Thirst	Try to gain some idea of how much water is being drunk. Excessive thirst may indicate impending pyometra, diabetes or a urinary tract infection.
	Behaviour	Take note of any abnormal behaviour that might indicate that your bitch is about to come on heat, has false pregnancy or the onset of some illness.
Weekly	Vulva	Look for wounds, signs of excessive licking or a discharge. Pay particular attention at the time the bitch is on heat and for the following 3 months.
	Mammary	Look for the presence of milk by gently squeezing the teats. Feel all the mammary glands for the presence of tumours and record their size. It is particularly important to carry out this examination when the bitch is on heat and weekly in the subsequent 3 months.

SECTION FIVE

SIGNS AND SYMPTOMS OF ILLNESS

Observing dogs for signs of illness

'What if my dog...?'

16
Observing dogs for signs of illness

> **Signs and symptoms**
>
> **Pain**

Introduction

Early recognition and treatment of illness is important, not only to save pain and suffering, but also because treatment is likely to be more effective.

The object of this chapter is to help the owner to recognise, identify and to describe accurately the signs of pain and illness in their pet and to know when to seek veterinary advice. The observant owner will then be able to supply an accurate and detailed history should veterinary treatment become necessary. An accurate history can be a crucial factor in helping the veterinary surgeon to arrive at a correct diagnosis and is thus a prelude to effective treatment. Your veterinary surgeon may appreciate having the history in writing.

Tips on observing dogs for signs of illness

- The concerned owner will spend time observing the normal habits, reactions and detailed appearance of their dog when in full health, so that any alterations which may be indicative of the beginnings of illness will be noticed quickly.
- Any small change in behaviour or any unusual physical sign should mean that the dog is kept under extra close scrutiny for a few hours, or a few days, until either more positive signs develop or the dog has returned to normal. A dog under observation for illness should not be given strenuous exercise nor should it be taken to a training class, a dog show or into any situation which may cause it stress.
- It may not be beneficial to seek veterinary advice in the very early stages of discomfort, as the vet will usually want some positive signs to develop before treatment can be started. The discerning owner should know instinctively when this stage is reached.
- Dogs, like humans, may have days when they feel 'off colour' for no obvious reason. If these episodes occur often in your dog, a note of days, times and associated circumstances should be made. Veterinary advice should then be sought in order to interpret the information collected in this way.
- Dogs may show signs of depression and illness in response to worry or grief affecting the owner or the household in which it lives. Human alterations in behaviour may be subtle, but the devoted dog recognises mood changes in its owner. The dog will return to normal when its owner is feeling happier and on no account should they be given anti-depressive drugs prescribed for human use.

Signs and symptoms

Most canine illnesses are shown by a combination of signs and symptoms.

Signs of illness
Objective evidence that something is wrong which is readily apparent to an observer, eg diarrhoea or coughing.

Symptoms of illness
A change in sensation of bodily function experienced by the patient, eg the pain caused by trying to put an injured foot to the ground. Symptoms are usually regarded as being subjective and applicable to people who can express what they are feeling. Although dogs are at a disadvantage in being unable to describe their symptoms they are nevertheless able to indicate in a number of ways what they are experiencing, but it is necessary to learn how to interpret these indications correctly.

It is important for the owner to keep an open mind about the nature of an illness during the early stages.
Not all cases of a particular illness show all the signs and symptoms associated with that illness. Furthermore, many signs are common to a number of different diseases. Jumping to the wrong conclusion too early may prevent help being sought at the right time and delay the start of proper treatment.

The significance of the various signs of illness shown by dogs will be found in Chapter 17. Suffice to comment here on temperament and behaviour changes and temperature taking.

Temperament and behaviour changes

Dogs are creatures of habit. Any marked changes not associated with changes in the household may be indicative of illness. However, allowance should be made for jealousy, resentment and pining, as well as undue persecution by a puppy, kitten or child, or the onset of heat, whelping or false pregnancy in bitches.

Temperature taking

The normal temperature of a newborn puppy is 98.6°F (37°C) and the normal adult body temperature of 101.5°F (38.5°C) is not achieved until the pup is about 4 weeks old. It is not wise or helpful for an inexperienced owner to take the dog's temperature unless specifically requested to do so by the veterinary surgeon – thermometers can be broken in the rectum all too easily! Furthermore, readings need skilled interpretation as any form of excitement can cause the temperature to rise by 2-3 degrees when the dog is in normal health.

Pain

Pain is probably the most significant symptom of illness or injury and it is important to understand the ways that dogs indicate that they are suffering from pain in a particular area or organ (see Table 16.1).

Two general signs of pain that are frequently shown by dogs are:

Crying
Dogs do not cry by means of tears, but they will utter a vocal cry at a sudden injury (such as being stepped on) or when an external injury or a painful internal organ is touched.

191

Unprovoked crying or vocalisation may indicate internal pain. Some dogs are more stoical than others and will endure considerable pain without any vocalisation.

Aggression

Any radical change in temperament may be a reaction to pain. A sudden tendency to aggression may be reversible when the pain is alleviated, so give the veterinary surgeon a full history before concluding that the dog has become vicious.

Table 16.1 Symptoms of pain in specific areas as indicated by tell-tale 'signs'

Area of pain	Signs that indicate that pain is felt
Head	Half-closed eyes coupled with persistent pressing of the top of the head into furniture, owner's lap or the flank of other dogs; gentle shaking of the head or vacant staring.
Eye	Pawing at eyes; rubbing eyes on furniture or on the carpet.
Ear/mouth	It is not always easy to distinguish between the two as the nerve pathways are very close. One ear may be carried low and the head inclined to the affected side. There may be drooling or excess saliva, reluctance to eat hard food or to take food from the hand. Dogs with mouth pain may yawn frequently and ear pain is usually accompanied by head shaking or gentle scratching at the ear.
Throat	Retching, drooling, stretching neck towards the ceiling (sore throat) and difficulty in swallowing shown by gulping.
Abdomen	Continual glancing round at the site of pain, biting and licking at the area. Lying in a curled up position, reluctant to leave its bed. The dog may hold itself in a hunched up position when standing, or may take up the 'prayer position' (down on forelegs with hindlegs standing). In some cases dogs with adbonimal pain will show persistent straining to pass a bowel movement.
Limb/joint	Dogs quickly adapt to carrying a limb which is giving them pain when weight is put on it. When the problem is on the foot or, in case of severe injury, the limb is usually carried high, but sometimes it is only partially elevated and the toes will be dragged along the ground. In other cases the dog will put the foot of the affected leg to the ground but will not put full weight on it. In such cases the dog's movement should be watched carefully, paying particular attention to the head and pelvis. A nodding action of the head or rump will be seen when the sound foreleg is put to the ground. Lameness associated with foot dragging is often indicative of nerve damage. A dog with arthritic pain in the joints will sometimes give a grunt or cry when settling into or rising from its bed. It is a useful diagnostic measure to know if the dog's pain eases when it has been moving about for a while, or whether exercise makes the pain worse. It is not always easy to decide which limb is lame, especially if more than one leg is affected. Bilateral hind leg lameness from severe hip dysplasia may not show on movement.
Spine	Sometimes a dog will appear lame when the actual site of pain is in the spinal column. Other signs of back pain are a resentment to touch or accidental knocks, trembling while standing, wasting of the upper thighs, humping of the centre back, difficulty in assuming normal defecation position, a staggering gait, collapse of hindquarters and incontinence.
Anal gland	Dragging the anus on carpet or grass is the dog's reaction to pain around the rectum. The dog may also turn round to inspect its back end frequently and suddenly, often accompanied by a yelp.
General internal	Being unable to settle down when all normal wants have been fulfilled may indicate internal pain or mental trauma.
'Hind end'	Frequent whirling round is the dog's response to 'hind end' discomfort from a burr or matt of fur in the region, or from blades of grass which have not been passed properly with a bowel movement and which are still protruding from the anus. As with anal gland pain the dog will also turn round suddenly and frequently to inspect the affected area, often with a cry.

17
'What if my dog...'

Introduction

This chapter seeks to answer the questions which worry dog owners when their pet shows signs which may indicate that it is ill. Each topic begins with the words 'What if my dog...?' and it is hoped that the details given will help owners decide whether:

- The sign is normal and no action is required
- Some simple 'treatment' is needed
- First aid action is indicated
- Veterinary help should be obtained and if so, how urgently it is needed.

Use the Index of Diseases and Conditions, the list below, or Figure 17.1 to identify the relevant number.

> Throughout the book are highlighted history tips. These show information which will be important for the veterinary surgeon to know when making a diagnosis. Usually this information can only be supplied by the observant owner and so you have a very important function to perform in contributing towards the restoration of your pet to perfect health. The history which you supply can be crucial in making a correct diagnosis and rapid recovery.

'What if my dog...?' – numerical index

1. eats grass
2. vomits
3. refuses to eat
4. is eating too much
5. is eating well but remains very thin
6. is drinking excessively
7. sneezes
8. has a discharge from its nose
9. has a dry and crusty nose
10. has a nose which has turned brown or grey
11. has runny eyes
12. has eyes that look abnormal
13. is blind
14. is shaking or scratching its ears
15. is holding its head on one side
16. is breathing abnormally
17. is shedding hair
18. is going bald
19. is scratching
20. keeps breaking wind
21. has noisy abdominal sounds
22. is biting its tail, scooting or rubbing its bottom on the ground
23. has diarrhoea
24. is passing blood in its faeces
25. is constipated
26. is eating its own faeces
27. is not passing urine
28. is incontinent
29. is passing blood in its urine
30. has a discharge from its penis or vulva
31. is mismated
32. is found to be pregnant unexpectedly
33. is pot-bellied

34. is limping
35. is coughing
36. is eating with difficulty
37. has bad breath
38. is having fits, convulsions or is twitching
39. has a lump or swelling
40. is wounded/cut/burnt/grazed
41. is licking itself excessively
42. is weak and lethargic
43. has collapsed and is comatose
44. is in pain
45. is losing weight, or is looking thin
46. is aggressive
47. is not breathing
48. is staggering and wobbly on its legs
49. appears deaf
50. is aborting
51. is nervous and over-excitable
52. has a depraved appetite
53. is salivating excessively
54. is over-sexed

1.   What if my dog eats grass?

Many dogs will eat small amounts of coarse couchgrass regularly, only for it to be vomited, covered in frothy saliva, a few minutes later. It is thought that the grass is eaten to relieve an excess of digestive juices which accumulate in the stomach when it is empty. If this habit causes inconvenience, it may help to give two or three small meals a day rather than one large meal, and to discourage the habit by using the behaviour control measures described in Chapter 4. Immediate, sharp punishment given consistently and in a planned way can be very effective.

Fine grass may be grazed by some dogs and digested. This will act as roughage in the diet.

* Grass eating is seldom harmful, provided the grass has not been sprayed with a toxic chemical. If grass eating is accompanied by prolonged or persistent vomiting, and particularly if the vomit contains blood, veterinary advice should be sought quickly.

2.   What if my dog vomits?

Dogs vomit easily and occasional incidents are to be expected and are unimportant.

* Vomiting is part of the defence mechanism of the body, enabling the stomach to get rid of an excess of food, water or unsuitable or decayed matter before it passes further into the digestive system and causes harm.
* Prolonged or persistent vomiting, particularly if the vomit contains blood, requires immediate veterinary attention.

There are three main types of vomiting listed here in order of the frequency with which they occur.

True vomiting

This involves movement of the muscles of the abdomen, chest or diaphragm (ie heaving) in order to eject the contents of the stomach.

The main danger of repeated or continuous vomiting is dehydration (loss of body fluids), so that the volume of circulating blood is decreased and the dog goes into a state of shock very rapidly. Dehydration can be recognised by picking up a fold of skin on the dog's back between your thumb and forefinger. If the fold remains 'tented' when you release it, dehydration is indicated.

Figure 17.1 What if my dog...?
Use this illustration to identify the relevant 'What if' number. The 'What ifs' are also listed numerically opposite. Alternatively, if you know the name of the condition, eg diarrhoea, constipation, etc, use the Index of Diseases and Conditions.

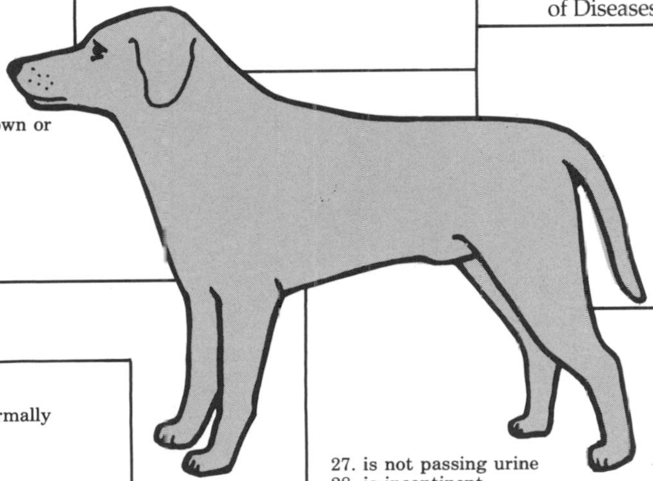

11. has runny eyes
12. has eyes that look abnormal
13. is blind
14. is shaking or scratching its ears
49. appears deaf
15. is holding its head on one side

1. eats grass
2. vomits
3. refuses to eat
4. is eating too much
5. is eating well but remains thin
36. is eating with difficulty
52. has a depraved appetite
53. is salivating excessively

6. is drinking excessively

7. sneezes
8. has a discharge from its nose
9. has a dry and crusty nose
10. has a nose which has turned brown or grey

37. has bad breath

21. had noisy abdominal sounds
20. keeps breaking wind

23. has diarrhoea
24. is passing blood in its faeces
25. is constipated

22. is biting its tail or scooting or rubbing its bottom on the ground

26. is eating its own faeces
39. has a lump or swelling
40. is wounded
41. is licking itself excessively
42. is weak and lethargic
43. has collapsed and is comatose
48. is staggering and wobbly on its legs
44. is in pain
45. is loosing weight or is looking thin

27. is not passing urine
28. is incontinent
29. is passing blood in its urine
30. has a discharge from its penis or vulva
31. is mismated
32. is found to be pregnant unexpectedly
50. is aborting
33. is pot-bellied
54. is over-sexed

35. is coughing
16. is breathing abnormally
47. is not breathing
17. is shedding hair
18. is going bald
19. is scratching
34. is limping
38. is having fits, convulsions or is twitching
46. is aggressive
51. is nervous and excitable

It is wrong to allow a vomiting dog to drink its fill of cold water as this often leads to further vomiting, but it is also dangerous to withhold water completely. Instead, very small amounts of water should be offered every half hour (see Chapter 13 on home nursing).

In cases of persistent vomiting where the dog is not eating, it may be helpful to dissolve one heaped tablespoon of glucose in one pint of boiled water (15 ml/550 ml) and to offer this in small quantities in order to supply the dog with the energy it requires. This is an emergency measure for use where veterinary advice cannot be obtained.

> If the vomit contains identifiable food, it may be helpful to trace the time it has been in the stomach. Note particularly whether the vomit consists of small food particles with a quantity of frothy saliva; or large quantities of recently drunk water plus yellow bile and stomach fluids.
>
> Make a note of how much water is given and when. Record how long it is retained.

Regurgitation

The second type of vomiting is regurgitation – a more passive action used to bring up sausage-shaped boluses of something recently eaten. When freshly eaten food is regurgitated the dog may eat it again at once, and this behaviour is so frequent as to be normal in some dogs, particularly when they bolt their food in competition with others or when persuaded to eat when they are not hungry.

It is normal for some bitches to regurgitate their own partially digested food for puppies to eat as they reach weaning age.

Persistent regurgitation in an older puppy or an adult dog may indicate some obstruction or malformation in the oesophagus and this condition warrants prompt veterinary advice.

> Note how much of the food given is being regurgitated and the time in relation to feeding.

Retching

The third type of vomiting is retching, an involuntary spasm of vomiting, possibly accompanied by a cough. There appears to be difficulty in swallowing food, which is then quickly brought back covered in saliva. The cause may be some obstruction in the mouth or throat, or retching may be associated with a cough or an acute sore throat. Veterinary advice should be sought at once if retching occurs frequently or is persistent.

The significance of true vomiting

Vomiting is associated with many **serious diseases** and conditions in the dog, particularly **canine parvovirus disease, haemorrhagic gastroenteritis, kidney disease** and **pyometra** in bitches. In these diseases vomiting will usually be accompanied by loss of appetite, depression and diarrhoea. Veterinary help is needed at once and must definitely not be delayed if there is blood in the vomit.

Vomiting may also be caused by **eating unsuitable or decayed material,** by eating poisonous substances or carrion or plant material which has been impregnated by poison; or by bad food, which irritates the stomach and intestines. In such cases the signs mentioned above may be accompanied by drooling from the mouth and signs of abdominal pain. Veterinary help is needed urgently.

If the dog is known to have eaten a poisonous substance, eg a garden chemical or slug bait, take the original container with you to the veterinary surgeon, as the manufacturer's analysis may be helpful in tracing an antidote to the poison.

Intestinal obstructions are a relatively frequent cause of vomiting in dogs, particularly puppies. Vomiting may result from stones, toys, bones and stolen objects becoming lodged in the digestive tract. Twists in the bowel, or the telescoping of one part of the bowel into another, as can occur in young puppies, will cause vomiting. In such cases true vomiting may be accompanied by frequent retching and the dog will become progressively more ill. If you suspect that your dog has swallowed some toy or trophy such as part of a ball or a bone, it is important to consult a veterinary surgeon *at once*, as surgery may be required and it is better done before the dog is exhausted by frequent attempts to vomit and has become dehydrated.

Projectile vomiting is used to describe a particular kind of vomiting action in which recently eaten food is ejected with some force, sometimes over a distance of several feet. It is seen most frequently in puppies from 6-16 weeks old, but may not be noticed until the puppy is separated from the rest of the litter. Vomiting of this type when only part of the food and liquid is retained is associated with failure of the stomach to empty its contents into the intestine, and is often associated with **pyloric stenosis** (a malfunction of the exit valve of the stomach). Seek veterinary help immediately, as surgical correction may be possible.

An estimate of how much food and/or liquid is retained is helpful, as well as daily weighing of the puppy, in order to monitor growth and weight gain.

Travel sickness may occur in dogs as it does humans. Many puppies are nauseated and drool and vomit when travelling in a car, possibly from a disturbance in the balance centre of the brain, or perhaps from stress associated with changing homes for the first time.

It is helpful for someone to hold the puppy securely so that it is not so affected by the movement of the car. Putting the dog into a wire mesh crate, perhaps covered with a light cotton material, may be helpful. Perseverance on the part of the owner – taking the dog out in the car *before feeding*, making journeys rewarding by including a walk etc, almost always allow the dog to grow out of travel sickness. Ideally, puppies should be introduced to car travel before they are 8 weeks of age and so before the 'fear period' in their development. If the puppy is not acclimatised and happy in the car by that age it is better to leave further introductions and the possible use of the methods described above until after it is 3 months of age. It is not desirable to give medication intended for travel sickness in humans. Specific, very effective, modern remedies designed for use in dogs are available from veterinary surgeons who will advise on their use in specific circumstances.

Unproductive attempts at vomiting can be serious. Sometimes a dog will be seen to try to vomit but will be unable to bring up any stomach contents. When this is associated with a rapid expansion of the abdomen (bloating), the condition is very dangerous indeed and needs veterinary help immediately.

3. What if my dog refuses to eat?

While inappetence may be the first sign of a major illness, it is also not uncommon for a healthy, well-fed dog to refuse a meal occasionally, often for the reasons listed below.

Common reasons for refusal of food in healthy dogs

Puppies
* Young puppies may refuse milky meals at around 6 months old.
* Puppies which have been on a four meals a day regime will begin to refuse 'breakfast' when the time has come to switch to three larger meals given at longer intervals.
* Puppies may refuse temporarily, to eat newly introduced foods.
* Puppies will often not eat if they are overtired.

Adults
* Refusal of food is normal and sensible when a dog is exhausted by vigorous exercise.
* Dogs will often refuse food when they have other things on their minds, for instance a bitch in season nearby.
* Inappetence may be due to environmental stress; guard dogs will not eat when strangers are present and pet dogs in boarding kennels may starve themselves for a few days.
* Most bitches will refuse food for a day or part of a day at certain stages of pregnancy, and usually for 24-36 hours before whelping. Appetite may be variable for a few days after whelping.

Persistent refusal of food, especially if accompanied by other signs of illness, needs careful monitoring. Veterinary help should be sought if a dog refuses all food for more than 24 hours in a young puppy or 48 hours in an adult, provided none of the situations mentioned above are pertinent. Advice on how to cope with *reluctant* eaters is given in Chapter 2.

Note particularly:
* How long is it since the dog ate a full meal eagerly?
* Whether the dog refuses all foods, or is selecting a certain type of food.
* Whether the dog is capable of swallowing, by offering small pieces of a favoured titbit.
* Whether or not the dog is drinking normally.
* If the dog is still passing motions at normal times and frequency; record their colour.
* If vomiting has occurred, record the frequency and type.

4. What if my dog is eating too much?

It is normal for dogs to 'gorge feed' if they have the opportunity and many dogs fill up their day by worrying for food which they do not really need. This habit is often intensified when there are other animals in the household.

The amount of food given to a house dog must always be in the control of the owner. While there are recommendations based on breed and weight on many commercial dog cans and packs, these are only approximations (commercial diets can vary by as much as plus or minus 20% in individual animals) and only the owner can gauge what is right for their dog.

Obesity is caused by giving too much food in relation to energy expended and, as in the human world, once too much weight is put on it is very difficult to take off again. Obesity is just as dangerous for dogs as for people, so take care not to overfeed. If it is difficult to limit the giving of titbits, cut the main meal down to compensate for the amount given between meals.

A dog that is frantically hungry and never satisfied and/or is willing to consume normally inedible things such as paper, plastic, soap, cardboard or stones, may be suffering from a specific disease or condition and veterinary help will be needed to diagnose the cause. See also Chapter 2.

> Note how long the condition has been apparent. What type of faeces are being passed (take a sample)? Note the stage of the oestrous cycle in a bitch. How much water is being drunk (take a urine sample as excessive hunger can be a sign of diabetes)? When was the dog last wormed, and what preparation was used?

5. What if my dog is eating well but remains very thin?

This is a normal situation in adolescent dogs of the larger breeds, especially where more than one dog is kept and there is continual activity. A dog which matures slowly is likely to have a longer life than one which is reared to make maximum growth as early as possible. Heavy worm infestations and a number of disease conditions can give rise to this sign. In either case it is best to seek veterinary attention since it is a waste of time and money to purchase medicines which may not be specifically for the particular problem.

> If the dog's condition is giving real cause for concern and veterinary advice is sought, a faeces sample should be taken and an estimate made of the volume of faeces passed daily. Note their consistency and frequency. It is helpful to provide a record of the food being given and if possible an additional list of what each item contains. This information is usually found on the can or bag.

6.   What if my dog is drinking excessively?

It is always useful for owners to have a note of what is normal for their own dog – any departure from normal which is not brought about by outside circumstances will then give rise to special observation to see if it has significance with regard to illness.

Common reasons for increased thirst in healthy animals

*   Polydipsia (excessive drinking) is normal in hot weather, after excessive exercise, after eating salt food or drinking sea water.
*   The lactating bitch needs to drink a lot of water in addition to any milk given.
*   Bitches with a false pregnancy may also consume more water.

Excessive drinking in other circumstances is a significant sign of illness, which should always receive veterinary attention, particularly in the case of a bitch which has recently been in season (see pyometra).

Make an estimate of how much the dog drinks during the day and whether drinking also goes on at night.

Measure the contents of the water bowl and take into consideration any other water to which the dog has access.

In bitches it is most important to know the date of the last heat. The most consistent sign of **pyometra** is increased thirst.

Be prepared to tell the veterinary surgeon about any change in behaviour and importantly let him know what medicines, if any, the dog is being given or has received lately.

Excessive drinking may be associated with diabetes or kidney disease, so it is useful to take a urine sample with you when consulting the veterinary surgeon.

7.   What if my dog sneezes?

It is normal for some dogs to sneeze two or three times when they wake up. An occasional bout of sneezing in dusty conditions, when being exercised on very dry ground, or when aerosol sprays or powders are being used is also normal.

A paroxysm of sneezing, accompanied by distress, shaking of the head, rubbing of the nose, with discharge or bleeding from the nostrils and noisy breathing may mean that a foreign body (a needle, grass seed, twig or blade of glass) is lodged in the nose.

Do not attempt any first aid but take the dog to the veterinary surgery at once since a proper diagnosis and *complete* removal of any foreign object is essential.

Sneezing, possibly with the addition of bleeding from the nostrils and perhaps with swelling and cuts on the face, may be caused by a blow to the nose, for example when the dog has run at speed into a hard object. Veterinary help will be needed to ascertain the extent of the injury.

Finally, it should also be borne in mind that sneezing may be a prelude to respiratory disease. If that is suspected, observe the animal closely for other signs that will indicate the need to seek veterinary help. Do not over-exercise such dogs.

Consider if the dog has been in an area where garden or agricultural sprays are being used, particularly where there is aerial spraying. Is anyone in the household using a more pungent perfume or aftershave lotion? Is a deodorant powder being used on carpets before vacuum cleaning? Many dogs have proved to be allergic to these powders.

8.　What if my dog has a nasal discharge?

It is normal for a dog to have a cool moist nose, but a warm, dry nose does not necessarily indicate illness..

It is normal for a small drop of clear watery mucus to accumulate at the nostrils, and this discharge may become temporarily more profuse when the dog is excited. Remove any excess discharge with moist cotton wool. If the discharge continues to be profuse for some hours, or if it becomes thick and contains pus, seek veterinary help at once as there may have been an injury to the nose, some foreign object may have become lodged in the nostril or the signs may be an indication that the dog is in the early stage of a major virus disease.

Note whether the discharge is worse at any particular time of the day or in special surroundings and whether the discharge continues at night and/or when the dog is asleep.

9.　What if my dog has a dry and crusty nose?

In some older dogs the black pigmented area of the nose becomes thickened and crusted, with deep fissures in which food particles can collect and cause infection.

If there is no sign of infection, the crusts may be softened with frequent applications of Vaseline or lanolin. If an infection is present, your veterinary surgeon will be able to provide a suitable dressing. Dogs that are suffering from, or which have recovered from **canine distemper** often develop thick crusty noses and pads. This is not usually too harmful in itself, but veterinary advice may be needed since some other signs may need treating or some medicament may be required to prevent the dog starting to show nervous signs.

Collie nose is an hereditary condition which affects mainly Collie and Shetland Sheepdog breeds. In affected animals the bridge of the nose become sore, ulcerated and weeping. Veterinary help should be sought promptly as a mild case can become very much worse, very quickly. Since the condition may be caused by exposure to sunlight, affected dogs need to be kept indoors during sunny weather and exercised only at night. In some cases the veterinary surgeon will advise the application of ointment containing sunscreens.

If the breeder can be contacted, it may be a good idea to ask if any of the dog's relatives suffer from **Collie nose**, as it tends to affect families within a breed. The nuisance to the owner and the discomfort to the dog should be taken into consideration if further breeding from the line is contemplated.

10. What if my dog has a nose which has turned brown or grey?

There is a tendency, said to be inherited, for the black pigmented skin on the nose to fade to brown or greyish pink periodically. The cause is not known and no disease is involved.

'Pink nose' is often associated with the anoestrus period in bitches, with the black pigment returning as they come on heat. 'Pink nose' can also occur in spayed bitches and in male dogs. This fading usually occurs in winter and the black pigment returns in warm weather. The condition does not respond regularly to the administration of extra vitamins and minerals or herbal cures. It is not a cause for concern, except for exhibitors in beauty shows. Seaweed and elderberry tablets from herbal suppliers have apparently improved some cases of 'pink nose'.

> In some cases loss of nasal pigment has been attributed to the use of plastic feeding and water bowls. You may wish to experiment with a change to pottery bowls.

11. What if my dog has runny eyes?

A slight, clear discharge from the eyes is normal in many dogs and in some breeds the shape of the face and eyelids make a slight overspill of tears inevitable. The discharge should be carefully removed with damp cotton wool once a day or as often as necessary.

Where there is a pronounced staining on the face which threatens to become sore or ulcerated, veterinary advice should be sought as it is possible that a correction to the drainage from the eye can be made. An unaccustomed smoky atmosphere, or riding with the head out of the car window, may also irritate the eyes and cause an excessive discharge. The latter habit is dangerous in more ways than one and should never be permitted.

If the discharge from the eyes is profuse, contains pus or is accompanied by persistent signs of pain, veterinary advice should be sought without delay, as any injury to the eyes can potentially inflict damage to the sight.

Persistent discharge from the eyes, associated with **conjunctivitis** and accompanied by other signs of systemic illness, may indicate that the dog is suffering from a major disease which requires prompt veterinary help. Conjunctivitis with a pus-like discharge often crusting the eyelids is caused by inflammation of the inside lining of the eyelids. The condition may be caused by a local infection, but it is also often linked with a major illness. Certain anatomical defects of the face and eyes will also cause chronic conjunctivitis. A dog's eyes are too important to risk delay or incorrect treatment, so veterinary consultation is always necessary and nothing but veterinary prescribed preparations should be used. Do not be tempted to use eye drops which have been prescribed for a previous condition.

Anatomical defects of the eye and face may be the root cause of runny eyes. Some breed standards actually call for a shape of eye or facial conformation which leads to an anatomical defect which will cause the dog pain. Some anatomical defects are inherited but some are acquired. Many cause an irritation of the eyeball which can become chronic and cause persistent runny eyes. Some surgical correction may be possible, but the veterinary surgeon is likely to require that the dog or bitch will not be used for breeding or showing subsequently.

Be prepared to tell the veterinary surgeon when the discharge started, whether it is worse at any time of the day or in any particular place and whether the dog has recently shown any other signs of illness.

12. What if my dog has eyes that look abnormal?

Once more an accurate study of the normal eye helps the owner to appreciate any changes quickly. The conditions listed in Table 17.2 will be noticeable to an observant owner.

Try to pinpoint the first time you noticed any change in the eye and whether at that time there was pain and irritation.

13. What if my dog is blind?

Many elderly dogs become partially or completely blind, but by using scent and hearing they can manage very well on familiar territory provided they are given a certain amount of consideration and unexpected hazards are not left in their path.

Loss of sight should not be a reason for having a well-loved dog destroyed when it is otherwise healthy.

Sudden blindness is a young or middle-aged dog needs immediate veterinary help. In a younger dog, veterinary advice should be obtained promptly as treatment may be possible, but only if the condition is recognised early.

Note when the condition was first apparent. Check whether blindness is total or partial. Observe whether sight is worse in dim light or in daylight. It is useful to teach dogs to catch titbits since their sight can be judged periodically by their ability to perform in this way. Any change should be noted.

Inherited eye defects

A number of eye defects which can lead to total or partial blindness while the dog is still quite young are known to be inherited. A large number of breeds and crosses or mongrels deriving from these breeds may also be affected (see Chapter 9).

In order to stop the spread of these degenerative diseases by breeding from affected stock, the British Veterinary Association, in conjunction with the Kennel Club, have set up schemes to screen males and females used for breeding.

- Do not buy a puppy of the severely affected breeds unless you are given a copy of current eye clearance certificates for both parents.
- Do not breed even one litter from your pet until a clear certificate has been obtained through an official examination.
- Do not breed at all from your dog or bitch if any inherited eye disease is present.

Your veterinary surgeon will be able to advise you on having your dog examined by an expert. See Chapter 9.

The common inherited eye defects are listed in Table 17.3.

14. What if my dog is shaking or scratching its ears?

It is important to be familiar with the appearance of your dog's normal, clean ear so that, when you make your routine weekly inspection, you will be aware of any changes taking place. A small amount of light brown waxy secretion is normal and necessary to the health of the ear but there should be no unpleasant smell.

Many dogs shake their ears quite violently when arousing from sleep, and may also occasionally scratch the ears, but repeated and violent head shaking is a sign that something is wrong.

Signs of ear disease

* Repeated scratching and head shaking.
* Head held with painful side downwards.
* Dark reddish-brown waxy deposit in the ear.
* An unpleasant smell from the ear.
* Inflammation – heat, swelling and pain in the canal and flap.

Treatment

Any disease of the ears must be properly diagnosed and treated without delay, as a simple condition may aggravate rapidly into a more complex situation which may become difficult and expensive to treat, and which may create a smell which pervades the whole house. In addition, the acute pain caused by ear disease may make the dog irritable and inclined to snap when the ears are touched.

No attempt should be made to treat ear disease with proprietary remedies which may be inappropriate or useless for the particular condition affecting your dog. Always seek veterinary advice early as delay could mean that an operation will be required to cure the condition if it has become chronic. Early treatment can save you time and money and prevent your dog suffering.

Tell your veterinary surgeon if you have other animals in the home, especially cats. Your cat may need treatment too. Even though it is not showing signs of ear disease, your cat could be the source of infection for your dog.

Avoiding ear disease

* Keep the hair in the underside of ear flaps combed free of burrs and tangles.
* Dry the dog's ears after bathing.
* Remove excess hair from inside the ears by plucking or clipping, but be gentle. Ask your veterinary surgeon to show you how to do this. Failure to keep the vertical ear canal clear, clean and properly ventilated is often the root cause of otitis externa.

- Do not attempt to clean deeply inside the ear. Wipe the surface only with cotton wool damped with a weak disinfectant solution. Use only your fingers, never any kind of instrument or probe.

Possible causes of ear disease—otitis externa (canker)

- **Ear mites**. Tiny mites living within the ear can cause acute irritation which makes the dog scratch and so damage the tissue of the ear. Treatment requires the use of a product that contains an ingredient that will kill the mites. Cats in the same household may be the source of the infestation.
- **A fungus or yeast infection in the ear.** This leads to intense itching, a reddish-brown discharge and an offensive smell. Specific medication from the veterinary surgeon is needed.
- **Foreign bodies.** It is common when dogs are running through long grass for the awns, or seeds, to lodge in the ear. Typically dogs that have a foreign body in the ear suddenly scratch violently, shake and often hold their head on one side. Do not attempt to remove the foreign body. Take the dog at once to the veterinary surgery, where treatment can be carried out, if necessary, under local anaesthetic or a strong sedative.
- **Allergy or an extension of skin disease.** Diagnosis and treatment by a veterinary surgeon is obviously required when these causes are involved.
- **Bacteria.** Most bacterial infection is secondary to some other initiating cause. The correct selection of an antibiotic is necessary to obtain a rapid and complete cure.
- **Ear conformation.** There is no doubt that the structure of the external ear can be an important predisposing factor for the development of otitis externa. Long, loosely-hanging, heavily feathered ear flaps prevent adequate ventilation, and excessively hairy ear canals, such as those occurring in Poodles and some Terriers, favour the retention of wax and debris – leading to inflammation.

15. What if my dog is holding its head on one side?

This sign usually indicates ear problems; see 'What if...' No. 14, but may also be caused by teething around the age of 4-6 months in a puppy, but toothache in an older dog (see 'What if...' No. 36) or by **tonsillitis** (see 'What if...' No. 35). Other causes may be **otitis interna** (inflammation of the middle ear – see Index of Diseases and Conditions) or:

Aural haematoma (a blood-filled swelling on the ear flap)
Signs:
A hot and painful swelling of the ear flap increasing slowly in size over a period of 2-3 days, probably accompanied by head shaking.

Cause:
A fight injury, or self-inflicted injury caused by aggressive scratching, or violent head shaking or banging often associated with **otitis externa**.

Action:
Consult the veterinary surgeon at once, as there is usually some underlying cause to make the dog injure its own ear and it is usually necessary for the swelling to be drained surgically.

> Has there been any recent injury or happening which has involved the ear flap? Possibilities are a fight with a cat, or being caught in a thorn bush. Have the regular checks of the dog's ears indicated any signs of **otitis externa**?

Damage to the area of the brain controlling balance
Signs:
Unsteady gait, circling towards the affected side, involuntary movement of the eyes from side to side.

Possible causes:
After-effects of epileptic fit; in this case the dog will return to normal within a few hours. **Otitis externa** leading to **otitis media**. Possibly poisoning, also brain damage due to trauma or neoplasia (growths and tumours).

Action:
Get a veterinary surgeon as soon as possible to diagnose the cause.

> It is important to recall any unusual behaviour or accident within the recent past.

16. What if my dog is breathing abnormally?

Dogs breathe through the nose when at rest, but through the mouth when running. Panting enables the dog to lose heat from the tongue and the lungs.

Deep compulsive panting when at rest is a sign of nervous apprehension, eg in a veterinary waiting room, or pain in the abdominal area.

Pregnant bitches may pant for up to 12 hours in the first stage of labour. Abnormal breathing is also associated with five important emergency situations:

* **Gastric dilation and torsion** – see 'What if...' No. 33.
* **Heat stroke** – see Chapter 13 (First aid).
* **Airway obstruction** – see Chapter 13 (First aid).
* **Eclampsia** (lactation tetany)
  This condition occurs in bitches, occasionally in late pregnancy, but most frequently during lactation when the puppies are making heavy demands on the bitch.

  Signs:
  Anxiety, hiding from light, leaving puppies, uncharacteristic behaviour, stiffness, muscular pain, panting, collapse and possibly convulsions or fits.

  Cause:
  Abnormally low calcium/glucose levels in the blood. This can occur even if a balanced diet including calcium is being given. Avoid supplementation of the diet in the late stages of pregnancy since that can make the occurrence of eclampsia more likely.

  Action:
  Contact veterinary surgeon immediately, day or night, as collapse, leading to death, can occur if the bitch is not treated immediately. The response to treatment is usually dramatic.

- **Chest injury**
  Signs:
  Sudden onset, distress, cuts and bruises, shock, weakness, pain.

  Cause:
  A fall, road traffic accident, or fight with a larger dog.

  Action:
  Gentle transport to veterinary surgery.

For other types of **abnormal breathing** see Table 17.4.

In all cases of abnormal breathing it is helpful to know if the onset of the sign has been a gradual (over 4-6 weeks) or a sudden occurrence. Was the abnormal breathing pattern seen first only after exercise? Does it happen even when the dog is resting? Has the dog been involved in any accident or trauma?

Note: with all breathing problems it is better to seek veterinary advice early, than regret it later.

---

17. What if my dog is shedding hair?

All dogs, with the exception of Poodles and Bedlington Terriers and Bichons, shed dead hair from the coat. Sometimes the shedding is seasonal, but some heavy coated dogs which originated in cold climates, for instance Labradors, shed all the year round if they are kept in a warm house. When a dog has started to moult, it is best to give it a thorough grooming out of doors to remove all the dead coat and allow the new hair to grow. German Shepherd dogs and other dogs with a dense undercoat shed large amounts of hair in the spring. Be prepared for this normal occurrence.

Other periods of hair loss are:

Post whelping and lactation in some bitches
Cause:
The cause of hair loss in these cases is simply the heavy demand made by the puppies on the bitch.
Action:
Worming, to remove any internal parasites that may be present, and early weaning will help reduce hair loss and speed recovery to normal. Consult a veterinary surgeon about diet and vitamin supplementation.

Post-infection/chronic infections. Diseases that affect the digestive system so that nutrients cannot be absorbed properly can cause hair loss. Frequently the coat does not grow normally for weeks or months after such an illness. Hair loss is often associated with chronic debilitating diseases. Consult a veterinary surgeon about the need for a more easily digested diet and vitamin and mineral supplementation.

Old age. A generalised hair loss is to be expected in extreme old age, as well as greying or whitening of coat colour, beginning on the muzzle and gradually extending right through the coat.

Poor diet. Dogs which have acute digestive problems, allergies or which have been kept on a poor or unsuitable diet may show a sparse, harsh, dry coat. This will improve when the cause is remedied.

Hormonal imbalance. Hair loss is quite often associated with hormonal imbalance or deficiency, eg in some spayed bitches and dogs with a thyroid deficiency. A veterinary examination, possible including the examination of a blood sample, is necessary to pin point the cause so that effective treatment can be given. See also 'What if' No. 18.

> A photograph of the dog when in full coat may be of help to the veterinary surgeon when estimating the amount of hair loss.

18.   What if my dog is going bald?

Symmetrical bilateral baldness is sometimes seen in older spayed bitches, particularly Boxers and Dachshunds. Typically, identical shaped bald patches appear on each flank. The cause of the condition is probably a hormone imbalance. Your veterinary surgeon will be able to help.

A more generalised progressive baldness may be associated with hormone deficiencies in entire animals, eg a lack of thyroid hormone. A veterinary consultation is certainly worthwhile as sometimes a few tablets daily will work miracles.

A few patches of baldness and dry skin situated on one area of the coat, typically on the spinal area, may be the result of an old scald or burn which was undetected at the time. It could also have been caused by some local skin infection or parasite infestation. Such areas should be observed closely and, unless they are showing signs of healing and new hair growth, veterinary advice should be sought so that the most appropriate medication can be given.

Large dogs often develop bare patches on their hocks and elbows through lying on hard surfaces. Your veterinary surgeon will give you some cream to help keep the skin supple but the dog should also, of course, be provided with soft areas on which to lie.

Note: Chronic demodectic mange may cause baldness in patches, particularly on the hocks and elbows. It is important not to let these lesions become chronic or erupt generally. Seek early veterinary help. Certain breeds of dog with short hair, eg Dobermanns, seem to be particularly prone to this condition.

19.   What if my dog is scratching?

Dogs, like humans, scratch because they itch. The nerve endings which transmit the itch sensation lie close to the surface of the skin. When the dog scratches the nerve receptors are damaged and no longer react. The mild pain which results is better tolerated than an irritation. A dog's strong nails and vigorous scratching action can cause considerable damage and open the way for bacteria to invade the broken skin, complicating the condition seriously.

Persistent scratching should not be allowed to continue. The main cause is parasites in the coat biting, sucking and causing damage to the skin. The most common parasites are fleas, lice, cheyletiella (the rabbit fur mite) and sarcoptic mange mites. Sometimes the cause is easily detected and can be treated simply but, if scratching persists, seek veterinary help. It is often cheaper in the long run to buy an effective anti-parasite treatment from the veterinary surgery. It is important to treat all other animals within the household with an appropriate remedy and also to take action to eradicate parasites from the dog's bed and the rest of the house.

Other causes of scratching include inflammatory conditions of the skin, caused principally by allergies or bacterial infections.

It will be helpful if you are able to decide if the scratching is becoming a compulsive behaviour. Will the dog stop scratching if you order it to? Does it scratch at only one area of its body or more generally? Is the scratching more intense at any particular time of day, in any particular surroundings, or when the dog is hot or cold? Is the scratching getting progressively more frequent and intense?

20. What if my dog keeps breaking wind?

Breaking wind, stomach rumbles (borborygmus) and flatulence are not usually associated with any specific major disease, and seldom seem to trouble the dog, although often cause considerable social embarrassment to the owner. Some possible simple causes are listed in Table 17.5.

Breaking wind and flatulence may also be associated with **pancreatic deficiency** and other general digestive upsets.

Experiment by giving the dog's largest meal earlier in the day. Change from dry to soaked biscuit or vice versa, or to boiled rice or bread as the carbohydrate element of the food, to try to reduce fermentation in the intestine. Make only one change at a time and continue with that regimen for 2 weeks. Observe the dog closely – does the flatulence seem to be causing any pain? If it still proves necessary to visit the veterinary surgeon, report the dietary changes you have made and the results.

A number of special diets are available through veterinary surgeons. It is always wise to consult your veterinary surgeon about your dog's diet when you visit for other reasons, as a dog's needs vary through its lifetime. An appropriate dietary adjustment could give your dog a new lease of life and increase its lifespan.

21. What if my dog has noisy abdominal sounds?

It is not uncommon for adult dogs to have an episode of making audible internal rumblings, possibly accompanied by refusal to eat, gulping and sometimes vomiting of small amounts of bile and saliva. The most likely causes are digestive problems of unknown origin, possibly due to stress, overeating, eating too rapidly or eating rubbish.

Treatment with children's antacid remedies will usually restore the dog to normal within a few hours. When calculating the dose to give, allow for the dog's size in comparison to a child. If episodes occur more often than once in 14 days, or if digestive remedies fail to improve the situation, or if the dog shows signs of pain, seek veterinary advice.

22. What if my dog is biting its tail, scooting or rubbing its bottom on the ground?

This behaviour is common in dogs and it is almost always due to anal gland problems. The popular notion that worm infestation causes irritation around the anus is generally unfounded. If this sign is caused by worms, you will see small worm segments, like grains of rice, around your dog's anus.

The anal glands situated on either side of the anus should empty every time faeces are passed, depositing their contents on the faeces as a scent marker. This was useful to the wild or wandering dog, but is largely obsolete for the household pet. A diet containing more bulk may serve to make the anal glands empty more regularly.

Anal glands which become overfull and are not relieved may abscess and burst, causing a malodorous wound. This condition can be prevented by having the glands emptied periodically at the veterinary surgery. In skilled hands this service is quickly performed and needs no anaesthetic.

For other conditions which may cause a dog to bite at its hind end, see Table 17.6.

> Try to observe how often scooting occurs. Is it a major behaviour pattern throughout the dog's day, or does it only occur after defecation? Is scooting compulsive or will the dog stop when commanded to do so?

23. What if my dog has diarrhoea?

Diarrhoea is defined as the more frequent passage of liquid faeces. It is always worthwhile taking note of the frequency with which your dog passes faeces and their consistency, type and amount, so as to be aware of any changes from normal. If a change is seen, close observation should be kept on the dog for other signs of disease, as diarrhoea is a common indication of many illnesses, some relatively trivial, but some of a serious nature.

Amount of faeces passed by normal dogs

Normal faeces contain the elements of food not used by the body, together with digestive juices, bacteria and the discarded cells of the gut lining.

A dog which is not eating at all will still produce a small amount of faeces from body waste.

Average amounts of faeces produced daily by dogs fed on canned foods are:

Miniature Dachshund	70 g
Beagle	190 g
Newfoundland	500 g

These amounts will be different if complete dry diets are fed. Modern dry diets such as Pedigree Chum Formula are especially formulated to reduce the amount of faeces produced.

It is normal for an adult dog to pass faeces once or twice daily but 4 times daily can be regarded as normal. Puppies defecate 2-6 times daily.

Colour of normal faeces

The colour of faeces is affected by the type of food being consumed. The faeces will be pale when white meat is fed, dark if raw meat is given and often dark red when the dog has eaten commercially prepared food.

Digested blood from the throat, stomach or small intestine produces a black stool. There may be streaks of fresh red blood on the faeces, in conditions where the lower bowel is damaged. Where as much as a teaspoonful of fresh red blood is passed with faeces, the veterinary surgeon should be consulted by telephone immediately as this sign is associated with the major canine diseases of **haemorrhagic gastroenteritis** and **canine parvovirus infection**; it may also occur in some cases of poisoning.

Diarrhoea is most frequently caused by digestive problems. The bowel looseness is likely to cease when the food which started the problem is withdrawn or if dietary changes are made gradually.

First aid treatment:

* Withhold food for 12 hours to rest the intestines.
* Water must always be freely supplied; diarrhoea cannot be 'dried up' by withholding water.
* Begin feeding again using cooked eggs, or fish, with plain boiled rice – fed in small quantities.

If diarrhoea persists, or if there are other signs of illness, contact a veterinary surgeon without delay, since it may be caused by bacterial or viral infection, or an enzyme deficiency. It may also be associated with an endoparasite infestation. Diarrhoea merits even earlier veterinary consultation in young puppies, as they quickly become dehydrated.

When giving the history of the case it is important to distinguish between the types of loose stool. Is the dog passing:
* a greater number of stools than normal, but of a normal colour and consistency?
* a normal number of stools, but very loose or accompanied by quantities of fluid?
* stools containing jelly-like mucus?
* foul-smelling, pale, bulky, fat-laden stools?
* very loose or watery stools, uncontrollably?
* blood-stained stools: how much and what colour?

Note: It can be helpful to take to the veterinary surgeon a small quantity of freshly passed faeces for examination. Pack the sample in a small carefully washed yoghurt pot or similar container and label with your name and the date. Be prepared to tell the veterinary surgeon whether the dog strains to pass the stools or whether they are produced relatively easily.

Other causes of diarrhoea

* Over-feeding in young puppies.
* Feeding liver and offal in large quantities.
* Too much milk – more than the equivalent of one pint (568 ml) to a Labrador. Some dogs may react to even very small quantities of milk.
* Lack of fibre in the diet may cause diarrhoea and constipation alternately.
* Raw eggs.
* Sugar and honey.
* Onions.
* Currants, sultanas and raisins.
* Nuts.
* Carrots and broad beans.
* Decaying or putrid food.
* Scavenging.
* Sudden dietary change.

Note:
Bitches that eat large numbers of afterbirths when whelping may have diarrhoea temporarily.

It is worth noting that diarrhoea may be associated with stress, particularly in dogs with a nervous temperament. The bowel of the dog reacts quickly to shock, fear and stress, and diarrhoea and failure to gain weight in an otherwise healthy dog may be due to nervous causes.

The tension of dog shows and obedience competitions, bullying by humans or other dogs, re-homing and even too great a desire to please the owner by instant obedience to demands, have been known to cause chronic diarrhoea in dogs. A peaceful, less demanding life without stressful episodes may be all that is required to effect a cure.

24. What if my dog is passing blood in its faeces?

Occasional, very slight streaks of fresh blood on the outside of the stool are likely to come from a small broken blood vessel around the anus and are unimportant provided the dog is otherwise well. If even this small amount of blood is seen persistently, veterinary advice should be sought. Any quantity of blood greater than a small fleck is a reason to seek veterinary advice urgently, even if the dog is otherwise well. This sign may be associated with a major canine disease, eg **haemorrhagic gastroenteritis** or **canine parvovirus infection**.

Polyps in the rectum are protruding growths which may accompany constipation or straining. They are common and may be the cause of blood-stained faeces. Although they are unlikely to be malignant, a veterinary surgeon should be consulted about their removal.

Be prepared to estimate the quantity of blood passed, its frequency and colour, fresh red or dark digested blood. Note also the colour and consistency of faeces. It can be helpful if a typical sample of blood-stained faeces is taken to the veterinary surgery.

25. What if my dog is constipated?

Constipation (difficulty and pain caused by trying to pass small, hard lumps of faeces) is not uncommon, especially in toy breeds. Constipation can result from the simple causes listed in Table 17.7 and may be cured by the administration of a small dose of liquid paraffin and some other simple actions, making a visit to the veterinary surgery unnecessary. However, if constipation continues and/or the dog is obviously in pain then veterinary attention should be sought.

Some other relatively common causes of constipation include:

Enlarged prostate gland in older male dogs. Dogs suffering from this condition will strain to pass faeces which are narrow and ribbon-like because the enlarged prostate bulges into the rectum blocking the passage of faeces. If these signs are seen in older dogs then veterinary help should be sought since if left the persistent straining may lead to a perineal hernia. Medication can help.

Stricture (narrowing of the rectum) is possibly congenital, but more often is caused by straining to pass sharp objects like splinters of bone. Typically, in these cases stools may be passed but only after considerable straining, and they may contain small amounts of fresh red blood. Seek veterinary advice without delay.

First aid tip
Where constipation is caused by the simple causes listed, such as inappropriate feeding, confinement in house, inactivity or travelling, medicinal liquid paraffin may be given at the dose of one dessertspoonful for a 30 lb dog (10 ml/13.5 kg). Giving too great a quantity is not harmful but the excess will probably leak from the anus and may soil the dog's fur and its bed.

Note:
When it seems that a dog or puppy is failing to pass any faeces, consider whether it may in fact not be constipated but consuming its own stools, or whether a companion dog may be doing this. See 'What if...' No. 26.

26. What if my dog is eating its own faeces? (coprophagy)

Eating the faeces of other animals, especially horse and cattle manure, is a natural animal behaviour which is, however, quite unacceptable in the companion dog. Not uncommonly the desire to eat animal manure extends to the dog eating its own faeces. It is a natural and normal behaviour in bitches to consume the faeces of their puppies until at least weaning time. Puppies will sometimes imitate the bitch in this behaviour, so it is essential to keep a sharp watch on them to ensure that this behaviour never starts, as it can be difficult to cure. In this condition especially, prevention is better than cure.

As a first step the dog's diet should be checked to see that it is receiving sufficient amounts of the essential nutrients, especially vitamins. If necessary, relevant adjustments should be made but care should be taken not to overdose with vitamins and minerals, otherwise problems could arise.

Faeces deposited in the garden should be picked up and disposed of promptly. this is far more effective than sprinkling the faeces with pepper, disinfectant powder etc. The dog should be called away from faeces passed while on walks and should be prevented from eating other animal manure as far as possible.

Coprophagy is often associated with boredom, when dogs are shut into a small run for a long time, and may also occur when thedog is left alone in the house. It has been noticed that some types of food seem to encourage the behaviour, while feeding a complete dry diet may make the faeces less attractive.

If the habit has become established, the behaviour control methods described in Chapter 4 should be used to cure this most undesirable trait.

Note:
If other signs of illness, such as diarrhoea or compulsive eating, occur it is wise to seek veterinary help initially before taking the actions mentioned above.

> Be prepared to describe to the veterinary surgeon exactly how the dog is fed and how it spends its day. Take a fresh faeces sample to the surgery with you.

27. What if my dog is not passing urine, or is straining to pass small amounts frequently?

It is important to distinguish between straining to pass urine and constipation; the straddle-legged stance adopted by bitches for both acts can appear similar. Not passing urine may be a voluntary decision on the dog's part. Bitches in particular are capable of withholding urine for as much as 24 hours when off their home territory but, if they are given as much opportunity as possible to use a ground surface similar to the one they use at home, they will usually oblige in the end.

It is useful, as an extension of house-training, to train dogs and bitches to urinate at the sound of an undulating whistle, or in response to some special word. Long confinement in a car or a crate can inhibit both sexes from passing urine when they do get the chance, but patience on the part of the owner will eventually get results.

In all other circumstances, failure to pass urine, or difficulty in doing so, is always a serious emergency and must certainly not be neglected if it continues for more than 24 hours. Be prepared to consult your veterinary surgeon earlier if other signs are present. The pain of a full bladder which cannot be emptied is agonising.

> Normal urine is yellow and clear, but certain drugs can alter the colour. Check with your veterinary surgeon if you notice any change in colour or smell of the dog's urine when on medication. If any urine is passed at all it is helpful to take a sample to the surgery at the time of consultation.

28. What if my dog is incontinent?

A distinction must be made between the puppy or adult which is not successfully house-trained and true incontinence, which is the dripping or dribbling of urine without the dog being aware of it. It is rare that a dog cannot be house trained, but in some individuals it has proved impossible. For example, older dogs which have lived in kennels all their lives can be very difficult to adjust to life in a house and this applies particularly to Beagles and Fox Hounds which are surplus to pack requirements and are offered as pets.

Territory marking in the male dog and bitches on heat should not be confused with incontinence. During illness and in extreme old age overnight incontinence should not be unexpected. Such dogs can be kept clean and comfortable by making up a bed on a sheet of plastic, topped with thickly spread newspaper over which is laid a polyester fur rug which allows urine to pass through rather than making the rug wet.

Arthritic dogs may also have difficulty in rising from bed to urinate, especially first thing in the morning.

One of the most troublesome demonstrations of incontinence is the very submissive bitch which dribbles urine when excited or when greeting people. See Chapter 3.

Incontinence is not an uncommon sequel to ovariohysterectomy (spaying), particularly in large bitches, and when the operation is performed in middle age. The condition can often be treated satisfactorily by giving hormone medication; your veterinary surgeon will advise. In some such cases the condition may need to be corrected surgically.

Incontinence in young puppies may be associated with a congenital defect in the urinary system which can often be corrected surgically. If your puppy drips urine constantly day and night, seek veterinary help promptly.

Incontinence is also associated with paralysis and with **cystitis**.

Any disease which causes excessive drinking will also lead to the more frequent passage of urine, see 'What if...' No. 6.

Incontinence is not in itself a serious sign since there are many simple causes. However, if other signs are present, or if the dog shows signs of discomfort or pain on passing urine, or if the urine contains blood, it is wise to seek veterinary help without delay.

> It is helpful to know if incontinence occurs every night, and/or during the day. Does urine dribble away all the time, or is the entire content of the bladder voided at long intervals? Can you relate any external circumstance to episodes of incontinence?
>
> Ask in advance at the surgery for a sterile container, so that you can take a fresh urine sample with you to the consultation, otherwise sterilise a small, well-washed bottle by boiling in water for 5 minutes, and allow to drain.

29. What if my dog is passing blood in its urine?

It is normal for a bitch on heat or a newly whelped bitch to have a bloodstained discharge from the vulva which will blend with the urine. In any other circumstances blood in the urine is a serious sign, so a veterinary surgeon should be consulted as soon as possible. It is helpful and saves time to take a urine sample with you, as it is often very difficult to persuade a dog or bitch to pass urine on the surgery premises.

> - Whether blood is present in the urine every time the bitch urinates.
> - Try to observe if blood is present in the first or last amounts of urine to be passed, or whether it is generally mixed with the urine.
> - Check whether the dog is having difficulty passing urine and whether urination is accompanied by pain before, during or after water is passed.

Blood in the urine is often associated with the following major diseases: **cystitis, leptospirosis, warfarin poisoning** (see index). Other possible causes include:

- **Growths and tumours** in the urinary or genital tract (these are rare)
- **Injury** to the urinary or genital tract following trauma, most frequently a road traffic accident,
- **Stones** (calculi) in the bladder.

30. What if my dog has a discharge from its penis or vulva (or licks excessively at its genitals)?

It is normal for male dogs to have a small amount of whitish, mucoid discharge from the prepuce, and bitch puppies also often have a drop of mucus at the vulva.

It is normal dog behaviour for both sexes to pay attention to cleaning the genital area. Bitches coming into season will pay extra attention to the vulva, and they will also do this after whelping. Male dogs may lick their genitals more frequently after mating.

An excessive amount of discharge, a foul-smelling emission, the presence of lesions on the genitals, or an obsession with licking them is abnormal and such dogs should be taken to a veterinary surgeon so that the cause can be diagnosed. A cause of this behaviour, which can be dealt with at home, is failure of the penis to retract into its sheath after mating.

Action
Bathe the penis with cold water, lubricate it with Vaseline, handcream or the like and pull the sheath gently forward over the top of the penis as it decreases in size. If the condition persists, seek veterinary help. Avoid over-enthusiastic use of disinfectants after mating.

Note:
A copious discharge from the vulva also occurs in cases of open pyometra. If a bitch has a severe foul-smelling discharge a few weeks after she has been in season, seek veterinary help immediately.

Dogs – It is important to relate the appearance of the sign to the last time the dog was used at stud. Before stating that the dog has never mated a bitch, consider if there is any possibility that the dog has escaped and had an opportunity for mating. It may be necessary to question other people who may have had charge of the dog within the past few months.

Bitches – The veterinary surgeon will want to know the date of the bitch's last season, if the season was normal, and if dogs are still paying the bitch attention.

---

31. What if my dog is mismated?

See Chapter 1 – The bitch.

32. What if my dog is found to be pregnant unexpectedly?

See Chapter 1 – The bitch.

33. What if my dog is pot-bellied?

It is normal for young puppies to show considerable abdominal distension after eating, but if the expansion is gross, consideration should be given to spreading the food intake over more, but smaller, meals. Adult dogs may also benefit from being fed two or more smaller meals a day, especially when high bulk, complete dry diets are used.

A pot-bellied puppy which is thin on the shoulders and hindquarters, with poor coat, is possibly suffering from an overburden of worms, see section on endoparasites, Chapter 7.

The most common cause of abdominal enlargement is:

Gastric dilation and torsion (bloat)

This is a sudden enlargement of the stomach which is usually full of fermenting food and gas. The condition is complicated when the stomach twists, blocking both the entrance from the throat and the exit to the small intestine. Dogs of 40 lb (18 kg) weight and upwards are most usually affected.

Signs

A sudden and noticeable enlargement of the abdomen, usually soon after eating. The stomach rapidly becomes grossly swollen and hard with a distension which is easily observed as it takes place very quickly. The dog is in great pain and distress, and has difficulty in breathing. There may be an attempt to vomit and pass faeces, but when torsion (twisting) has taken place nothing can pass.

Cause

No definitive cause has been found. Suspicion has fallen on violent exercise after feeding, copious drinking on top of dry meals, blockage of the stomach exit by indigestible material, excess fermentation in the stomach and overloading the stomach with one large meal.

Action

This is one of the true veterinary emergencies. Releasing the gas and emptying the stomach by mechanical means is imperative as this condition can be fatal within a very short time. Make contact with a veterinary surgeon at once, day or night, and be prepared to drive the dog to the surgery immediately.

Prevention

Your vet will advise you about the preventive measures which may help to avoid a recurrence of the condition.

Other causes of pot-bellied appearance which are not due to overfeeding are heart disease, pregnancy and false pregnancy, pyometra (pus in the uterus), some hormone disorders and other major abdominal diseases which are accompanied by fluid retention (see Chapter 1, The bitch). If in doubt, seek veterinary attention.

> **Worms** – Take a fresh faeces sample with you to the surgery if you suspect the condition is due to worms in a puppy or young dog.
>
> **Bloat** – When a dog is frequently subject to painful gross enlargement after meals, it is helpful to keep a record of the normal post-feeding enlargement, by measuring round the widest part of the abdomen with a tape-measure. It is then easier to assess whether the dog is enlarging more than normal and is in danger of bloating, so that rapid action to get veterinary help may be taken when needed.

34. What if my dog is limping?

Dogs limp because of pain or a 'mechanical' problem in the leg. It is not always easy to find out which leg is causing pain but it helps to watch the dog moving across in front of you, as well as coming towards and going away from you.

A dog may often take the weight off the injured leg when standing still and, when moving, may nod or drop the head as the weight goes on to the sound foreleg. Similarly the hindquarters will be dropped when the sound hindleg is placed on the ground. If a dog is holding its leg off the ground the problem is most likely to be in the foot. It if places its foot gently to the ground or drags the leg, the injury is likely to be higher up.

Very often an acute limp is easily diagnosed and can be cured by first aid. Look at the food to detect impaled thorns, stone chippings, balls of tar, or snow wedged between the pads, which are common causes of limping in dogs.

Examine the rest of the leg for signs of injury, such as swelling, deformity, pain, loss of function or a break in the skin. In most cases it is sensible to seek veterinary advice promptly but if the dog is otherwise well, is eating, and the pain is not severe, then such action can be delayed for 24 hours. It will be helpful to your veterinary surgeon if you have already managed to identify the painful area or locate some injury.

Other causes of limping may be:

Arthritis

Cause
Inflammation of a joint which may be caused by infection, a previous injury, or hereditary joint deformity.

Signs
Chronic pain, difficulty in rising from bed, reluctance to walk, but may ease after some movements are made.

Action
Many new products are available to veterinary surgeons which can ease the pain, but continual medication may be needed. In some cases, surgery may be required.

Bone fractures

Cause
Usually the result of road traffic accidents or falls.

Signs
Severe pain of sudden onset; inability to put weight on the leg which may be visibly deformed.

Action
Contact a veterinary surgeon quickly for diagnosis and fixation of the fracture. Repair is usually good. See Chapter 13 for advice on care and transport to the surgery.

Dislocations

Cause
The displacement through accidental injury of one or more bones which form a joint.

Signs
Sudden onset of pain; limb cannot be used and may be noticeably different in length from the sound leg.

Action
Veterinary consultation at once as there may be internal bleeding or an associated fracture. Generally, correction of a dislocation is more likely to be successful if it is carried out without delay.

Sprains

Cause
Damage to a ligament or tendon by being overstretched or torn through wrenching or twisting.

Signs
Sudden pain occurring while running or playing, followed by inability to use the leg; swelling and tenderness when the area is touched. There may be swelling around the injury. The most common joints to be affected are the shoulder, the stifle, the carpus or the tarsus.

Action
Put a cold compress on the leg to reduce the swelling and pain. Prompt veterinary consultation is necessary to assess the extent of the damage and commence treatment.

Strains

Cause
Damage to the muscles. Muscles are most often torn or damaged by a sudden wrench or twisting movement, particularly in racing dogs.

Signs
Usually a sudden pain while running followed by swelling and loss of power..

Action
Complete rest of the limb and prompt veterinary advice for differential diagnosis and further treatment.

Interdigital cysts (painful inflammed swellings between the toes)

Cause
Some dogs are subject to a succession of these cysts. The cause is thought to lie in the sweat glands in the foot. The cysts may become infected by bacteria and may contain grass seeds.

Signs
Lameness; red swollen area between the toes on the upper side of the paw.

Action
Veterinary consultation for immediate treatment and future prevention, which may involve long-term treatment with antibiotics.

35. What if my dog is coughing?

It is normal for a dog to cough occasionally, particularly after a bout of barking, or after vigorous play. Any dog which suddenly begins to cough persistently should be segregated from other dogs, kept very quiet and taken to the veterinary surgeon promptly. Even if the cough is occasional and not severe, if it persists for more than a week the cause should be investigated.

Do not take a coughing dog into the waiting room at the veterinary surgery, as many coughs are infectious. Telephone for a special appointment or leave the dog in your car and ask the receptionist what to do next.

Coughing is associated with the following major diseases and conditions (see Index of Diseases and Conditions):

- **Canine distemper**
- **Kennel cough**
- **Heart disease**
- **Respiratory disease**
- **Endoparasite infection** (worms) (*Oslerus (Filaroides) osleri* – see Chapter 8)
- **Poisoning** (warfarin and paraquat)

For other possible causes, see Table 17.8

36. What if my dog is eating with difficulty?

Decaying teeth and gum disease are common causes of difficulty in eating. The study and practice of veterinary dentistry is enlarging all the time and much can be done to avoid discomfort and preserve the teeth without the need for extraction. Missing teeth prevent dogs getting show prizes. Seek veterinary advice promptly if in doubt, but much can be done to prevent the need for dental treatment – see 'What if' No. 37.

Other causes of difficulty in eating include:

Neoplasia (growths and tumours in the mouth)

Signs
Visible swellings around flews and gum line, offensive breath.

Action
Veterinary consultation as soon as possible with a view to removal of the growth. Treatment can be very successful.

Foreign body lodged in mouth

Signs
Sudden onset of foul breath, gagging, retching, drooling or foaming at the mouth; pawing and rubbing the mouth.

Cause
Typically, a piece of bone or stick lodged across the roof of the mouth, between the upper carnassial teeth; cotton or wire wound around the teeth.

Action
It is best not to persist in trying to remove the obstruction, if it does not come away easily, but to take the dog to the veterinary surgery. A sedative may be needed while the obstruction is removed.

Broken teeth
From time to time dogs' teeth break, often because they are asked to catch hard balls or even stones. The nerves inside the tooth are exposed once a tooth is broken. This appears as a pink or red spot but eventually the nerve dies and looks black. There is no way the nerve can heal.

Initially a broken tooth is likely to be painful to the touch but once the nerve is dead the pain subsides. An abscess often develops inside the jawbone leading to more pain.

All veterinary surgeons agree that the most important step to take in dogs with broken teeth is to eliminate the pain and infection. A root filling can do this. It is a delicate procedure that may be far more desirable and less traumatic than an extraction especially when key teeth, like the canines, are involved. Skill and expertise are essential and your dog may need to be referred to a specialist.

Crooked teeth
Most of the irregularities of a dog's bite are inherited and correcting the problem will not prevent them being passed to future generations. If the condition is causing pain or preventing the dog from eating properly, corrective treatment is acceptable, but ideally the animal should be neutered at the time and not allowed to breed. As with people, braces can sometimes be devised to move the teeth into a better position.

Sometimes milk teeth are not lost at the correct time and this may guide the permanent teeth into a poor position. The extraction of milk teeth to prevent problems and pain is sensible. Your veterinary surgeon will be glad to advise and remove the teeth if necessary. Many dental surgeons and most veterinary surgeons agree that orthodontic treatment for appearance and show purposes is unethical and unacceptable.

37. What if my dog has bad breath?

Mild cases of **halitosis** (bad breath) are often associated with what the dog eats. For example, a large quantity of fish meal incorporated in a complete dry diet will give a characteristic fishy smell. Scavenging and the eating of horse or rabbit droppings (see also coprophagy, 'What if' No. 26) will also render the breath unpleasant.

The mouth harbours many naturally occurring bacteria that can stick on the teeth to form plaque. This can calcify to form calculus (tartar – hard deposits on the teeth). It is the activity of the bacterial deposits that leads to mouth odour.

Most pet dogs in this country are fed a well-balanced diet but it is often given in a form and consistency that requires very little chewing. As the bacteria are not disturbed, they continue to live and breed. The poisons they release can cause serious gum disease (gingivitis) associated with bleeding and loose teeth.

Dogs and wolves in the wild and in zoos don't usually suffer from gum disease. Their mouths smell and look clean because they have to tear up their food and chew at large pieces of tough meat. This has a cleansing action, removing the bacterial deposits from around the teeth. To limit mouth odour in your pet dog, add large pieces of tough meat to its diet occasionally. The pieces should be so big they cannot be swallowed whole but have to be 'worked on' first.

Many owners think giving bones will help keep their pet's teeth clean. This is a fallacy and can be harmful as chewing bones can lead to broken teeth. Rawhide chews and some of the treats designed especially for the purpose can help prevent gingivitis.

Brushing your dog's teeth 2-3 times a week can help keep its mouth and gums clean and healthy. Toothpaste and toothbrushes specially designed for dogs are available. Don't use human toothpaste as it is too frothy and strongly flavoured for animals and as they are unable to spit it out, swallowing it can upset their digestion. Never use salt or baking soda either as this can be fatal, especially for an older animal with a heart condition.

Where the odour is persistent and very noticeable, it is wise to have the dog examined by a veterinary surgeon.

Other possible causes of bad breath include:

Periodontal disease

Cause
Inflammation of gums associated with the accumulation of tartar deposit. This is by far the most common cause of loss of teeth in dogs.

Comment
Common in old age.

Action
Regular tooth brushing and possibly visits to the veterinary surgeon for scaling can be enormously beneficial for the dog's health and comfort. Feeding hard, crunchy food can help prevent the condition occurring.

Foreign body lodged in mouth
See 'What if' No. 36.

Tooth decay

Signs
Difficulty in eating. Possible swelling and abscess formation over the root of the tooth. The upper carnassial tooth is most often affected and leads to a swelling in the cheek, often called a facial abscess, just below and in front of the eye. This can burst, leaving a discharging painful sinus.

Comment
Tooth decay is most common in the toy breeds and some may have lost nearly all their teeth by the time they are 4 years old. Such dogs can usually deal with hard foods despite having no teeth.

Action
While it is sometimes possible to fill or replace teeth which are decayed it is hardly practical, and painful teeth are usually extracted, under anaesthesia by the veterinary surgeon.

Other possible causes
Bad breath may be associated with the following major diseases: kidney disease and liver disease.

38. What if my dog is having fits, convulsions or is twitching?

It is normal for newly born puppies to twitch frequently when resting and older dogs may twitch and whimper during their sleep while dreaming. These twitching episodes are very different from a true fit or convulsion. A fit is a convulsive seizure, occurring typically while the dog is relaxed or asleep and never while the dog is active. The first fit which an owner observes usually occurs when a dog is between 1 and 3 years of age. A fit usually begins with a period of rigidity (tonic phase) which is followed by shaking and spasm of the muscles,which progresses to involuntary paddling with the paws (clonic phase). There may be involuntary passing of faeces and urine. The fit may last only a minute or two and the dog may recover quickly and appear perfectly normal. In other cases the fit may be more prolonged and the dog may appear dazed and disorientated for some hours after the convulsions have stopped. Sight seems to be the last sense to return fully. Dogs often eat ravenously after a fit. In severe episodes, one fit may lead very quickly to several more.

Although it is unlikely that the dog will harm humans or itself while in a fit, it is wise to be cautious. The type of first aid treatment given to human fit victims is inappropriate for dogs, and no attempt should be made to force anything into the dog's mouth.

While the fit lasts, do not touch the dog, but remove anything lying nearby which could cause it injury and gently move the dog by using a blanket if it is lying in a dangerous place such as the top of the stairs. Turn off radios and the TV and keep the room dark and quiet (see also Table 13.3).

Make a note of the progress and duration of the fit and the circumstances which preceded it. **There is no point in asking the veterinary surgeon to make an urgent visit to the dog,** as it will almost certainly be normal by the time help is obtained. Once the dog is out of the fit, report to the veterinary surgeon on the telephone. It will probably be wise not to attempt to make a surgery call the same day, as the dog is best kept quiet for some hours following a fit.

Puppies may react to severe pain, especially of an abdominal nature, by having convulsions. Veterinary diagnosis and treatment of the underlying cause will be needed.

Epilepsy, often showing for the first time at around 2 years old, is a relatively common condition in dogs, but this condition can often be controlled by medication so that the dog lives to a full lifespan. Since fits may sometimes be associated with brain tumours, previous traumas, inherited conditions such as hydrocephalus (water on the brain), canine distemper and liver disease or eclampsia, always seek veterinary attention since an accurate diagnosis of the cause is essential before any medication is given.

Rabies, in countries where the disease is endemic, would have to be considered as a possibility but this is extremely likely to be the case in Britain, unless the dog has only recently been released from a quarantine kennel, or has been bitten by a dog or cat which has been illegally smuggled into the country. If you have any suspicion that this may be so, tell your veterinary surgeon so that he can report the matter to the Ministry of Agriculture, Fisheries and Food, Rabies Division, immediately. Even if your fears may be unfounded, where this deadly disease is concerned it is better to err on the safe side.

It will be helpful to the veterinary surgeon if you can recall any traumatic incident in the dog's life, eg a fall, being dropped or hit by a car, which may have caused brain damage not perceived at the time. The breeder may also be able to contribute some information on the dog's early life and whether similar signs have been shown by related animals.

39. What if my dog has a lump or swelling?

Any lumps or swellings which do not appear within a few days should be investigated by a veterinary surgeon. This is particularly important for the early recognition of abscesses and to identify tumours early in their development. It is common for the large breeds to develop swellings on their elbows or hocks; the risk of this can be minimised by ensuring that the dog has an adequate number of soft areas where it can lie.

Types of swelling include:

Abscess

Cause
Swelling beneath the skin caused by bacterial infection. Often the result of a bite or puncture wound.

Signs
Pain, heat and swelling developing over a few days probably with subsequent bursting and discharge of pus. Abscesses may occur anywhere on the body.

Action
Contact the veterinary surgeon promptly as the condition may need surgical drainage and medication with antibiotics.

Puppy head gland disease (juvenile pyoderma)

Cause
Unknown but thought to be due to a hypersensitivity reaction. Occurs in puppies of many breeds under 4 months old.

Signs
Sudden painful gross swelling around eyes and on head, which may spread to the whole body. The swellings eventually burst and drain pus. The puppy may, surprisingly, remain otherwise well and reasonably cheerful.

Action
Veterinary advice immediately for appropriate medication. A very prolonged course of treatment is usually required. With careful nursing the puppy is likely to recover but there may be subsequent scarring.

Salivary cyst

Signs
Sudden appearance of a large swelling under the tongue and at the angle of the jaw causing drooling and sometimes displacing the tongue to one side of mouth so that it protrudes.

Action
Seek veterinary advice at once; surgery may be required.

Cysts

Sign
Smooth slow-growing swelling under the skin, anywhere on the body.

Action
Urgent veterinary advice if the cyst ruptures or starts to bleed. Otherwise keep the cyst under observation for any changes.

Interdigital cysts

Signs
Painful swellings between the toes. See 'What if' No. 34.

Papillomas and warts

Cause
Unknown but may be due to a virus infection. Often occurs on smooth-coated dogs.

Sign
Painless dark coloured projections from the skin (tags), usually small.

Action
Seek veterinary advice if the wart is increasing in size rapidly, otherwise, mention the wart at the next routine consultation.

Comment
A number of warts caused by a virus infection sometimes occur in the mouths of young puppies.

Ulcers

Cause
Various.

Sign
A red, ulcerated area occurring on any part of the body.

Action
Seek veterinary advice without delay.

Haematoma (blood or fluid filled swelling)

Cause
The result of an injury to blood vessels, or to drainage of fluid post-operatively. The ear flap is a common site. See also 'What if' No. 15.

Signs
Soft swelling and distortion of the area – sometimes painful but not usually so to the touch.

Action
Consult your veterinary surgeon as surgical treatment may be required. A post-operative haematoma may require a support bandage which the veterinary surgeon will show you how to put on.

Tender area at an injection site

Cause
A local irritant reaction to a component in the injection.

Signs
Pain and swelling and possibly heat. If the injection has been given into a leg muscle, possibly lameness.

Action
Further treatment seldom required unless the dog is in a lot of pain but the matter should be reported to the veterinary surgeon.

Stings and insect bites

Sign
Very sudden swelling which may be severe, and dangerous if the face and mouth is affected, especially in short-nosed breeds.

Action
See Chapter 13 but contact veterinary surgeon immediately if breathing or swallowing is impeded.

Bruising after injury

Sign
Pain and heat in the affected area which may also be grazed and bleeding.

Action
Seek veterinary advice if pain is severe.

Lumps and swellings may also be associated with urticaria and possibly tumours, the most common being mammary tumours and testicular tumours (see Index of Diseases and Conditions).

> In the case of non-urgent lumps and swellings, make a note in the dog's record to remind you when the swelling was first noticed, where it is, and the size now (in centimetres measured with calipers). It is also a good idea to compare it in size and shape with a common object, eg a golf ball, a coin, etc. Subsequent measurements will provide vital information on the rate of enlargement, a possibly crucial factor in deciding whether surgery will be necessary.

40. What if my dog is wounded/cut/burnt/ grazed?

See Chapter 13.

41. What if my dog is licking itself excessively?

Licking is part of the normal cleaning procedure in dogs, to clean dirt off coat or paws, to clean a wound, or to remove excess secretions.

Bitches will lick the vulval area when coming into season and during oestrus. Stud dogs lick their genitals after mating.

Many dogs will attend to wounds on their companion animals and will also clean the vulval and rectal area on puppies.

If a dog is seen to be licking excessively at one area of the body, check for some unsuspected injury, insect sting or thorn embedded in the flesh. Continual licking can cause additional damage to the skin and so should be investigated.

Excessive licking may be indicative of:

Lick granuloma

Cause
Often a self-inflicted injury through boredom, frustration or nervousness.

Sign
A sore, thickened, red area of skin on a place the dog can reach easily, often a paw (carpus).

Action
Veterinary advice for medication, as constant licking can lead to an intractable sore. Also re-think the dog's day and lifestyle to improve its outlook and provide more activity and interest.

42. What if my dog is weak and lethargic?

It is normal and sensible for short-faced dogs, elderly dogs and pregnant bitches to be lethargic in hot weather, but general weakness and lethargy accompany many serious illnesses. There will usually be other more prominent signs, but if you feel that your dog is less active than it should be, it is always wise to seek veterinary attention.

Lethargy and obesity may be associated and be a consequence of each other – see Chapter 2.

Other causes of lethargy include:

* **Diabetes mellitus**
* **Anaemia**
* **Heart disease**
* **Hypothyroidism**

(See Index of Diseases and Conditions).

A bitch which is experiencing a false pregnancy, see Chapter 4, will often appear to be lethargic, as she has the instinct to remain with her imaginary puppies.

> Dogs can become acutely depressed when some element that they particularly value is removed from their lives. Where there are no other clinical signs of illness, try to relate this behaviour pattern to any deprivation of person, activity or location which is causing the dog to sulk or pine.

43. What if my dog has collapsed and is comatose?

The terminal stages of any serious illness or death from extreme old age will include collapse.

Any disease or condition which makes breathing difficult may cause a dog to collapse temporarily. Heat stroke, which frequently occurs when dogs are confined in stationary cars, causes collapse – see section on First Aid, Chapter 13.

Short-nosed dogs (Boxers, Pekingese, Pugs, Bulldogs) taking violent exercise may faint through lack of oxygen. A few minutes rest, plus dousing the head with cold water will generally restore the dog to normal, but the rest of the walk should be controlled on the lead. It is wise to take the dog to the veterinary surgeon to be checked if the problem arises on more than one occasion.

When a dog which has been previously healthy and is not stressed for air, collapses suddenly, ensure that mouth and nose are clear of discharges and obstructions, keep the dog warm and seek veterinary advice urgently.

A conditions associated with Cavalier King Charles Spaniels causes them to spin round and collapse momentarily unconscious, usually while walking on the lead. No satisfactory explanation has been found, and the dogs usually recover quickly, but the episode is likely to be repeated.

Other causes of collapse include:

Hypoglycaemia (low blood sugar) causing malfunction of the central nervous system. The condition is seen most frequently in puppies of the toy breeds or in hard-working gun dogs.

Cause
Irregular feeding times, distress, exhaustion.

Action
Feed something sweet at once, a Mars bar or the equivalent is ideal.

'Slipped disc' (dislocation of the cushioning disc between the vertebrae). This condition occurs most frequently in short-legged, long-backed breeds, Dachshunds and Pekingese predominantly.

Sign
Intense pain, weakness and unsteadiness in the hind or all four limbs or absolute paralysis of hind limbs. Alternatively there may be no pain, but complete loss of all sensation and power below the injured area. There may also be loss of bladder control.

Action
Keep the dog still, transport the dog to the veterinary surgery on a flat board to avoid causing it pain.

Hypothermia (following exposure to intense cold)

Action
Apply gentle warmth, keep the dog loosely covered, until you reach the veterinary surgery. Give warm milk if the dog is able to swallow; do *not* give brandy or other spirits.

Shock (following road accident or serious haemorrhage)

Signs
Cold, limp, lifeless, with rapid shallow breathing. Lips and gums and eye rims (conjunctiva) very pale.

Action
Seek nearest veterinary surgeon immediately. Give nothing by mouth, cover the dog loosely and keep warm.

Collapse may also be associated with the following major diseases:

- **Diabetes mellitus,** particularly following an overdose of insulin
- **Heart disease**
- **Kidney disease**
- **Poisoning**

(See Index of Diseases and Conditions.)

> Be prepared to tell the veterinary surgeon the exact circumstances surrounding the collapse, ie relationship to feeding time or exercise, any trauma which occurred, the dog's behaviour just before the collapse, and the time it took for the dog to return to normal.

44. What if my dog is in pain?

Some dogs, especially the Bull breeds bred for guarding, such as Dobermanns, and Hounds, are very stoical about pain and although they may be badly injured or very ill they will give little, if any, indication of the site of the pain.

Other dogs, usually of the smaller breeds, can be very babyish and make a great fuss over a mild inconvenience, so it is important to know your own dog's character.

If a minor accident, such as stepping on a paw, appears to have caused pain which has not subsided within a few hours, seek veterinary advice.

Occasionally pain may appear generalised and difficult to locate. If pain is persistent, always seek veterinary diagnosis. Dogs may show signs of pain before other signs become apparent.

Where the location of the pain is obvious, eg in teeth, ears, abdomen or from an abscess, consult the relevant 'What if'.

Other causes of severe pain may be **arthritis, canine parvovirus infection, cystitis, haemorrhagic gastroenteritis, infectious canine hepatitis, leptospirosis** and **Poisoning** (see Index of Diseases and Conditions).

Another cause of severe and sudden pain is:

Cramp

Cause
Inflammation of muscles, often following strenuous exercise especially when a dog which has been hot becomes quickly chilled, eg through jumping into cold water.

Signs
Acute pain, probably vocalisation at least once, muscle tremor.

Action
Protect dog from any danger, if in water take steps to bring it to land. Massage of the affected limb, keep warm, rest. Consult the veterinary surgeon if pain persists.

Myositis
Inflammation of the muscles may follow unaccustomed strenuous exercise. Affected dogs show signs of acute pain particularly affecting the back or hind legs and they resent being touched. If persistent or if the dog is in great pain, seek veterinary advice.

45. What if my dog is losing weight or is looking thin?

Young adolescent dogs in the larger breeds often remain very thin, although they are well fed. Dogs of this age, particularly where two are kept together, often burn off all the food they are given through constant activity. This is good and will help ward off obesity in middle age. It is better to make no strenuous attempt to artificially fatten or cram a dog just to appease criticism or in order to compete in the show ring, provided it only looks thin and is not actually losing weight.

Male dogs will lose weight dramatically when they are close to a bitch in season, and many dogs will lose weight in boarding kennels although they appear to eat well. Nervous anxiety will lead to lost weight very rapidly and the dog will not utilise its food intake properly until the cause of its distress is removed.

Bitches may lose weight when feeding a large litter, as they cannot process enough food through their bodies to maintain their own weight as well as producing enough milk for the puppies. They will usually recover quite quickly if they are given increased amounts of high quality food after the puppies are weaned. Worming 2-3 times at two-weekly intervals while the bitch is suckling and after the puppies are weaned may help the bitch regain her normal weight more quickly.

If there is any doubt whether a dog is being fed sufficient food of good nutritional quality, consult Chapter 2 and/or seek veterinary help.

Where an adequate diet is provided and none of the circumstances apply but the dog still loses weight, this is an indication that disease is present. Since the cause of the weight loss may be obscure and associated with many major disorders, professional help should be sought.

> Before going to the surgery, write out the dog's menu giving weighed quantities of all the food eaten and milk drunk. If you are using a commercially formulated food, take a package or label with you so that the veterinary surgeon may see the manufacturer's analysis of the contents. It can also be helpful to take fresh faeces and urine samples with you when you go to the surgery.

46. What if my dog is aggressive?

Aggression, even in the smallest dog, is always dangerous, as it is a cumulative habit, and a dog which shows aggressive tendencies usually becomes increasingly fierce, unless the cause can be found and some strategy used to correct it. See Chapter 4.

47. What if my dog is not breathing?

Lay the animal flat on its side, open its mouth, pull the tongue forward and check that there is nothing obstructing the throat. See Table 13.3. Contact the veterinary surgeon urgently and take the dog to the surgery quickly if it is possible to do so.

48. What if my dog is staggering and wobbly on its legs?

During the recovery period from an anaesthetic, or during convalescence, hind leg weakness is to be expected, as it is in very old dogs.

During the recovery stage from a fit, gait may be uncertain and wobbly. In any other circumstances, lack of a firm and steady hind leg movement is abnormal and, as this sign may be associated with serious conditions, veterinary help should be sought promptly.

Other possible causes of staggering gait include:

Slipped disc (disc protrusion)
See 'What if' No. 43.

Cerebral haemorrhage (stroke, CVA)
May occur in older dogs. This condition has been observed to occur more often in winter and may be triggered by turning an old dog out into a very cold atmosphere.

Signs
Confusion, dilated pupils, lack of response to owner, head tilt, circling, sudden blindness. Any combination of these signs may appear suddenly, but may gradually improve.

Action
Veterinary advice as soon as possible to confirm diagnosis and as medication may be needed.

German Shepherd syndrome (CDRM – Chronic Degenerative Radiculomyelopathy)
This breed in particular is associated with a condition of increasing weakness in the hind legs of older dogs, with a tendency to collapse when turning corners, and to drag the hind paws which may become grazed. Pain is not a sign in this condition. Consult the veterinary surgeon to obtain advice on how best to cope with the problem and to prevent secondary complications developing. The condition is, unfortunately, progressive, despite treatment.

Wobbler syndrome
Inherited or congenital damage to the vertebrae results in pressure on the spinal cord causing ataxia (a wobbly gait) and poor position sense, usually in animals 10-24 months of age, although the signs may not develop until the dog is 5-6 years old. The wobbler syndrome is seen particularly in Great Danes and Dobermanns but other large breeds are also affected. The condition has also been reported in Basset Hounds.

Consult a veterinary surgeon as soon as any signs are noticed, as rest and medication may bring about an improvement. Surgery may be necessary in some cases.

Hypertrophic osteodystrophy (skeletal scurvy)
This is a complex condition that affects rapidly growing puppies (3-6 months of age) of the larger breeds, and particularly Boxers, Dobermanns and Afghans.

Signs
Pain and swelling of the joints of the legs, staggering gait, unwillingness to walk, acute pain on being touched. Possibly bleeding from the gums.

Cause
The cause of this condition is an imbalance of vitamin C metabolism. The condition may be associated with cramming growing puppies with food and with an excess of vitamins and minerals in an effort to put weight on what should naturally be a lean, lithe frame.

Action
Veterinary consultation promptly for accurate diagnosis, probably via X-ray, and medication to relieve pain. Subsequently a balanced and moderate diet must be devised and the pup allowed to grow normally. Rest is also important.

Be prepared to lead the dog up and down for some time so that the veterinary surgeon may have the opportunity to observe the gait. Make a note of whether the staggering gait is consistently bad or whether the dog is better at some times of the day or before or after exercise. Be prepared to tell the veterinary surgeon about the onset of staggering – was it sudden or progressive?

---

49. What if my dog appears deaf?

Congenital deafness is often associated with white coat colouring, and is known to occur in Dalmatians, Bull Terriers, White Boxers, Cocker Spaniels, Border Collies and several small Terrier breeds.

Deafness in puppies does not become apparent until about 5 weeks of age, and breeders should test each puppy individually at this time. Deafness may not be recognised in situations where affected puppies can copy the actions of other litter members.

Congenital deafness cannot be treated and it is usual for affected puppies to be painlessly destroyed by a veterinary surgeon, as acute hearing is of vital importance to a dog for self-preservation, interaction with other dogs, and obedience to its owner's commands. It is no kindness to a dog to attempt to rear a deaf puppy and furthermore such dogs could be the cause of serious accidents involving people.

Elderly dogs often become progressively deaf, but as by this age they have learnt to comply with their owner's wishes and they are not violently active, deafness is not such a handicap to them provided the owner bears their disability in mind. It is worth asking the veterinary surgeon's advice to check that there is no underlying disease causing the deafness and which could be treated.

Loss of hearing in adult dogs may be associated with growths in the ear canal or disease of the various parts of the ear, so when there is any indication that the ears are being affected in any way it is important to seek advice promptly.

An avoidable cause of progressive deafness may be:

Carbon monoxide poisoning

Cause
Inhalation of toxic fumes from solid fuel boilers, or from a leaking car exhaust system, causing a lack of oxygen to reach the lungs and blood system.

Signs
Excessive sleepiness, bloodshot eyes, or, in extreme cases, collapse with blue-tinged tongue and mucous membranes.

Carbon monoxide poisoning can occur at low level where a dog is kept at night in an airtight boiler room where the atmosphere is tainted by fumes from the boiler, and also where a dog is made to ride in a car boot, or on the floor, without adequate ventilation.

In an acute situation, carbon monoxide poisoning will kill a dog in a very short time.

Action
Acute: See 'What if' No. 47 and 14.
Mild: Take steps to improve the dog's location in house and car and have boilers serviced regularly. The latter action will also of course avoid danger to humans.

Test the dog with an ultrasonic (silent) whistle and low frequency sounds to see if anything at all can be heard. Be prepared to say when you first notice signs of deafness and whether you can associate this sign with any trauma or ear disease which may have since cleared up. Test the dog's response, in the quiet of your own home before going to the surgery, to loud and soft noises, close to and far away, and in each ear. Be prepared to tell the veterinary surgeon the results and your conclusions.

---

50. What if my bitch is aborting?

Canine pregnancy lasts on average 63 days (range 57-69 days), so an early whelping is not necessarily an abortion which is, incidentally, not a common condition in bitches.

Where an abortion does occur in a breeding kennels it is always a good idea to have the bitch, and any dead foetuses which are salvaged, tested for the presence of any infection which may affect other bitches. Since the bitch will often eat the expelled foetuses, it is not always possible to know when an abortion has occurred.

Causes of abortion may be: **hormonal imbalance, bacterial infection,** and in imported bitches, **brucella canis infection.** The latter is an important cause of abortion in the USA and a few cases have occurred in the UK. It is important to have this cause investigated, as it is infectious to other dogs, including any stud dogs used on the affected bitch.

Abortion is also more rarely associated with accidental injury to bitches and also to fighting between bitches. Toxoplasmosis (see Chapter 8) may also be a cause of abortion in bitches.

It is important to be able to tell the veterinary surgeon the day the bitch's heat started, the day of mating, whether one or more services were given and at what intervals, whether the bitch escaped during heat, whether the pregnancy was normal before the abortion occurred, and whether previous pregnancies were normal. It may be helpful also to ask the breeder about the whelping record of your bitch's dam.

---

51. What if my dog is nervous and over-excitable?

Variations in temperament are inevitable in any litter. A tendency to nervousness may be inherited, from sire to dam or earlier ancestors, or it may be learned from the dam in very early life.

A confident puppy may become nervous through lack of understanding in the home to which it was sold, and a 'rescued' dog may have become nervous through past experiences.

Dogs which have been in road accidents or similar traumatic happenings may be nervous in the same surroundings for many years afterwards.

Nervousness at dog shows may occur when a young male is benched next to a mature, very dominant dog, so that the younger animal is in a stress-inducing situation for many hours.

Some dogs show exaggerated fear of some specific noise, eg thunder, but this fear will be frequently found to be generated by the humans the dog is with. Dogs are very quick to pick up tension and fear from their owners.

For programmes to improve difficult behaviour patterns see Chapter 4.

Puppies go through a 'fear period' between the ages of 8 and 12 weeks, when the puppy is very sensitive and impressionable about new experiences. Great care should be taken during this time to make the puppy feel secure and protected while behaviour training starts.

Failure to allow a puppy sufficient rest and quiet away from the stimulation of human attention is a common cause of development of nervous temperament.

Hyperexcitability can be induced in *adolescent dogs* by encouraging them to play roughly and in physical combat with owners. Great care must be taken in this respect especially in the case of guard dogs like Rottweilers, Dobermanns and Boxers.

Clinical causes of nervousness and excitability may include:

* **Onset of oestrus** and/or whelping in the bitch.
* **Eclampsia**, see 'What if' No. 16.
* **False pregnancy** and the frustrations of guarding an invisible litter.
* **Hypersexuality** in the male. See 'What if' No. 54.

Nervousness may also be associated with the secondary stage of **canine distemper, diabetes** and **rabies** in countries where the disease is endemic.

> It will be helpful if you try to associate episodes of excitability with particular happenings in the household, or with the presence of particular people. Some people's voices, or manner with dogs, creates over-excitability in dogs, whether they mean to or not.

52. What if my dog has a depraved appetite?

It is normal for the wild or free-running dog to eat decomposing bodies and the faeces of other animals, and sometimes their own faeces. Pet dogs will also do this if they have the opportunity. See 'What if' No. 26.

Puppies will explore the edibility of practically any substance, and may eat leaves, earth and stones, paper etc. This habit is usually grown out of by the time the puppy is 9 to 10 months old. Take steps to actively discourage the habit – see Chapter 4.

When an older dog chooses to eat earth, gravel, stones etc, regularly, it is as well to check with the veterinary surgeon that there is nothing wrong. If you happen to notice your dog eating rubbish or decaying matter, giving it a dose of liquid paraffin (1 teaspoonful/5 ml to 1 tablespoon/15 ml) can often prevent a digestive problem occurring.

> Try to recall when the behaviour started, and look for other signs of illness, eg compulsive drinking. It can be helpful to take fresh faeces and urine samples with you when you go to the veterinary surgery.

53. What if my dog is salivating excessively?

It is normal for dogs with loose lower lips to exude more saliva than those with tight mouths. It is also normal for a dog to drool when eagerly awaiting food, and stud dogs will drool in the presence of an in-season bitch. Fear and anxiety give rise to drooling and over-production of saliva is a frequent prelude to car sickness. Where none of these explanations applies, excessive and continual salivation should prompt a visit to the veterinary surgeon.

Excessive salivation may be associated with problems in the mouth which may cause difficulty in eating. See 'What if' No. 36, and also the following major conditions: neoplasia and poisoning.

54. What if my dog is over-sexed?

Sex drive in the dog is expressed in mounting behaviour, territory marking, roaming, excitability, and aggression to other dogs. Males of the small breeds and mongrels up to medium size tend to hypersexuality more than males of large and giant breeds, which are often reluctant to mate even when required for stud work.

It is normal for a healthy, young male dog to have a vigorous sex drive, especially if he is kept with or near entire bitches coming into oestrus.

Many adolescent males go through a short period of hypersexual behaviour at puberty (6-14 months), but in most dogs this behaviour is short-lived.

It is a common error to believe that the dog 'needs a bitch' at this time and that being used at stud will cure the behaviour – it is in fact more likely to encourage this undesirable tendency in the pet male. It is far preferable never to use a companion dog at stud and not to keep him with brood bitches unless there is the prospect of regular stud work for him.

For corrective treatment of hypersexuality in the male, see Chapter 1 (Male dogs) and Chapter 4.

Your veterinary surgeon may also be able to help with medication and, if necessary, eventually with castration, but where mating behaviour has been learnt, or even it if has not, the dog may still 'go through the motions' when extremely stimulated, but will not, of course, be fertile. It is a mistake to assume that castration will cure all hypersexual activity since that is not the case and castration may cause the dog to increase in weight and change its character in other ways.

Note whether the hypersexual behaviour is regular or intermittent. If the trait occurs irregularly try to observe some pattern in the episodes of hypersexual behaviour. Does it occur, for instance, after boisterous play with children or adults? Are the episodes linked with visits to specific places?

Table 17.1 Common ocular defects which cause runny eyes

Condition	Description	Breeds particularly affected
Distichiasis	Extra hairs on the margin of the eyelid point inward and irritate the surface of the eye	Sheltie, Cocker, Poodle, Pekingese, Mini-Longhaired Dachshund
Entropion	In-turning eyelids which cause the eyelashes to rub on the cornea	Chow-Chow, Cocker, Labrador, Retriever, Golden Retriever
Extropion	The lower eyelid is turned outwards, leading to inflammation of the conjunctival sac	Basset Hound, St Bernard, Bloodhound
Trichiasis	Facial hair causing irritation to the cornea	Pekingese

Table 17.2 Conditions which cause dogs' eyes to look abnormal

Sign	Comment
Dislocated eyeball (eye hanging out of its socket)	Generally due to trauma but may be spontaneous. An emergency, see first aid section in Chapter 13.
Bulging eyeball (see also table of inherited eye defects)	May be a sign of glaucoma, an acutely painful and serious condition. Consult veterinary surgeon immediately. Note, however, that certain breeds like Pekingese and Cavalier King Charles Spaniels have bulging eyes normally.
Swelling of eyelids and surrounding facial area	May be due to an allergy or an insect sting. Probably quickly alleviated by a visit to the veterinary surgeon.
Inability to raise upper eyelid (ptosis)	Associated with conditions affecting nerves of the head and also possibly with generalised illness. If not already receiving veterinary treatment for the illness, an immediate consultation is necessary.
Hair loss around the eye	Bare skin around the eye rim can be an early sign of demodectic mange, which may become generalised if neglected.
An opaque patch on the surface of the eye	Possible causes are: a film over part or all of the cornea caused by inflammation (keratitis) or by a failure in tear production (keratitis sicca — dry eye). A corneal ulcer, usually caused by a direct injury to the cornea, eg being struck by the end of a lead. An indolent ulcer, seen most frequently in spayed Boxer and Corgi bitches, possibly caused by low oestrogen levels in the blood. In all cases veterinary consultation is urgent as sight may be damaged if treatment is delayed.
Blue eye, almost overnight the whole of the cornea becomes opaque pale blue	Seen mainly in puppies, following infection with infectious canine hepatitis, or possibly about 10 days after vaccination against this disease. The eye colour usually reverts to normal in time. See infectious canine hepatitis, Chapter 7. In advanced cases of glaucoma the surface of the eye becomes a blue-green colour. Dogs with such signs should be taken without delay to a veterinary surgeon.
Cataract (an opaqueness within the eye)	The lens *lying behind the iris* becomes opaque and as a result vision is affected. Indeed, the first signs may be that the dog starts bumping into objects in its path or loses the ability to catch a ball. The condition may affect one or both eyes. Some cataracts are inherited. Visit a veterinary surgeon without delay as in some cases treatment is possible.
Third eyelid prolapsed	In some dogs the third eyelid is always prominent and particularly noticeable because it is darkly pigmented. When the third eyelid is more prominent than usual in an individual dog, it is often because fat has been lost behind the eyeball through illness and poor condition. Severe dehydration can give the same appearance. If the dog is not already under treatment for illness, consult a veterinary surgeon without delay.
Enlarged Harderian gland (a red lump protruding at the inner corner of the eye), also known as 'cherry eye'	The Harderian gland is on the inner surface of the third eyelid. It can become swollen so as to protrude past the third eyelid. Veterinary attention should be sought without delay.
Dilated pupils in daylight	This sign may be associated with several serious eye conditions and hereditary defects such as PRA. See 'What if' No. 13.

Table 17.3 Inherited eye defects

Disease	Sign	Breeds chiefly affected
Progressive retinal atrophy (PRA) — progressive destruction of light-sensitive tissue at the back of the eye	Failing sight in dim light leading to total blindness. May start at any age so annual examination necessary. No treatment, no cure	Collies, Shelties, Cockers, Mini-Longhair Dachshunds, English Springers, Irish Setters, Poodles, Golden Retrievers, Labradors, Briards, Tibetan breeds and crossbreds
Hereditary cataract — loss of transparency of the lens of the eye	A bluish clouding of the lens causing blindness. Common in the older dog but in badly affected breeds can occur at less than 2 years of age. Surgical correction may be possible	Staffordshire Bull Terriers, Afhans, American Cockers, Bedlingtons, Bostons, Golden Retrievers, Labradors, German Shepherd Dogs, Welsh Springers
Collie eye anomaly (CEA) — an eye defect very widespread in Collie breeds	A canine ophthalmologist can distinguish this defect in puppies of 6-8 weeks old. While the defect does not cause blindness, it can lead to other painful eye conditions. Affected puppies are acceptable as pets but should not be used for breeding. Do not buy a Collie puppy which has not been screened for CEA. The condition cannot be treated but seek veterinary advice about management of affected dog	Rough Collies, Smooth Collies, Border and Working Collies, Shetland Sheepdogs and crossbreds
Glaucoma — increased fluid pressure within the eye	A fixed cloudy, bulging, staring eye with wide-open pupil, usually only in one eye at first. Veterinary attention is needed immediately	American Cockers, English Cockers, Welsh and English Springers, Beagles, Basset Hounds, small Poodles
Lens luxation — weakening or rupture of one or more of the ligaments holding the lens in place	Probably suddenly failing sight will be the only sign the owner can recognise. Affected animals lose the ability to catch titbits and knock into objects in unfamiliar places. Surgical correction may be possible and veterinary advice should be sought before other complications set in	Wire-haired and Smooth Fox Terriers, Jack Russell and similar terriers, Tibetan Terriers

Table 17.4 Abnormal breathing — signs and symptoms

Sign	Possible cause(s)	Action
Snorting, reverse sneezing Very noisy snorting and inability to breathe properly, often occurring when the dog is first let out of the house or taken for a walk.	Believed to be brought about by a temporary spasm of the throat muscles possibly caused by excitement or sudden encounter with cold air.	None needed beyond soothing the dog, as the spasm soon passes and the dog returns to breathing normally. No treatment is required.
Roaring Occurs when the normal airway is obstructed and is seen most frequently in short-faced dogs but may occur in other breeds.	Elongated soft palate in short-faced dogs may block the airway especially when they are being exercised in hot weather. In other breeds, collapse of the larynx can cause obstruction to the airway.	Veterinary consultation and diagnosis. Remedial surgery is often possible. A minor form of roaring will occur sometimes when dogs lean their heads on someone's knee or the arm of a chair. No action is required in such cases.
Shallow breathing The inspired breath is not deep enough to expand the rib cage. Signs of distress and collapse are also usually present.	Pain on taking a deep breath, due to pneumonia or fracture of the ribs after a fall or road accident.	Careful removal to veterinary surgery.
Wheezing Wheezy breathing possibly since birth and accompanied by exercise intolerance. The puppy may fail to eat and grow properly.	In short-faced breeds, collapse of cartilage tissue in the nose and narrowing of nostrils restricts air intake.	Veterinary consultation at once, as remedial surgery should be performed as early as possible.
Rapid breathing A dog normally breathes at between 10 and 30 times a minute when at rest. Fast, shallow breathing indicates something is wrong.	Pain, stress, fever, shock, heat stroke, haemorrhage, dehydration, poisoning.	Veterinary consultation.

Table 17.5 Possible causes of flatulence

Possible causes	Comment	Action
Unsuitable diet	Some dogs cannot tolerate diets based on soya or other beans.	Take advice on a more easily digested diet.
Sudden diet change	The villi in the intestine need time to adjust when a radical diet change takes place, eg from a complete cereal diet to meat and biscuits.	Change diets gradually over at least 4-5 days.
Feeding household left-overs	Highly seasoned and spiced foods create digestive problems in dogs.	Avoid feeding spiced foods.
Scavenging	Dogs are attracted to the smell of decaying flesh and will eat putrid carcasses.	Keep the dog under stricter control.
Constipation	Low fibre diets will contain very little residue and faeces may be difficult to pass.	The addition of 10% bran to the diet may help. A special diet may be needed. Your veterinary surgeon will advise.
Old age	Lack of muscle tone in the digestive tract and a reduced ability to digest protein, fat and carbohydrate.	Try giving four small easily digested meals a day. Your veterinary surgeon may advise you to use a diet specially formulated for elderly dogs.
Pregnancy	The digestive organs may be displaced and cramped by the full uterus.	Charcoal granules on the food or charcoal biscuits may help.
Enforced inactivity	A bitch nursing a litter or a dog on cage rest while recovering from injury inevitably lacks exercise.	Give 4-6 small meals a day plus a human digestive remedy such as Bisodol, Asilone or Milk of Magnesia tablets. Give one quarter to a whole child's dose according to size of dog.

Table 17.6 Conditions which may cause a dog to bite at its hind end

Condition	Comment
Anal furunculosis Sore skin around the anus with open wounds discharging pus, originating from infected anal glands.	Almost exclusive to German Shepherd Dogs (Alsatians) and Belgian Shepherd Dogs. The anal glands can be removed surgically if trouble persists.
Anal adenomata Lumps (benign tumours) around the anus.	The surface of the tumour can become raw and ulcerated through pressure and contact with the ground. Seek veterinary advice at once as the area is unlikely to heal naturally.
Tail chasing Seems to have no physical cause.	May be an attention-attracting behaviour or a nervous aberration.

Table 17.7 Some common simple causes of constipation

Cause	Comment
Low residue, all meat diet	Change the diet to contain some carbohydrate, eg add biscuit or rusk plus 10% bran. Special diets which can help in chronic cases are available from veterinary surgeons.
Feeding bones	Fine bone chips can impact in the colon to cause cement-like faeces which are difficult and painful to pass. Bones are unnecessary and cause many problems so they are best omitted from the dog's diet. Chicken bones and other bones that can splinter or be eaten whole must on no account be given to dogs.
Feeding meat sawdust	This meat product, although cheap, contains large quantities of very finely ground bone and is, therefore, not recommended. Very hard, white faeces result.
Dog left indoors all day	House training may override the urge to defecate. Dogs should have the opportunity to go outside every 4 hours at least, during the day time.
Travelling by car and attending dog shows	Dogs may refuse to pass faeces if their eating pattern is upset, little exercise is given or the surroundings are unfamiliar.
Matted fur beneath tail	Hair matted with faeces can block the anus, making the passage of faeces impossible. The surrounding skin also becomes very sore. Long-haired dogs should be groomed thoroughly and regularly, especially around the anal area and, when necessary, the fur on the hindquarters should be washed and dried. If severe matting has already occurred it may be necessary to have the dog clipped at the veterinary surgery. In some cases an anaesthetic will be required so that the job can be properly accomplished.

Table 17.8 Possible causes of coughing

Condition	Signs	Action	Comment
Breathing of irritants (fine dust, paint fumes, aerosol sprays)	Rapid and exaggerated breathing, watering eyes, depression.	Telephone veterinary surgeon for advice on first aid treatment.	Prevention is much better than cure.
Injury to chest	Rapid breathing, bruising or pain over the ribs.	Seek veterinary help without delay.	Many road accidents cause some degree of lung haemorrhage.
Pharyngitis, laryngitis and tonsillitis	Depression, fever, loss of appetite, coughing and retching.	Prompt veterinary consultation as this condition responds well to treatment.	It is as well to remember that *tonsillitis* is often an early sign of a major infectious disease and it should not be treated lightly. Some breeds of dog seem especially susceptible to recurrent bouts of tonsillitis.

Index of Diseases and Conditions affecting dogs (IDC)

The major diseases and conditions affecting dogs are listed alphabetically in this index, which shold be used in conjunction with the general index.

Disease/Condition		Disease/Condition
Abcess	A septic region caused by bacterial infection, which consists of a pool of pus surrounded by a wall of fibrous tissue.	See 'What if' No 39
Abortion	Loss of puppies (foetuses) while still in the womb, possibly as a result of trauma, hormonal imbalance or an infection.	See 'What if' No 50
Abrasion	A superficial wound.	See Chapter 13
Acanthrosis nigricans	A chronic black/brown inflammatory condition of the skin beginning in the armpit. Especially common in Dachshunds.	
Achondroplasia	An inherited condition leading to a failure of the long bones to grow. It has been recorded in Scottish Terriers and Poodles.	
Acne	An accumulation of 'spots' and pustules in the skin.	
Addison's disease	Failure of the adrenal cortex to produce hormones leading to vomiting, weakness, diarrhoea, excessive thirst and increased frequency of urination.	See 'What if' Nos 17 and 18
Agalactia	Failure to produce milk possible caused by hormonal imbalance, stress mastitis or generalised disease.	
Allergy	Hypersensitivity to various allergens which may be contained in food, environmental objects, or in the air, may be manifest as skin disease or haemorrhagic gastroenteritis.	
Alopecia	Hair loss, which can result from a great number of causes.	
Anaemia	Reduced number of red cells in the blood. There are many causes and diagnosis can be difficult.	
Anal adenomata	Knobbly tumours situated just under the skin around the anus in older dogs.	See 'What if' No 22
Anal furrunculosis	Sinus formation around the anus probably from an infected anal sac.	See 'What if' No 22
Anaphylaxis	Hypersensitivity to injected foreign material (usually shown as shock).	
Anorexia	Inappetence — failure to eat.	See 'What if' No 3
Apnoea	Cessation of breathing.	See 'What if' No 47
Arthritis	Inflammation of a joint.	See 'What if' No 34
Ascarid infestation	Roundworm infection.	See Chapter 8
Ascites	Accumulation of fluid in the abdominal cavity mostly associated with heart disease or liver disease.	See 'What if' No 48
Ataxia	Unco-ordinated gait.	
Atelectasis	Rupture of the small sacs up the lung leading to chronic coughing.	
Aujeszky's disease	A disease which, in dogs, is characteised by intense itching with self-mutilation, fever, dullness, salivation, facial oedema, convulsions and death. Caused by a virus infection, usually from contact with infected pigs.	

Auto-immune disease	A condition where the body rejects its own tissues. The basic cause is a failure of the dog's immune system.	See Chapter 2
Avitaminosis	Vitamin deficiency.	See 'What if' No 30
Balanitis	Inflammation of the sheath which covers the penis.	See 'What if' No 30
Balanoposthitis	Inflammation of the sheath which covers the penis, and the penis itself.	See 'What if' No 11
Blepharitis	Inflammation of the eyelids usually secondary to conjunctivitis.	See 'What if' No 12
Blue eye	Cloudyness of the cornea associated with infectious canine hepatitis (p 136).	See 'What if' No 33
Bloat	Accumulation of gas in the stomach and/or intestines. A true emergency.	See 'What if' Nos 15 and 48
Brain lesion	Brain damage — see also CVA.	See 'What if' No 35
Bronchitis	Inflammation of the bronchi. See kennel cough (p 140).	See Chapter 10
Brucellosis	Infection with the bacterium *Brucella canis* resulting in possibly neonatal puppy deaths, abortion and infertility.	
Bruising	A contusion (wound) caused by a blow from a blunt object inflicting damage to the tissues under the skin.	See Chapter 13
Burn	An injury caused by dry heat.	See Chapter 13
Bursitis	Inflammation of a bursa, a fluid-filled sac which is present to protect a vulnerable part, usually a bony structure, eg the elbow, from trauma.	
Calculus (plural calculi)	A stone which has formed in the urinary bladder or gall bladder.	See 'What if' No 29
Campylobacteriosis	An infectiou with campylobacer organisms. The most common sign of this infection is profuse diarrhoea but often the infection does not cause any obvious signs.	
Canine distemper	A serious, highly contagious virus disease of dogs (hard pad is a form of canine distemper).	See Chapter 7 & 'What if' No 9
Canine parvo-virus infection	A virus disease of dogs which emerged suddenly in the late 1970s.	See Chapter 7
Canker	A lay term which used to be used for inflammation of the ear (otitis externa).	See 'What if' No 14
Carbon mono-xide poisoning	A form of poisoning caused by breathing carbon monoxide gas.	See 'What if' No 49 and Chapter 14
Cardiac arrythmia	Irregular heart beats.	
Cataract	An opacity of the lens in the eye.	See 'What if' No 12 and 13

Index of diseases and conditions

Disease/Condition	Disease/Condition	
CDRM	See German Shepherd syndrome.	See 'What if' No 48
Cheyletiella infestation	An infestation of the skin with *Cheyletiella parasitavorax*, the rabbit fur mite.	See Chapters 8 and 10
Chorea	Nervous twitching; usually a sequel to canine distemper infection.	See Chapter 7
Coccidiosis	An infection with coccidial parasites resulting in diarrhoea.	
Colitis	Inflammation of the colon.	
Collie eye anomaly	A congenital disease of the eye.	See 'What if' No 13 and Chapter 9
Collie nose	Lesions on the bridge of the nose probably from exposure to sunlight.	See 'What if' No 9
Coma	Unconsciousness.	See 'What if' No 43
Congestive heart failure	Chronic heart disease associated with breathlessness, coughing, exercise intolerance, fluid in the abdomen and weight loss.	
Conjunctivitis	Inflammation of the conjunctival sac in the eye which may be caused by virus or bacterial infections, foreign bodies or malformed eyelids.	See 'What if' No 11
Constipation	Failure to pass faeces. There are many causes of this sign.	See 'What if' No 25
Contusion	A bruise caused by a blow with a blunt object which leads to rupture of the small blood vessels under the skin.	See Chapter 13
Coprophagy	Eating own faeces.	See 'What if' No 26
Corneal ulceration	Ulceration of the front of the eye — the cornea.	See 'What if' No 12
Coronovirus infection	A virus infection which causes, principally, diarrhoea.	
Cramp	An uncontrolled contraction of a muscle.	See 'What if' No 44
Cushing's syndrome	Excessive production of the hormones produced by the adrenal cortex causing increased thirst, more frequent urination, enlarged abdomen, symmetrical hair loss and skin changes. Similar signs may be produced by prolonged medication w ith corticosteroids.	
CVA	Cerebro-vascular accident — a blood clot in the brain as a result of rupture of a blood vessel.	See 'What if' No 48
Cystitis	Inflammation of the urinary bladder usually as a result of bacterial infection.	See 'What if' Nos 28 and 29
Cysts	Swelling, usually under the skin, which contains fluid.	See 'What if' No 39
Dehydration	Water and salt depletion in the body.	See 'What if' No 2

Index of diseases and conditions

Disease/Condition		Disease/Condition
Impetigo	A superficial pustular skin inflammation mostly associated with bacterial infection.	See 'What if' No 28
Incontinence	Involuntary passage of urine.	See 'What if' No 48
Inco-ordination	A staggering gait — ataxia.	See 'What if' No 12
Indolent ulcer	Cloudy patch on the eye not caused by injury. Common in Boxers.	See Chapter 7
Infectious canine hepatitis	A viral infection of dogs. The acute form is sometimes referred to as Rubarth's disease.	See Chapter 7
Infectious canine tracheobronchitis	The technical name for kennel cough.	See 'What if' Nos 34 and 39
Infertility	Inability to reproduce.	
Interdigital cysts	Cysts between the toes.	See 'What if' No 2
Intussesception (intestinal)	Telescoping of one section of the intestine into another often as a result of severe enteritis.	
Jaundice	See icterus.	See 'What if' No 39
Juvenile pyoderma	Also called juvenile cellulitis, 'puppy strangles' or puppy head gland disease. A swelling of the whole head in puppies of 6-12 weeks of age, probably caused by a hypersensitivity reaction.	
Kennel cough	An infectious cough mainly affecting kennelled dogs.	See Chapter 7
Keratitis	Inflammation of the cornea.	See 'What if' No 12
Laceration	An irregular shaped wound with jagged edges. Often with a loss of skin. Often caused as a result of road traffic accidents.	See Chapter 13
Lactation tetany	See eclampsia.	
Lameness	Inability to put a leg on the ground or to bear full weight on it.	See 'What if' No 34
Laryngitis	Inflammation of the larynx often associated with generalised disease.	See 'What if' No 35
Lens luxation	Dislocated lens in the eye.	See 'What if' No 13
Leptospirosis	A disease of dogs caused by the bacteria *leptospira canicola* or *Leptospira icterohaemorrhagiae*.	See Chapter 7
Lice infestation	Infestation with lice (pediculosis).	See Chapter 8
Lick granuloma	A chronic wound produced by continued licking.	See 'What if' No 41
Mammary neoplasia	Tumours in the mammary glands. Such tumours often spread secondarily to the lungs in bitches.	See Chapter 1 (The bitch)
Mange	A parasitic skin disease of dogs caused by various mange mites.	See Chapters 8 and 10

Glossary

What did the veterinary surgeon mean?

Inevitably veterinary surgeons will use long or difficult words to describe various conditions and procedures. This glossary is provided to help dog owners understand what is meant. It should be used *in conjunction with* the Index of Diseases and Conditions affecting dogs.

Aberrant	varying from the norm
Acute	severe and short course — applied to the disease or condition
Adhesions	the joining together of tissues, usually applied to organs in the abdominal cavity and may occur after an operation
Aetiology	the cause (of a disease or condition). Sometimes spelt etiology
Afterbirth	the membranes (placenta) expelled with the puppies during birth
Anabolic steroid	a hormone which promotes growth. Anabolics are used only in very specific situations by veterinary surgeons
Anaerobes	bacteria which like to grow in the absence of air. They may occur in the uterus and are often associated with inflammation of the gums
Analgesic	a medicine which relieves pain
Aneurysm	a dilated sac on a blood vessel
Anoxia	lack of oxygen
Anthelmintic	a worm remedy
Antibiotic	a substance, eg penicillin, produced by micro-organisms which inhibits the growth of, or destroys, bacteria. They may be given by injection, by mouth or applied locally.
Antihistamine	a medicine which counteracts the effect of histamine, a substance released locally in insect bites or stings and which causes inflammation in the tissues.
Antiseptic	a substance that kills or inhibits the growth of micro-organisms.
Antiserum	blood serum containing high levels of antibody — used as a treatment for virus infections, eg canine distemper.
Aural resection	An operation to open up the external ear canal to allow exposure to the air — used to cure chronic ear disease
Auriscope	an instrument used for looking into the ears
Autogenous vaccine	a vaccine prepared from a micro-organism isolated from animals affected by an outbreak of disease
Bacteria	unicellular micro-organisms
Benign	not malignant, recurring or spreading. Usually applied to tumours
BHS	Beta-haemolytic streptococci — round-shaped bacteria which may cause tonsillitis or fading puppies

Glossary

Biopsy	a minor operation to take part of an affected tissue to diagnose the cause of a lesion and reach a prognosis
Cachexia	debility and wasting
Callus	the swelling which develops around a fractured bone as part of the healing process
Carcinogenic	cancer producing
Carcinoma	a type of malignant tumour
Cardiac	pertaining to the heart, eg cardiac failure
Cautery	the destruction of tissue, usually to prevent bleeding, by applying a caustic substance or a hot instrument
Chorea	involuntary muscle twitching — most commonly as a sequel to canine distemper
Chronic	persisting over a long period of time, applied to a disease
CNS	central nervous system
Coitus	sexual intercourse
Congenital	present at birth
Contagious	capable of being transmitted from one animal to another. Applied to a disease
Corticosteroids	medicines which mimic the action of the steroid hormones produced by the adrenal cortex. They are used most frequently for their anti-inflammatory action
Cryosurgery	the application of intense cold to destroy diseased tissue
Cutaneous	appertaining to the skin
Cyanosis	used to describe tissues which have turned purple or black due to an inadequate blood supply
Cyst	a closed cavity filled with fluid, eg sebaceous cyst
Dew claw	an extra claw near the carpus or below the hock, may be removed when puppies are a few days old
Diathermy	the destruction of tissue, usually to stop bleeding by using a high frequency electric current to generate heat
Diuretic	a medicine which increases the production of urine
Dys-	a prefix meaning painful or difficult,
Ecbolic	a medicine which makes the uterus contract
E. coli	a bacterium, present in the intestines, which may become pathogenic
Electrocardio-gram (ECG)	a record, made by an electrocardiograph, of the heart's performance
Electroenceph-alogram (EEG)	a record, made by an electroencephalograph, of brain function
Electrolytes	substances that split up into ions when dissolved in water. Electrolyte solutions are often used as transfusions in dehydrated animals
Embolism	a plug, usually a blood clot, blocking a blood vessel
Emaciation	excessive thinness or wasting
Endemic	usually applied to a disease which is present in an area at all times. Endemic is truly a medical term — the veterinary equivalent is enzootic

Endocrine glands	glands which secrete hormones into the blood to act as chemical messengers
Endoscope	an instrument for looking inside the body, usually through a natural opening, eg the vagina, but possible through an artificial opening, eg a surgical wound
Enterotomy	an operation involving cutting into the intestines
Etiology	see aetiology
First intention	applied to a wound that heals promptly
Fistula	an abnormal opening or duct leading into a natural canal, hollow organ or other part of the body
Fomites	particles in the air or environment which may act as carriers for infectious agents
Furunculosis	a bacterial infectiou of the skin whereby there are multiple openings in the skin surface through which pus drains, eg anal furunculosis
Gangrene	death and putrefaction of tissue
Gestation	period of development of the young in the womb
Granulation tissue	tissue containing large numbers of blood vessels which occurs when wounds fail to heal promptly. It is seen particularly in large open wounds which need to heal from the bottom.
Haematology	examination of the blood
Hormone	a chemical messenger transported by the blood and produced by an endocrine gland
Hyper-	a prefix to mean excessive, eg hyperthyroid, hyperactive
Hyperplasia	excessive growth of tissue
Hypertrophy	increase in size of an organ or tissue
Hypo-	a prefix to mean deficient or low, eg hypothyroid
Hypotension	lowered blood pressure
Hypothermia	lowered body temperature
Iatrogenic	caused by medication
Idiopathic	of unknown cause
Immunisation	to make an animal resistant (immune) to disease
Infectious	caused by disease producing micro-organisms. Infectious diseases are not necessarily contagious
Intra-articular	given into a joint cavity. Not commonly used nowadays
Intramuscular	given into muscles. Intramuscular injections are usually given into the hind leg. This route is used generally where a quick action is required
Intranasal	through the nose. This route is used for vaccines designed to give local protection of the respiratory tract
Intraperitoneal	into the abdominal cavity. This route is very infrequently used
Intubation	placing a tube in the trachea to facilitate breathing while under an anaesthetic
Larva	an immature stage in the development of an insect or worm
Lesion	a pathological change to a tissue, eg a wound
Lipoma	a benign tumour of fat cells

Glossary

Malignant	severe, life threatening, capable of spreading. Applied to tumours
Metastases	tumours arising as a result of malignant cells spreading to other parts of the body
Mucus	fluid produced by a mucous membrane, eg the lining of the vagina
Necropsy	a post-mortem
Neonatal	newborn
Neoplasia	formation of a neoplasm or growth (tumour)
Ophthalmo-scope	an instrumet used for looking into the eyes
Oral	pertaining to the mouth, given by mouth
Orthopaedics	treatment of bones and joints
Paraplegia	paralysis of the rear end of the body
Paresis	partial paralysis
Parturition	giving birth
Pericardium	the membrane that encloses the heart
Perinatal	in the period around birth
Pheromone	a chemical substance secreted externally by an individual, the odour of which causes a response in other members of the same species, eg pheromones shed by bitches in season will stimulate others in close contact to also come on heat
Photophobia	fear or intolerance of light
Placenta	see afterbirth
Prognosis	the expected outcome of a disease, condition or operation
Prolapse	protrusion, to the outside, of an abdominal organ, eg vagina or bladder
Prophylaxis	prevention of a disease
Prosthesis	an artificial part, eg hip joint
Purulent	containing pus
Pus	a secretion from inflamed tissue, usually sticky and creamy, which contains white blood cells, serum and bacteria
Put down	to painlessly destry (also: put to sleep)
Pyrexia	raised body temperature, fever
Renal	pertaining to the kidney, eg renal failure
Sepsis	bacterial infection usually causing pus to be formed
Septicaemia	blood poisoning by bacteria and their toxins
Serology	the examination of blood for the presence of antibodies to disease
Sporadic	occurring occasionally
Staphylococci	bacteria which commonly occur, particularly in association with skin disease
Stenosis	narrowing of a canal, eg the intestines
Streptococci	commonly occurring bacteria which affects dogs, particularly following a virus infection. Often a cause of tonsillitis
Subacute	between acute and chronic

Subclinical   applied to a disease in which the signs are not obvious by clinical examination

Subcutaneous under the skin. Subcutaneous injections are used very commonly where a rapid effect is not required since this route of administration tends to be less painful

Sulphonamides chemical compounds which are used to kill or suppress the growth of bacteria in the body

Superficial   on the surface. Often applied to a wound

Suppurative   producing pus. Applied to a wound

Syndrome   a set of signs which occur together indicating a particular condition or disease

Synergistic   acting together to increase the effect, eg penicillin plus streptomycin

Tachycardia   increased heart rate. The opposite is bradycardia

Tachypnoea   increased rate of breathing

Teratogenic   capable of producing abnormalities in puppies int he woumb, applied to a medicine, eg thalidomide

Thrombus   a blood clot occurring in a blood vessel or the heart

Tissue   an aggregation of similar cells in the body, eg a muscle

Toxaemia   the spread of bacterial products (toxins) in the blood from a source of infection

Trauma   injury, wounding, shock

Tumour   a growth, neoplasm

Ulcer   break in the surface of an organ, eg corneal ulcer

Umbilicus   the point on the abdominal wall where the umbilical cord emerged

Villus   small, finger-like processes projecting from the wall of the intestine

Virus   a sub-microscopic agent which infects animals, plants and even bacteria

Viscus   any large internal organ (plural — viscera)

Wood's lamp   a lamp that emits ultraviolet light. Used to diagnose some forms of ringworm

Zoonosis   a disease that can be transmitted from animals to man

Index

For specific diseases and conditions, see separate index starting on page 244.

Record of illness and medication*

Date	Signs shown/ diagnosis	Medication given/ surgical procedure	Comments

Ask your veterinary surgeon to write down the name of the injections or tablets prescribed.

* To include medication given for treatment and prevention of disease, ie antibiotic injections, chemical control of heat, worm doses etc.

Record of illness and medication*

Date	Signs shown/ diagnosis	Medication given/ surgical procedure	Comments

Ask your veterinary surgeon to write down the name of the injections or tablets prescribed.

* To include medication given for treatment and prevention of disease, ie antibiotic injections, chemical control of heat, worm doses etc.